Ads, Fads, and Consumer Culture

Ads, Fads, and Consumer Culture

Advertising's Impact on American Character and Society

THIRD EDITION

Arthur Asa Berger
With illustrations by the author

ROWMAN & LITTLEFIELD PUBLISHERS, INC.
Lanham • Boulder • New York • Toronto • Plymouth, UK

ROWMAN & LITTLEFIELD PUBLISHERS, INC.

Published in the United States of America
by Rowman & Littlefield Publishers, Inc.
A wholly owned subsidiary of The Rowman & Littlefield Publishing Group, Inc.
4501 Forbes Boulevard, Suite 200, Lanham, Maryland 20706
www.rowmanlittlefield.com

Estover Road, Plymouth PL6 7PY, United Kingdom

Copyright © 2007 by Rowman & Littlefield Publishers, Inc.

British Library Cataloguing in Publication Information Available

Library of Congress Cataloging-in-Publication Data

Berger, Arthur Asa, 1933–
  Ads, fads, and consumer culture : advertising's impact on American character and society / Arthur Asa Berger ; with illustrations by the author. — 3rd ed.
    p. cm.
  Includes bibliographical references and index.
  ISBN-13: 978-0-7425-5443-6 (cloth : alk. paper)
  ISBN-10: 0-7425-5433-0 (cloth : alk. paper)
  ISBN-13: 978-0-7425-5444-3 (pbk. : alk. paper)
  ISBN-10: 0-7425-5444-9 (pbk. : alk. paper)
  1. Advertising—United States. 2. Popular culture—United States. 3. Consumer education—United States. I. Title.
  HF5823.B438 2007
  659.1'0420973—dc22

                                                              2006100596

Printed in the United States of America

⊗™ The paper used in this publication meets the minimum requirements of American National Standard for Information Sciences—Permanence of Paper for Printed Library Materials, ANSI/NISO Z39.48-1992.

Some measure of greed exists unconsciously in everyone. It represents an aspect of the desire to live, one which is mingled and fused at the outset of life with the impulse to turn aggression and destructiveness outside ourselves against others, and as such it persists unconsciously throughout life. By its very nature it is endless and never assuaged; and being a form of the impulse to live, it ceases only with death.

The longing or greed for good things can relate to any and every imaginable kind of good—material possessions, bodily or mental gifts, advantages and privileges; but, beside the actual gratifications they may bring, in the depths of our minds they ultimately signify one thing. They stand as proofs to us, if we get them, that we are ourselves good, and full of good, and so are worthy of love, or respect and honour, in return. Thus they serve as proofs and insurances against our fears of emptiness inside ourselves, or of our evil impulses which make us feel bad and full of badness to ourselves and others.

—Joan Riviere, "Hate, Greed and Aggression"

CONTENTS

FOREWORD

Fred S. Goldberg

I spent thirty-four years in advertising: the first fifteen at what was then, arguably, the finest of the large traditional Madison Avenue agencies (Young & Rubicam, NY); the next nine years at arguably the finest creative agency in the country at the time (Chiat/Day, LA); and the last ten founding and managing my own agency (Goldberg Moser O'Neill, San Francisco). This experience provided me with a unique overview and insight into the business of advertising.

When you study advertising and advertising impact, it helps to understand the context within which advertising messages are developed, produced, and aired. Many of the print ads and commercials that consumers ultimately see could have been demonstrably different, were it not for the conflicting interests that went hand in hand with their development.

In theory, advertisers hire advertising agencies to create ads that will break through and impact their customers and potential customers. They hope to maximize the effectiveness of often limited media and promotional dollars, achieve a competitive edge, and gain extra mileage from each advertising message.

Yet, because of the nature of the industry and the agency and client relationship, a series of conflicts often prevents this from happening as frequently as it should. And this explains, at least in part, why there is so much advertising that is spurious, curious, muddled, and jumbled. The impact that it all has on the American character and culture, as explained in this book, is partially the result of the conflicting way advertising gets developed. One can only wonder what the ads, and their effect, would be if self-interest was removed along the way.

These conflicts have a numbing consequence on the impact of clients' advertising dollars and the subsequent success they have in the marketplace selling their products or positioning their companies or causes. The advertising business is unique and particularly difficult because it is fraught with these conflicts which very often result in a dumbed-down final product.

Trying to represent what is best for the client, while still trying to make a profit, is sometimes a challenge for an advertising agency. It's easy to profess, as advertising agencies are prone to do, that their recommendations are impartially formulated only to drive a client's business, but that is not always the case. In fact they are influenced by the existence of various agendas operating at different levels of management in an agency and in different departments. Similar agendas may exist on the client side.

Advertising executives may believe that they are providing complete objectivity, but at the end of the day they can be often prejudiced, partial, and biased. One example that Arthur Berger observes in this book is that for various reasons it is important that the advertising agency recommend only one campaign. It must be made to seem to be the only answer to the company's problems. This practice provides fertile ground for conflicts of interests and less-than-complete objectivity.

Why does this happen? One reason is conflicts between departments. On the one hand, Account Management representatives may be trying to support the client's view and interest within the agency, while other departments are developing recommendations that may or may not reflect the client's actual needs. Or vice versa. The Account Planners are supposedly trying to represent the consumer; the Creative people are representing their ad; and the Client is concerned about his brand. This leads to internal agency debate, to compromises, and ultimately to a finished product that often depends on who made the strongest argument or had the most authority.

This is all further complicated, as Berger accurately points out, in that people in advertising agencies need to sell both themselves and the products they have been engaged to advertise. This can, in and of itself, create a conflict.

There is another conflict where many advertisers rely on creative testing to help them make a decision. They rely heavily on the often-spurious conclusions, and this conflicts directly with implementing work that can truly break through and impact the consumer in a highly competitive manner. In client organizations, testing is a political tool as often as it is a learning device. It helps protect people's decisionmaking, particularly in the context of a large organizational framework, as much as it does to determine the worth of a particular message or idea. When a test shows an idea to be normative, then the decision to use it can be more easily justified. In other words, one's backside is adequately covered in the event of a failure.

Finally, there is the conflict in trying to develop truly unique and creative solutions to business and communication problems. It is my experience that, generally, opposition to a creative solution grows greater in direct proportion to its uniqueness and lack of familiarity. This is true for people within an ad agency, the client organization, and even potential customers, all of whom are asked to judge things that are new and different.

I was personally involved in what may have been one of the great advertising lessons of all time, exhibiting all of these various conflicting forces. It was for Apple Computer—a commercial known as "1984." This was the introductory commercial for Apple's Macintosh and was one of the most memorable, most persuasive, most effective commercials ever created.

However, the commercial, after being fully produced, was rejected by then–Apple CEO Steve Jobs, after it was inordinately criticized by Apple's board of directors just prior to airing. They argued that it was an extravagance and did not appropriately communicate Apple's persona as a serious business computer company to stockholders, investors, and the consumer. They worried that Apple would look "insane" and "out of control" if the commercial aired.

A test of the commercial supported the board somewhat, although they never saw the results. It indicated that the commercial was well below established averages in its "effectiveness," scoring only a 5 against a norm of 29 for thirty-second business-directed commercials. The commercial was actually sixty seconds, and should have scored all that much higher.

The commercial was to air during the Super Bowl. Because the advertising agency was not able to resell the media time they had purchased for it, Steve Jobs ultimately gave his approval to run the commercial in lieu of forfeiting the money for the time which had already been committed. This was done despite internal protestations at Apple.

History was made. The personal computer industry is entirely different today because of this single "conflicted" advertising decision. The commercial was recalled the day after it ran by 78 percent of viewers; Apple sold $3.5 million worth of Macintosh computers within six hours the next business day and $155 million over the next one hundred days. Today, Apple's revenues are $25 billion and it has a market capitalization of $59 billion, arguably because of the airing of one single commercial.

This is but one eye-popping example of why advertising is such a unique business among businesses.

The manner in which advertising is developed and implemented, and the incredible influence it has on our culture and consumers, is profound. *Ads, Fads, and Consumer Culture* delves into this and other matters. Arthur Berger provides fresh insights and explanations on various aspects and issues of the industry and the ads, and the impact on all of us. On the very first page he identifies one of the critical issues: "Advertising agencies are forced to talk out of both sides of their mouths at the same time."

When one considers the enormous impact advertising has on millions of people every day, and upon our culture, it is mind-boggling that so many arbitrary factors and self-interests can shape the communication development process. Reading Mr. Berger's book in this context makes many of his analyses and conclusions that much more surprising, insightful, thought provoking, and entertaining.

The author specifically discusses and analyzes the Apple "1984" commercial in depth in the last chapter. It's amazing that this advertising had such a profound impact on products and people's lives when one considers the agony and irony involved in giving birth to a genuinely new idea.

On the other hand, maybe it's not so amazing. Maybe most advertising works, whatever the development process, just because all advertising works.

PREFACE TO THE THIRD EDITION

It is a great pleasure for me to offer this new edition of *Ads, Fads, and Consumer Culture* to my readers. The advertising industry is one in which there is constant change, as new technologies develop, new products are created, and new services are offered. For example, the Internet has become a major new source of advertising revenue, as anyone who has used search engines such as Google or Yahoo knows. And bloggers have become increasingly important. Advertising companies are now studying what bloggers say about new movies, video games, and other products to gain added insights into consumer behavior.

There is a good deal of debate in academic circles and in the government about the role of advertising in American society. Does advertising for fast foods and junk food play a role in the rapid growth of obesity in America and in a number of other countries? If so, how big a role has it played and what should be done to remedy this situation? Has advertising for expensive consumer drugs had a negative impact on the medical profession and upon the health of Americans? As I write, there are efforts being made to modify the way drug companies can advertise their products. Are young children being taught to be self-indulgent and materialistic as they are "branded" by advertising? If so, how do we counter this development?

Has advertising shaped, in important ways, the way individuals perceive themselves and the way we perceive one another? If this is the case, how can people defend themselves against the way they are being affected or even "manipulated" by advertisers? These are only a few of the topics I deal with in this book.

HIDDEN PERSUADERS

Whatever else it might be, advertising is a form of mass persuasion, and we must wonder about the social, psychological, and cultural impact of this industry that plays so large a role in our media and everyday lives. In 1957, Vance Packard wrote a book, *The Hidden Persuaders,* that alerted his readers to the role advertising was playing in American society. He wrote (1957:3):

> This book is an attempt to explore a strange and rather exotic new area of American life. It is about the way many of us are being influenced and manipulated—far more than we realize—in the patterns of our everyday lives. Large-scale efforts are being made, often with impressive success, to channel our unthinking habits, our purchasing decisions, and our thought processes by the use of insights gleaned from psychiatry and the social sciences. Typically these efforts take place beneath our level of awareness; so that the appeals which move us are often, in a sense, hidden.
>
> Some of this manipulating being attempted is simply amusing. Some of it is disquieting, particularly when viewed as a portent of what may be ahead on a more intensive and effective scale for us all. Co-operative scientists have come along providentially to furnish some awesome tools.

The impact of this use of psychoanalytic and other methods has led advertisers to more effectively sell us (1957:3) "products, ideas, attitudes, candidates, goals or states of mind." Packard wrote his book some fifty years ago. Since then, the advertising industry has developed incredible new means of understanding our thought processes and ways of shaping our behavior.

It has also extended its reach, and uses "product placements" to put certain products in television shows and films and now shows commercials on cell phones. In some cases, one product placement in a television show or film can lead to huge increases in the sales of that product. In addition, since films with product placements in them are widely distributed abroad, it gives products placed in films a global reach. Sometimes, products sold in a foreign country are substituted for the original product placements in films. Thus, in *Spider-Man 2*, Dr. Pepper was shown in the film in the United States but Mirinda was shown overseas.

We can say, without stretching the truth too much, that, with few exceptions, wherever in the world there are flat surfaces, such as sides of buildings, cars, buses, and screens of all kinds and sizes, advertisers will find a way to use them for their purposes.

BRAIN SCANS AND CONSUMER BEHAVIOR

There is now experimentation in using brain scans to see which parts of the brain are activated by exposure to advertisements. Advertisers have moved beyond surveys, focus groups and depth interviews and now are experimenting with by-passing people's explanations of why they do things to see, more directly, how specific images, bits of dialogue and music passages stimulate certain parts of our brains. If advertisers are able to figure out how to bypass our consciousness by using information learned by studying brain scans, they will be even more powerful than they already are.

Sigmund Freud, the father of psychoanalytic theory, had suggested that material stored in the unconscious elements of our psyches, areas we cannot access and of which we are unaware, is often responsible for our actions. Many advertising agencies use this notion to convince us to purchase the goods and services they are selling. The Russian psychologist Pavlov showed how dogs could be trained to salivate on command by being given certain stimuli and some advertisers have attempted to use this stimulus-response theory to attempt to shape our consumption behavior. Now, advertising agencies, using information derived from neurological studies of brain activation, may move beyond Freud's theory and develop strategies that can only be described as Orwellian in their implications.

So there is much to discuss in this new edition and I hope that you will find this book helps you understand the role advertising plays in American culture and society and in giving you notions about who you are, what is important in life, and what role you should play in society. Advertising pervades our everyday lives. How advertising effects our psyches, our society and our culture is a question that demands continual study and attention. This book will help you learn how to analyze print advertisements and television commercials, as a means of gaining a bit of control over this subtle and all-pervasive force in American culture and other societies as well.

A NOTE ON THE ADVERTISEMENTS
USED IN THIS BOOK

Advertising campaigns come and go so quickly that it is impossible to keep up with the newest ads and commercials, and there is really no need to do so. Most advertising is undistinguished, at best. And the "life expectancy" for any advertisement or commercial or campaign is, generally speaking, not very long. One exception to this fact is the Absolut campaign, which lasted for twenty-five years before the company decided on a new campaign.

Thus, for my chapters on analyzing print advertisements and commercials I have chosen texts (the terms we use in academic discourse for advertisements, films, television shows, and so on) of great interest and ones that are considered classics. They are also very useful since they are extremely rich in symbols and cultural significance and allow for a great deal of analysis.

The Fidji advertisement was the main subject of a major study of perfume advertising at INSEAD, The European Institute of Business Administration, one of the most important business schools in the world. I didn't know about the INSEAD study when I wrote my analysis of the advertisement. I was captivated by the complex symbology in the advertisement. The Macintosh "1984" commercial was voted the second best advertisement in the 1980s (the first was the famous "fast talker" commercial for Federal Express by Ally & Gargano) by The One Club for Art and Copy, an organization that evaluates advertising in the advertising industry.

So I have chosen texts for these two chapters, and in a number of other places, that are extremely interesting and useful for analysis. Choosing more up-to-date advertisements and commercials for my chapters on methods of analyzing print advertisements and television commercials, from my perspective, would serve no useful purpose, for it is the application of the techniques of interpreting and analyzing advertisements and commercials that is critical, not the texts themselves. However, I have inserted new advertisements in various places in the third edition, though what is really important is the degree to which the reproduced advertisement reflects some topic of interest dealt with in the book, not when it was made.

PREFACE TO THE SECOND EDITION

It's always a pleasure to introduce the second edition of a book, for it means that the first edition of the book has found an audience. Whatever else you can say about writers, one thing is certain—writers like to have their books read. My sins may be scarlet (to paraphrase a wit of a while back), but my books are read. So I'm very happy that I've found enough readers to warrant a second edition of *Ads, Fads, and Consumer Culture*.

In this second edition, I have added material to flesh out a number of topics and added new theoretical material in various places. Since I wrote the first edition of this book, a faltering economy has caused the advertising industry to fall on hard times. To cite a rather extreme example of this matter, consider this. In 1998 I spent three weeks as a visiting professor at Goldberg Moser O'Neill, a midsized advertising agency in San Francisco. The agency, at that time, had 280 employees and billings of around $500 million or so. It now has somewhere around sixty employees. The agency was sold and taken over by a different management, lost several very large accounts, and was hit by the slump in the advertising revenues. For one reason or another, it is only a shadow of its former self. Most of the advertising agencies in the United States and abroad lost business, but not like Goldberg Moser O'Neill. Things are getting better now and the industry is making something of a comeback.

Although *Ads, Fads, and Consumer Culture* is the only book I've written on advertising, I've been fascinated by advertising for many years and have chapters on advertising in a number of my books. In 1970 I testified before a United States Senate subcommittee on advertising and drug abuse. And I've written articles on advertising that have appeared in a number of magazines. Those of you who might be interested in my adventures at Goldberg Moser O'Neill in 1998 and at a large advertising agency in London in 1973 might wish to consult my book *The Agent in the Agency*. It has a long ethnographic chapter about my "secret agentry" in these two advertising agencies.

I hope readers of this edition of *Ads, Fads, and Consumer Culture* will find this book to be, as advertisers often put it, a "new and improved version" and one that will help readers understand advertising and its impact on their psyches, their personal identities, their friends and families, and American society even better than the first edition did.

I STINK, THEREFORE I AM

A number of years ago I wrote an article about deodorant advertising entitled "I Stink, Therefore I Am!" My thesis in this article was that our bodies, which give off odors, confirm our existence and that deodorants, which mask our bodies' odors, reflect an unconscious desire to be "perfect," to escape somehow from the physical aspects of our existence. The title is a parody of René Descartes's famous statement, "I think, therefore I am." It is humorous because I have used and subverted, to an extent, Descartes's words. I have not abandoned my interest in smells. In this book I deal with a fascinating advertisement for Fidji perfume. I think you will be interested in all the things I find in this advertisement.

TO BUY IS TO BE PERCEIVED

I also wrote an essay on advertising based on another well-known quotation from a philosopher. The great Irish philosopher George Berkeley once wrote, "To be is to be perceived." I "adapted" that idea and wrote, "To buy is to be perceived," explaining that one reason people buy things is that when they purchase products or services, salespeople pay attention to them. Salespeople confirm, if only for a brief moment, our existence when we buy something. And as soon as we're done, they tend to ignore us and pretend we don't exist. The bill in the mail or on the list of credit-card purchases is an additional confirmation of our existence. We are not conscious of these things, of course.

We do not recognize the "real" reason we do any number of things. If we did, we wouldn't need all the psychiatrists, psychotherapists, sociologists, psychologists, anthropologists, and others who spend a great deal of their time trying to figure out:

1. what people do and
2. why they do what they do.

People are very complicated, and there are no easy answers to these questions.

MY AMBIVALENCE TOWARD ADVERTISING

I must admit to a kind of ambivalence about advertising. (The convention is that commercial messages in print are called advertisements and those on radio and television are called commercials.) Many advertisements and commercials are brilliant works of art: They are funny; they are moving; and they use avant-garde cinematic techniques. But their purpose, generally speaking, is to get people to buy products and services, and thus there is an ethical problem connected with the advertising industry: People are not treated as ends in themselves but as means to an end—consumption, doing what the advertisers want them to do. In some cases, such as with cigarettes, people who work in advertising agencies have a real ethical dilemma to deal with.

In this book I consider the matter of the degree to which people can resist advertising. We may think we are not affected by advertising, but we may be wrong. As Leo Bogart pointed out many years ago in *Strategy in Advertising*:

> The real significance of advertising is its total cumulative weight as part of the culture—in the way in which it contributes to the popular lore of ideas and attitudes towards consumer products. The information and impressions which people have about branded goods represent folk wisdom: they are part of the landscape of symbols with which people are familiar from childhood on, and which they play back to each other in the discussions that precede a major purchase. (1967:78)

That is, advertising is an important part of our culture, and many of our ideas and notions have been influenced by the enormous amount of advertising we are exposed to as we grow up.

There's also a great deal of interest in advertising itself. If you call up Google (www.google.com) on your computer and type in the word "advertising," you would get 35,800,000 web sites that mention the word "advertising" on them. Here are the figures, as of April 17, 2003, for some aspects of advertising:

Topic	Number of Web Sites
"Television Advertising"	119,000
"Magazine Advertising"	107,000
"Radio Advertising"	71,600
"Newspaper Advertising"	138,000
"Advertising Research"	41,500
"Advertising Publications"	6,350

In addition, I searched www.amazon.com and found that there are 6,881 books dealing with advertising, from a variety of perspectives, listed on Amazon's web site.

Just before I wrote this preface, I happened to meet a neighbor in a supermarket. He told me about the problems his son was having with his wife—she could not stop buying things, and this was causing them all kinds of problems, because she was spending more money than they could afford to spend and going into debt. My neighbor wondered whether his son's marriage would last much longer. "They get along OK," he said, "but she just can't seem to understand that they have limited finances." This story is not unusual. And I'm not suggesting that advertising is the villain that might lead to the breakup of this marriage or other marriages. But advertising plays an enormous role in our society of consumption, and young people are trained, one might say, by the advertising industry to be consumers.

THE GOALS OF THIS BOOK

I wrote this book to do a number of things:

1. to teach you something about how advertising works,
2. to suggest how advertising has affected American society and culture, and

3. to help you learn to analyze and interpret advertisements and commercials in more interesting and profound ways. This should help you learn to resist them better.

Since advertising is so pervasive in our culture, this book deals with a number of different topics—sexuality, politics, market research, consumer culture, and many other things. I hope you, my reader, will find it interesting and useful and that it will help you see the role advertising has played, and is playing, in your life.

ACKNOWLEDGMENTS

My list of topics to consider on print advertising and television commercials draws upon, but is a modification and enhancement of, material in my book *Seeing Is Believing: An Introduction to Visual Communication* (1998). In *Ads, Fads, and Consumer Culture* I focus on a more general analysis using some of the basic critical techniques. The interpretive techniques I use in the Fidji analysis are dealt with in more detail in my books *Media Analysis Techniques, Cultural Criticism, Seeing Is Believing: An Introduction to Visual Communication,* and *Signs in Contemporary Culture: An Introduction to Semiotics.* They offer more amplified discussions of the various methodologies and concepts I will be using here, and they also have bibliographies for those interested in pursuing these interpretive methodologies in more depth. The glossary is an adaptation, revised and tied to advertising, of my glossary in *Essentials of Mass Communication Theory.*

I am grateful to Transaction Publishers for giving me permission to reprint my article on the "1984" commercial and to Sage Publications for giving me permission to reprint my analysis of the Fidji advertisement. I have revised both of these articles considerably for this book. I also want to thank the Advertising Education Foundation for granting me a visiting professorship in 1999 that enabled me to spend three weeks at Goldberg Moser O'Neill advertising in San Francisco, and Fred Goldberg and all his colleagues for making my stay there so enjoyable and useful and for allowing me to use a number of their advertisements in this book.

Advertisements sanctify, signify, mythologize, and fantasize. They uphold some of the existing economic and political structures and subvert others. Not only does advertising shape American culture; it shapes Americans' images of themselves.

—Katherine Toland Frith, *Undressing the Ad:*
Reading Culture in Advertising

The loyal customer is worth more than the sum of her purchases. A faithful General Motors customer can be worth $276,000 over her lifetime, including the 11 or more vehicles bought plus a word-of-mouth endorsement making friends and relatives more likely to consider GM products.

—Greg Farrell, "Marketers Put a Price on Your Life"

1

ADVERTISING IN AMERICAN SOCIETY

Advertising is really quite puzzling. It is a $200 billion a year industry in the United States and employs a goodly number of the brightest and most creative people in American society and other societies as well (often at very high salaries, to boot). Curiously, people who work in the industry have difficulty proving that it works—especially in the long term. The word *advertising* means "to make known," and generally is understood to refer to public—now we would say mass mediated—announcements of products and services that are for sale. The Latin root of the word is *advertere*, which means "to pay attention to." This word can be broken down further: *ad* means "toward" and *vertere* means "to turn." So advertising attempts to turn our attention toward something—namely the announcement of some product or service. There is logic, then, to the first rule of advertising, which is, attract attention. If people aren't paying attention to a print advertisement or a radio or television commercial, you can't persuade them to do anything.

ADVERTISING AS A PUZZLEMENT

One advertising executive told me that "half of the money people spend on advertising is wasted . . . but we don't know which half." Also, advertising agencies are forced to talk out of both sides of their mouths at the same time. They have to convince clients that advertising is really effective—in generating sales, holding on to the customers a company already has, or attracting new customers. But when governmental agencies or consumer groups ask advertising agencies about what they do when it comes to advertising products such as cigarettes and alcohol, for instance, the advertising agencies argue that they have very little impact on people.

The situation seems to be that although nobody in the business world is certain how advertising works, there is a consensus that it is necessary and

1

Insights from Advertising Agencies

The psychological profile of people in advertising is that they love the drama involved in working in agencies and the excitement generated by making ads and commercials. Also, planning is about demonstrating that it's not just about logic. It's not a linear process. In the United States, business people are rewarded for being extremely logical and having statistics to back themselves up. This produces dreadful advertising that often fails to make any impact. Advertising agencies are refuges for people who don't think only in a linear fashion and who recognize that other people—consumers of advertising—don't think that way, either.

---

that campaigns are worth the enormous amount of money they often cost. Thus, for example, commercials broadcast during the 2005 Super Bowl cost $2.4 million for thirty seconds and the cost of the commercials during the 2006 Super Bowl was $2.5 million for a thirty-second spot. This is a great deal of money but there are reasons why companies pay that amount of money to show commercials during the game. I will discuss Super Bowl advertising in more detail shortly.

    We must always keep in mind the difference between the cost of making a nationally broadcast television commercial and the cost of purchasing airtime to show a commercial. The cost of making a standard thirty-second nationally broadcast television commercial is between $300,000 and $400,000 now, though some commercials can cost a good deal more than that. A typical "Got Milk" commercial costs around $370,000 (figure 1.1). Purchasing the airtime might run into the millions of dollars. Naturally, advertisers want to run effective commercials, so it's worth spending a bit more money for a commercial that will work. The campaign for "Got

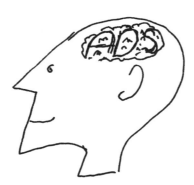

The Cost of a Typical Commercial

These figures represent a breakdown on the cost of a thirty-second "Got Milk" commercial. They were supplied by a former student of mine who works at the advertising agency that created the commercial. A typical thirty-second spot costs between $300,000 and $400,000; this spot cost $363,000.

$281,000	Television Production
$45,000	Television Postproduction (editing)
$6,000	Music (usually much higher)
$1,000	Sound Effects Search/Narration
$11,000	Talent Fees (3 principal actors, 5 extras, including voice-over)
$1,000	Tapes and Dubs
$1,000	Legal Clearances (often much higher)
$1,000	Shipping
$16,000	Agency Travel, Casting, Callbacks, Pre-Pro Edit
$363,000	Total

Figure 1.1

Milk" attracted an enormous amount of attention and has spawned many "Got . . . " imitations. Of course, advertisers and advertising agencies never know which commercials will be effective and why they are effective. Though there is often an enormous amount of data about target audiences "behind" a given commercial, all the data in the world doesn't mean anything when it comes to making a commercial that is effective.

If we believe what advertising agencies (and the companies they make advertisements and commercials for) tell us, we have to conclude that advertising works in strange and mysterious ways and that although nobody is sure precisely how it works, it does have an impact—though its power to shape any given individual's behavior is (or seems to be) really quite minimal.

We each like to think we (perhaps "uniquely") can resist advertising and it has no impact on us. This notion, which I will discuss in more detail in chapter 3, makes light of the power of advertising and helps us preserve our sense of autonomy and individuality. Others are brainwashed by ads and commercials, but not us, we think—as we find ourselves purchasing products we feel, somehow, we must have. Thus, we play into the hands of advertisers who use our illusion that we are not affected by advertising against us. As the president of a large advertising agency told me, "Even lousy advertising works!"

We cannot show that a given commercial or campaign makes a given individual buy a product or service being advertised—or is the primary force in shaping that person's behavior—but we can see that advertising has a collective impact; that is, it affects people in general. Corporations don't spend hundreds of billions of dollars a year because they are Good Samaritans who want to make sure that radio stations and television networks are very profitable. And politicians, who spend millions of dollars on their election campaigns, aren't Good Samaritans either.

I believe that advertising is a very powerful force, one that plays a major role in the economy (it has replaced Puritanism in motivating people to work hard so that they can earn money and be able to buy things) and, increasingly in recent years, the political sphere. Advertising has the power, I believe, to influence and, in some cases, shape people's behavior, broadly speaking.

For example, in the 1994 campaign by forces against the Clinton health-care plan, the "Harry and Louise" commercials are credited with eroding support for the plan by approximately twenty percentage points. In these commercials, Harry and Louise criticized the Clinton plan for making major changes in the medical system and lamented the way big government would be telling them who their doctor had to be and would be depriving them of their freedom to make decisions about medical matters. I'm not suggesting that campaigns always work or that they always work the way advertisers and advertising agencies imagine they will. But if we take a broad look at human behavior in the long run, it seems quite obvious that advertising exists and has been flourishing because, somehow, it works—that is, it works a good deal of the time the way those paying for the advertising want it to work.

DEFINING ADVERTISING

This is the way the advertising industry works, most of the time:

1. Advertising agencies purchase space for print advertisements in newspapers, magazines, or other kinds of publications, or time to broadcast commercials, made for companies selling products or services. Some organizations and corporations do their own advertising, but this is not usually the case. There are other ways of advertising, such as putting ads on billboards, in bus shelters, on buses and taxicabs (figure 1.2), using the Internet, sponsoring events, and placing products in films and television shows.

Figure 1.2

2. These commercials or print advertisements are generally designed to attract the attention of people with suitable demographics and the proper psychographics—values and lifestyles—for some product or service. Advertising agencies tend to concentrate on people, roughly speaking, from 18 to 49—assuming they are the ones who buy most of the products and services advertised. Certain products are aimed at children and others at older people, but most advertising is aimed at the 18 to 49 cohort, give or take a few years on either end.

3. Advertising tries to attract attention to, create the desire for, and stimulate action that leads to the purchase of products and services advertised on the part of those reading print advertisements, listening to radio commercials, or watching and listening to television commercials. That is, advertisers hope to convince, to persuade, to motivate, and most importantly, to get people to act, to *do* something. This something generally involves moving from the desire for products and services to the actual purchase of the products or services.

There are, as I pointed out earlier, a number of different forms and genres of advertising. Advertising pervades the American media and our lives—from the billboards on our highways to the print ads in the publications we read, the commercials on radio and television, and the designer logos on T-shirts and other kinds of clothes we wear. Advertising is also used by charities, labor unions, and organizations of all kinds to get their messages to the public. In consumer cultures, it seems fair to say that just about everyone is advertising, which creates a major problem—clutter. There are so many messages being sent to us that sometimes, as the result of information overload, we get them all mixed up.

The box that follows (figure 1.3), which I wrote in 1978, deals with many of the issues about advertising that have occupied my attention, as you can see, for a number of years. It shows the problems one faces in trying to live according to the dictates of competing advertising campaigns.

If you look at the advertising for such products as athletic shoes, razors, perfumes, beer, automobiles, you find advertising agencies fighting, desperately, to hold on to their segment of the market and, if possible, to gain market share. They use every editing technique they can think of to make their commercials visually more memorable and every trick of language and narrative structure to gain our attention and divert our attention from the advertising of competitors.

One of the problems advertisers face is that of clutter—the enormous number of advertisements we are exposed to on a given day, which leads to information overload and in many cases, paralysis. So advertising agencies knock themselves out to differentiate their campaigns from other campaigns and get the attention of the target audience they are attacking. A remarkable Honda commercial, made in England, cost six million dollars to make and involved 606 takes and took three weeks, shooting nonstop day and night, to film and three months to make. It is two minutes long, as well, which means it costs an enormous amount of money to air the commercial on television. But the commercial has attracted an enormous amount of attention and interest and thus, Honda no doubt believes, it was worth doing.

Many Americans report that they are annoyed by all the advertising to which they are exposed. A 2004 survey by Yankelovich Partners, done for the American Association of Advertising Agencies, reported the following:

69%   expressed interest in products that would block advertising
66%   felt they are constantly bombarded by advertising
61%   described the amount of advertising to which they are exposed as out of control
60%   felt their opinion of advertising is more negative than before
54%   said they avoid buying products that advertise too much (www.medialiteracy.com/stats_advertising.jsp)

So there is a good deal of hostility in the American public about the amount of advertising to which they are exposed, and that is an additional problem the advertising industry faces.

"Don't Go Away, We'll Be Back with More Ads"

(*The Chronicle Review*, November, 13, 1978)

As I sit at my typewriter, considering the commercials on television this fall season, I find myself possessed by an overwhelming urge to make a long-distance phone call and join the Navy. Who can resist a bargain like being able to call anywhere in the continental United States and talk with "loved ones" for only 85 cents for five minutes (as long as you place the call at the right time—mostly the wee hours of the morning)? And who doesn't want a life of "adventure and excitement" instead of just a job?

I had always thought that sailors spent most of their time with mops and buckets, but that must have been the old Navy. The new one seems as technologically advanced as "Battlestar Galactica." And "Homeward Bound," the new Navy's new commercial, scripted to the tune of the old Simon and Garfunkel song, is one of the more interesting and attractive advertisements on national television this fall. The commercial plays very cleverly on our romantic attitudes about the sea and our fascination with futuristic technology.

While "Ma Bell's" appeal to our homing instinct is equally clever and imaginative, the campaign is cloying in its not-so-subtle attempts to make us feel guilty for failing to "keep in touch" often (monthly, weekly, daily perhaps?) with all of our relatives and each of our old college pals.

Of course, such efforts to make us, the viewers, feel guilty for not using a given service or buying a certain product are nothing new to the world of the TV commercial. Because of their televised pitches, I know that "sooner or later" I will own General tires, that my next television set probably will be a Zenith System 3, and that I simply must get my hands on a Toyota.

In my mind's eye—and in yours—flit hundreds and hundreds of broadcast-advertising images, impinging upon one another in a cluttered mosaic of mediated desire: of beautiful young women blazing with sexual passion generated by Old Spice, of gorgeous damsels sensuously smoothing baby oil over their childlike skins, of nondescript homemakers in wonderment about how to get their husbands' underwear whiter-than-white, of rugged men joyful in their new cars, of modish kids on souped-up motorcycles. I find myself drooling slightly—and who doesn't—as colorful images of sizzling steaks, thick slabs of rare roast beef, and even humble hamburgers with secret sauce flash before me in my living room.

(*continued*)

Figure 1.3

The current battle of the light beers is one in which the advertising industry has shown considerable success, as well as imagination and inventiveness. Taking a drink that bombed when it was first marketed a number of years back as a kind of diet (read: ladies') beer and selling it to men by giving them super-masculine tough-guy role models is quite an achievement. The Miller Lite beer slogan—"Everything you've always wanted in a beer . . . and less"—has a nice touch of irony about it. I also like actor James Coburn's cheeky commercial for Schlitz Light. He gives an image of menacing machismo to this beer and in just a few seconds projects a steel-like hardness as he sidles up to the bar, his face grim and resolute. The other male figure in the commercial, spellbound and overcome with admiration, orders the same beer—and so, by implication, should we. There aren't many Westerns on television anymore, and fans of the genre have to be grateful to Coburn, who seems to condense an hour's worth of adventure into an entertaining half a minute.

There are several other excellent, action-packed ads for light beer, featuring heavyweight boxers and huge football players who rip open beer cans as if they were hand grenades. Thus we males are reassured that drinking a light beer will not make people think we are sissies. The massive authority of the National Football League and assorted toughs from boxing, the movie industry, and the world of accounting all guarantee our masculine identity and virility.

The guarantee seems to be working wonders on the typical male ego, for the market share of the various light brands has been growing by staggering proportions. Although there certainly are viewers of both sexes who find the macho thrust offensive, the tough-guy commercials also seem to be having what the advertising industry refers to as a "tag-along" effect on many women.

Could it be that these rough-and-tumble beer commercials are so effective because they provide more arresting entertainment than do today's criminally boring police-action shows? I have been asking myself this kind of question often since deciding to take a close look at the genre of the TV commercial.

I also find myself faced with many dilemmas. Should I be drinking the beer of kings or the king of beers? Should I feed my dog nutritionally balanced crunchy nuggets or nutritionally balanced soft 'n' chewy morsels? Should I combat the anxiety and pain generated by all the conflicting commercials with 100 percent aspirin or with a product that has no "upsetting" aspirin? (Will I ever discover what it is that Anacin has more of than any other leading pain remedy? Or should I use Bufferin, which promises me "protection" as well as relief?)

Figure 1.3 cont.

Theoretically, I suppose, like the donkey caught equidistant between two stacks of hay, I should be immobilized. But life doesn't seem to work that way, and, even with the commercials that fight it out in the open with their competitors, I find myself choosing sides. And sometimes for the underdog food.

The commercials I like most reflect my "seduction" by such elements as interesting dialogue, humor, beautiful images, clever cutting, fine acting, and so forth—including subliminal factors of which I may not be conscious. Among the fall season's entries, those I favor include: the Boeing 747 Japanese kite flyers, Juan Valdez picking Colombian coffee beans, Perrier water bubbling up from God-knows-where, United Airlines' Barry Fitzgeraldian Irish priest, the inner workings of La Machine by Moulinex, the Harlem Globetrotters' Sherwin Williams paint extravaganza, the Berlinetta "heartbeat" ad, Tuborg's vikings "going for the gold," the Make That Dessert spoof of game shows, the Porsche ad with the bored young woman, and (on the West Coast) most Wells Fargo Bank bits of Americana.

Some of the current commercials I hate, because they are dull, unimaginative, crude, sexist, vulgar, trite, obnoxious, and/or irritating are: Geritol's she-takes-it-because-she-loves-me campaign, National Rent-A-Car's "Green Team," Gillette Trac-2, Stovetop Stuffing, Special K, Brush Your Breath With Dentyne, That's My Dodge, Kentucky Fried Chicken's "It's so nice to feel so good about a meal," and Kenner Toys' "Baby Heart Beat." I could go on almost endlessly here.

Like other television viewers, I long resented having to watch commercials and considered them pernicious and, at times, dangerous to our mental health and general well-being. But many commercials are works of art—mini-dramas created to persuade and convince—that use the talents of some of our most imaginative and creative writers, photographers, directors, lyricists, and actors. In thirty seconds or so, they have to engage our interest, tell us some kind of a story, and leave us with a resolution to do something. They must accomplish all this by overcoming our inattention, our desire not to be bothered by them, and the clutter of competing commercials. They cost an enormous amount to produce, often many times that of regular programming on a cost-per-minute basis, and they cost a great deal more to air.

When I started watching television for the commercials it carries rather than the programming (or "fill" between commercials), I felt uncomfortable. The programming itself became a source of irritation to me, and I found myself anxiously waiting for the next commercials to

(continued)

Figure 1.3 cont.

come on. There seemed to be enormous gaps between commercials, and during them I reached an important insight.

I think we've been watching television the wrong way. Since advertising is the source of the television medium's profits and much of
its artistic experimentation, we should face up to reality and watch TV
primarily for its commercials. When we regard the commercials as the
essence of television and the programs as mere interruptions, the
medium takes on an entirely different dimension. The absurdity and
triviality of most television programs becomes understandable.

Who knows—we might all be better off if we went to the bath-
room and ran for snacks during the program and returned only for the
commercials. We might even have time to read a few more books and
magazines.

Figure 1.3 cont.

This book focuses on print advertisements and television commercials
and the role they may play in stimulating the consumption of products and
services by people. Traditionally we call sales messages in print "advertisements" and sales messages on electronic media, that use sound effects, music, and actors, "commercials." Originally, most of the sales messages on the
Internet were little more than print advertisements. Now, with new technological developments, we find pop-up screens, cartoon animations, and
other ways of attracting the attention of people using the Internet. The
methods of analysis I discuss can be used on all forms of advertising.

It is worth noting some of the ideas mentioned in the most common
definitions of advertising. We find such terms as "arouse" and "desire,"
which suggest there are very powerful "affective" and perhaps even unconscious or "irrational" elements at work in advertisements.

In his book *Visual Persuasion: The Role of Images in Advertising*, Paul
Messaris suggests that there may be certain kinds of hard-wired responses
in human beings that function as a result of visual cues to which they are
exposed. He discusses the work of a number of researchers in this area
and writes:

> When we look at the world, we are strongly predisposed to attend to cer-
> tain kinds of objects or situations and to react in certain kinds of ways.
> These predispositions reflect the influence of culture, but . . . they have
> also been shaped to a certain extent by biological evolution. In short,
> real-world vision comes with a set of built-in response tendencies. Con-

sequently, to the extent that a picture can reproduce the significant visual features of real-world experience, it may also be able to exploit the response tendencies that are associated with those features. (1997:4)

Messaris offers as an example of these "response tendencies" the use in magazine ads, and other kinds of advertising, of having someone—spokespersons in television commercials and models in magazine advertisements—look directly at the viewer or reader. In real life, we have a natural tendency to look back at someone when they look at us, and advertising agencies can exploit this in attracting our attention to their advertisements and generating emotional responses to them.

Later in the book I will quote from an article that makes an even stronger argument, namely that the famous experiment in which Ivan Pavlov was able to train dogs to act in certain ways when special cues were given to them is the basic metaphor for understanding how advertising works. That is, advertising conditions us—as individuals and as members of society—in the same way that Pavlov was able to train dogs.

In this chapter I do a number of things. Having broadly defined advertising, I offer a brief look at advertising agencies, followed by a model of advertising that deals with advertisements and commercials in terms of their cultural impact rather than their effects on individuals. Then I discuss how advertisers attempt to deflect criticism and tie this in to "weak" and "strong" theories of the media offered by communication scholars. Next I discuss the techniques used in commercials, which I consider to be the most powerful form of advertising. Finally, I relate commercials to "teleculture" and argue that television has become the dominant means of socialization in American culture and many other societies as well. We must always keep in mind that from a business point of view, what television does is deliver audiences to advertisers.

ADVERTISING AGENCIES

Advertising agencies, we must remember, are media businesses, and like all businesses they have human resource departments, accounting departments, production departments, and various levels of management (such as chief executive officers, chief financial officers, executive vice presidents, senior vice presidents, and ordinary vanilla vice presidents). They also have huge account management departments, with account supervisors, account directors, and many, many account executives. The job of account executives, generally speaking, is to look after the agency's clients. Some cynics have suggested that what account executives do best is take clients out to lunch.

But the most important employees of advertising agencies, I would suggest, are what are generally called the "creatives." The creatives are the creative directors and their teams of copywriters and art directors (and sometimes others), who turn all of the data provided by the marketing researchers into print ads and radio and television commercials. The creatives think up campaigns like "Got Milk" or the Absolut vodka advertisements and are the "stars" in any agency—the people who bring fame and fortune (in the form of new billings) to their agencies. Like all important creative artists, they are given a great deal of freedom. There are numerous awards given by organizations in the advertising industry and some creatives have dozens of awards to their credit.

Interestingly enough, for an industry seen as glamorous by most people, advertising doesn't always pay that well. The top management of big advertising agencies make a great deal of money, and the creatives do well, but most of the other people in advertising agencies aren't as well paid, as shown in table 1.1.

The figures in the table (taken from Salary Wizard) for small, medium sized, and large agencies are rounded off and very approximate. To understand the significance of these salaries you have to realize that a very good secretary might make $50,000 or $75,000 a year. Entry level positions in advertising are very low because there is a great deal of competition for what are thought to be "glamour" jobs. In addition, women everywhere are generally paid considerably less than men for doing the same job, though that is changing slowly.

Salaries are also affected by the size of the agency one works in and the location of the agency. Thus, in a major market such as the San Francisco Bay Area, account executives might earn around $75,000 and art directors around $115,000 or more, and workers in smaller agencies in smaller markets would earn considerably less. Salaries in big New York agencies are also

Table 1.1. Total Pay, 2005

Position	Size of Agency		
	Small	*Medium*	*Large*
Account Executive	$55,000	61,000	74,000
Creative Director	$81,000	85,000	111,000
Art Director	$78,000	97,000	115,000
Copywriter	$67,000	72,000	85,000

Insights from Advertising Agencies

The *Advertising Age* salary numbers are terribly misleading and have never reflected the reality of the workplace. These numbers have always been way understated. For example, an average Art Director would easily make $75K, a good one $150+. Associate Creative Directors make upwards from $150K. Creative Directors make far more money than indicated. This data does not include bonuses, which could be up to 50 percent, and other rewards like stock, etc. One of the reasons this data is distorted is because it is not a proper statistical sample and tends to reflect the smallest agencies with the fewest people. The larger and medium-sized agencies don't bother to respond. If you're in advertising and if you're good, you can make a lot of money. You do have to work your ass off and you do tend to be underpaid at the start for a fair amount of time. (Fred Goldberg, retired chairman and CEO of Goldberg Moser O'Neill)

---

considerably higher, while salaries in small, southern agencies are a good deal lower than those in the chart. But there are also bonuses that people who work in agencies get and other rewards, as well.

During my three weeks at Goldberg Moser O'Neill I interviewed people involved in every aspect of the advertising business and everyone intimated that it was *their* job that was absolutely crucial and that without them the place would fall apart. I found the people in these agencies to be, as a rule, very intelligent and extremely hardworking. The work is so demanding that advertising agencies have very high turnover rates; I was told by the GMO human resources director that the average advertising agency loses something like a third of its employees from burnout and other factors in a given year. In some cases people move to better jobs in other agencies, and others leave advertising for another career.

A PSYCHO-CULTURAL PERSPECTIVE ON ADVERTISING

The model many social scientists have used in studies of the impact of advertising is a psychological one (or perhaps a social-psychological one). People are tested to see whether they recall advertisements or whether their attitudes or opinions have been changed by having been exposed to advertisements. Figure 1.4 shows the social-psychological model.

Exposure to advertisement or commercial

↓

Recall, attitude change, opinion change

Figure 1.4. Social-Psychological Model

This approach, which often is quite sophisticated in terms of research design, frequently indicates that advertising has little or no effect on respondents. Or, to be more precise, none that can be detected or measured . . . or, in some cases, no long-term effects that can be measured.

I would like to suggest a different model (see figure 1.5), which focuses not upon attitude or opinion change but upon the effect upon the culture of advertising in general and in some cases, of a particular campaign.

Figure 1.5 focuses not on opinion or attitude change but instead on two different matters: One can broadly be defined as cultural behavior and the other as people's or perhaps the collective unconscious. Focusing on individuals or groups of individuals in test studies frequently concludes that advertising plays no significant role in decision making. An examination of advertising as a cultural phenomenon, on the other hand, suggests something quite different, a conclusion that might explain why revenues for advertising keep growing and why businesses continue to advertise.

RUNNING IT UP A FLAGPOLE
TO SEE IF ANYONE SALUTES

Corporations and organizations that advertise are not irrational; they do not spend money "running flags up flagpoles to see if anyone salutes" out of idle curiosity. (On the other hand, while companies that advertise may not be irrational, they assume people are irrational. More precisely, they assume that people respond to messages that avoid ego-dominated "ra-

People's psyches (the unconscious)

exposed ↓ *to*

Advertising

↓

Cultural behavior of people

Figure 1.5. Psycho–Cultural Model

tional" decision making, that have an effect on unconscious elements in their psyches that often shape their behavior.)

In his structural hypothesis, Sigmund Freud suggested that the human psyche was composed of three elements: the id, which represents drives (and says "I want it now"); the superego, which represents moral sensibilities and conscience (and says "don't do it"); and the ego, which has the task of perceiving and adapting to reality and mediating between the id and the superego. Freud described the id in his *New Introductory Lectures on Psychoanalysis*:

> We can come nearer to the id with images, and call it a chaos, a cauldron of seething excitement. We suppose that it is somewhere in direct contact with somatic processes, and takes over from them instinctual needs and gives them mental expression, but we cannot say in what substratum this contact is made. These instincts fill it with energy, but it has no organization and no unified will, only an impulsion to obtain satisfaction for the instinctual needs, in accordance with the pleasure principle. (quoted in Hinsie & Campbell, 1970, p. 372)

Thus, advertisements appeal to id elements in our psyches and our desires for gratifications of all kinds ("I want it now"), and seek to avoid the strictures of the superego ("you can't afford it and you don't need it") and the mediating efforts of the ego ("maybe you ought to think a bit before buying it").

The devaluation of the power of advertising by advertising agencies and by businesses that use advertising is generally an attempt to escape from regulation by governmental agencies and to escape from criticisms of being manipulative and, in some cases, antisocial, by consumer groups and other interested parties. Communication scholars, I might point out, have wavered in their assessments of the power of media. Thirty years ago, scholars concluded that the media were powerful; then they changed their minds and concluded that they are weak. (A famous scholar said something to the effect of "Some media sometimes have some effects on some people.") Now, it seems, the notion that the media are powerful is once again gaining acceptance.

Given this situation, when the media were seen as weak, advertisers could argue that advertising was relatively trivial—a service to inform or entertain the public, but little more than that. Yet at the macro level, when, we look at collective behavior, it seems that advertising does have power. *It is advertising's role as a cultural and political force that is significant.* We may lack the tools in the social sciences to show how advertising affects specific individuals or small groups of people in tests, but when we look at advertising as a social and cultural phenomenon, the situation is strikingly different.

One argument that advertising people use to defuse criticism is the *post hoc, ergo propter hoc* argument. Just because something happens *after* something doesn't mean it was *caused* by it. That is, just because Y follows X does not mean that X caused Y. Thus, if Lisa sees a beer commercial on television and then drinks a beer, it does not mean the commercial caused Lisa to drink the beer. Nobody can argue with this. But when you move to the collective level, and have lots of people drinking beer after having seen lots of beer commercials, there is good reason to believe that the beer commercials might have played some role in the behavior of the beer drinkers.

That is, commercials for alcoholic beverages may not be the sole causative factor responsible for people drinking, but they may play an important contributing role. Since the public airways are held "in trust," so to speak (and are supposed to broadcast "in the public interest"), by television stations, the question we must ask is whether this trust is being abused.

One reason it is so difficult to establish via experimental methods a direct causal link between television commercials and consumption is that television is so ubiquitous that it is very difficult to find a "control" group, a group of people who are not exposed to television. That is why I think the anthropological model is more useful than the social-psychological model.

COMMERCIALS AS MINI-DRAMAS AND WORKS OF ART

Commercials—in my opinion the most interesting and powerful form of advertising—should be seen as works of art that have their own conventions; they might best be thought of as mini-dramas that employ all the techniques of the theater and the cinema to achieve their aims. At their best, they use language brilliantly, they are dramatic, they employ the most sophisticated techniques of lighting and editing, they have wonderful actors who use body language and facial expressions to get their messages across, and they often cost enormous amounts of money, relatively speaking, to produce—many times, the production costs (on a per-minute basis) outstrip those of the programs during which they are shown.

The power of the human voice is well-known. When it is added to strong narratives, music, sound effects, and superb writing, it is easy to see why the commercial is such an incredible means of persuasion. Commercials (and advertisements in print and other media, to an extent) also make use of many of the following:

Heroes and Heroines

Young people often identify with heroes and heroines and try to emulate their behavior, their "style," or their images—if not in the real world, then in the world of consumption. Some of these heroic figures are showbusiness personalities—singers, dancers, comedians, actors, and athletes.

Sexuality

Many commercials overtly connect sex and consumption (figure 1.6). These commercials often feature extremely beautiful women; they are shown as an integral part of the consumption experience. One hopes, in one's unconscious, that by purchasing the product, one will get the beautiful woman (or some beautiful woman) as well—or in some cases, an attractive man. In recent years, advertising has used homoerotic appeals for gay men and lesbians. I talk at length about sexuality in advertising in Chapter 5.

Figure 1.6

Humor

At one time, advertisers were afraid of humor. Now they realize that humor sells, and many commercials are extremely funny (figure 1.7). This humor generates what might be called a "halo effect," a feeling of well-being that becomes attached to the products being advertised.

Since there is so much hostility toward advertising in the general public, many companies that use advertising are turning to humor as a means of entertaining viewers of their commercials and thus eliciting some good-

Figure 1.7

Table 1.2

Language	Logic	Identity	Action
Allusion	Absurdity	Before/After	Chase
Bombast	Accident	Burlesque	Slapstick
Definition	Analogy	Caricature	Speed
Exaggeration	Catalogue	Eccentricity	
Facetiousness	Coincidence	Embarrassment	
Infantilism	Comparison	Exposure	
Insults	Disappointment	Grotesque	
Irony	Ignorance	Imitation	
Misunderstanding	Mistakes	Impersonation	
Over literalness	Repetition	Mimicry	
Puns & Wordplay	Reversal	Parody	
Repartee	Rigidity	Scale	
Ridicule	Theme & Var.	Stereotype	
Sarcasm	Unmasking		
Satire			

will. Mirthful laughter generates endorphins in our brains that make us feel good and some of this may also rub off on the product being advertised. Humor also is a way of establishing relationships with others, so there is a value in using humor as long as it doesn't offend people and get in the way of the persuasive part of the advertisement.

A number of years ago I did some research on the techniques that generate humor in plays and other texts. I found that the techniques I discovered formed four different categories of humor. The list appears in table 1.2; you can use it to analyze humor in print advertisements and commercials, and all kinds of other works.

There is considerable disagreement among scholars about the definition of some of these terms, such as satire and parody, but most of them are more or less self-evident.

Fun

Jean Baudrillard, a French sociologist, argues that in modern consumer societies we now feel obliged to have fun. He writes in *The Consumer Society: Myths & Structure* (1998:80):

THE FUN SYSTEM OF FORCED ENJOYMENT

One of the strongest proofs that the principle and finality of consumption is not enjoyment or pleasure is that that is now something which is forced upon us, something institutionalized, not as a right or a pleasure but as the *duty* of the citizen. . . . Consumerist man . . . regards *enjoyment as an obligation*; he sees himself as *an enjoyment and satisfaction business.* He sees it as his duty to be happy, loving, adulating/adulated, charming/ charmed, participative, euphoric and dynamic.

This represents a reversal, Baudrillard adds, of the old Puritan ethic of hard work and abstention for the glory of God. It is now our "duty" to have fun, and we do this, to a great degree, by being a member in good standing (and good purchasing) of our contemporary consumer culture.

Success

In many commercials, we see (and it is suggested we emulate) people who use a given product or service and who are successful. One aspect of being successful is knowing what to consume—having "product knowledge," which has replaced regular knowledge in all too many people in America. They don't know history, are not well-read, have no appreciation of art, music, philosophy . . . you name it. But they have incredible product knowledge; that is, all they know is what they can buy.

I used to play a learning game in which I asked students to determine what products Americans would likely purchase based on their class makeup. I used a well-known classification system by sociologist W. Lloyd Warner, elaborated fifty years ago, that suggested we have six classes in America:

Class	Percentage of Population
Upper-Upper	1.4 percent
Lower-Upper	1.6 percent
Upper-Middle	10 percent
Lower-Middle	25 percent (common man and woman level)
Upper-Lower	35 percent (common man and woman level)
Lower-Lower	25 percent

These percentages still apply, generally speaking, with minor modifications. The percentage of wealth of the top 1 percent has increased considerably over the years and the number of people falling into poverty has also increased. The top 1 percent of Americans own 33 percent of the wealth in America, the same amount as the bottom 90 percent.

What I discovered is that my students were able to make a large number of very subtle distinctions about which products people in the various class levels might consume. There was a considerable debate among them about whether Lower-Upper class people would or should purchase a BMW or a Mercedes and which particular model of each car they would buy. They debated endlessly whether an entry-level BMW had more status than an entry level Mercedes. What this demonstrated to me is that my students had an enormous amount of what I call "product knowledge," based on their constant exposure to advertising in print and electronic media.

 Reward

Purchasing various products—such as soft drinks and automobiles—is often shown as a "reward" for people who have worked hard and who therefore "deserve" their drinks and sports utility vehicles. This appeal works at both the blue-collar and at the white-collar levels. The rewards one gets are fun, comradeship, pleasure, and sex. Especially sex. Our print advertisements and television commercials are pervaded by sex, and most Americans live in a sexually saturated media environment, where men and women are used as sex objects to sell everything from trucks to cruises.

TELECULTURE

The term "teleculture" suggests that our culture is, to a large degree, shaped by television. Thus, television is not a simple medium for entertainment, which merely reflects the culture in which it is found. Television does, of course, reflect culture, but the important thing to keep in mind is that it also profoundly *affects* culture. It does this, in part, by focusing attention on certain aspects of culture and not paying attention to others, by creating certain kinds of heroes and heroines and neglecting other kinds.

Insights from Advertising Agencies

We try to make ads that evoke an emotion—humor is often useful in this respect. We brainstorm together about ideas that might be used for an ad. Usually, we come up with three or four ideas for a spot. We're looking for the single most compelling idea to communicate.

In my opinion, television is the most powerful socializing and encul-turating force in society. It not only entertains us but also instructs us, even when it is not trying to do so. Thus, it has usurped the roles formerly played by other actors who used to be dominant figures in the socialization process. Let me list them below.

Parents

With the changes that have taken place in the family structure and the breakdown of both the family (due to the high numbers of divorces) and parental authority in America, the role of the parents in socializing young people has greatly diminished. Many children are now raised in one-parent families or in blended families.

Priests, Ministers, Rabbis

Nowadays the clergy also has a diminished role, though some of the priesthood has discovered television and now uses it for its various purposes. The use of television by the clergy, however, tends to be associated with fundamentalist sects (and, in some cases, charlatans) and not, in large mea-sure, with mainstream religious organizations.

Professors

At one time, teachers and other academics played a significant role in socializing young people, and in many cases they still do. But this role has also been diminished. This is because teachers cannot compete with popu-lar culture and in fact have to spend a good deal of their time doing what they can to counter the power of the media and popular culture.

Peers

It is widely known that children and adolescents are particularly sus-ceptible to peer pressure, and at various stages in their developmental cycle, peer pressure is much more significant to young people than parental pres-sure. What about these peers? Who or what, may we ask, socializes peers? Where do these peers get their values and attitudes? They, too, like the opinion leaders who allegedly affect the beliefs of older generations of peo-ple, are socialized by the media.

Pop Culture

It is, of course, simplistic to claim that popular culture and the mass media are the only determinants of behavior, but it probably is correct to argue that the media play a major role (or, at least, an increasingly important role) in the socialization of young people. And it is television that is of major significance here—for it is television that broadcasts (and affects, as well) much of our popular culture.

The most important genre on television is, of course, the commercial. Teleculture is, in large measure, commercials and thus plays an important role in creating and maintaining consumer cultures.

Baudrillard devotes the last section of his book *The System of Objects* to advertising. He makes an interesting point in his analysis:

> Neither its rhetoric nor even the information aspect of its discourse has a decisive effect on the buyer. What the individual does respond to, on the other hand, is advertising's underlying leitmotiv of protection and gratification, the intimation that its solicitations and attempts to persuade are the sign, indecipherable at the conscious level, that somewhere is an agency . . . which has taken it upon itself to inform him of his own desires, and to foresee and rationalize these desires to his own satisfaction. He thus no more "believes" in advertising than the child believes in Father Christmas, but this is no way impedes his capacity to embrace an internalized infantile situation, and to act accordingly. Herein lies the very real effectiveness of advertising, founded on its obedience to a logic which, though not that of the conditioned reflex, is nonetheless very rigorous: a logic of belief and regression. (1968:167)

This is an important insight to keep in mind. Baudrillard doesn't think advertising works by use of conditioned reflexes, but by regressing people to infantile states. It may be that advertising uses both *conditioning* (think of Pavlov here) and *regression* (think of Freud here) in accomplishing its mission.

In 1951, Marshall McLuhan wrote a pioneering book, *The Mechanical Bride,* which was devoted to understanding the role that popular culture, the media, and, in particular, advertising played in shaping people's consciousness. The book analyzes the symbolic and cultural significance of comic strips and the front pages of newspapers, but most of *The Mechanical Bride* is devoted to advertisements that McLuhan mines for their cultural importance.

He explains the problems caused by entertainment and pop culture and his method of operation in the Preface to the book (1951:v):

> Ours is the first age in which many thousands of the best-trained individual minds have made it a full-time business to get inside the collective public mind. To get inside in order to manipulate, exploit, control is the object now. And to generate heat not light is the intention. To keep everybody in the helpless state engendered by prolonged mental rutting is the effect of many ads and much entertainment alike. . . . The present book likewise makes few attempts to attach the very considerable currents and pressures set up around us today by the mechanical agencies of
> . the press, radio, movies, and advertising. It does attempt to set the reader at the center of the revolving picture created by these affairs where he may observe the action that is in progress and in which everybody is involved. From the analysis of that action, it is hoped, many individual strategies may suggest themselves.

It is McLuhan's aim to waken people from the collective dream in which they find themselves by using the methods of art criticism and literary analysis to show how advertising agencies manipulate people and strive to obtain the effects they seek—shaping consumer taste and behavior.

Each of the short chapters in the book contains an image—usually of some advertisement—and some elliptical questions, and his analysis, often written in a rather jazzy style, of the social, psychological, and cultural significance of the language and images in the advertisement.

THE SUPER BOWL

The 2006 Super Bowl, held on February 5th, attracted an audience of something like 90 million people in the United States and hundreds of millions of people in more than 200 other countries. There are a number of reasons why companies advertise during the Super Bowl, even if the cost of doing so is very high in dollar terms. First, there is a good deal of prestige connected with having a commercial shown during the game. Companies recognize that having a commercial during the Super Bowl attracts a great deal of interest in the media, as well as the general public.

In addition, because Super Bowl commercials are "showcase" advertisements, which are specially designed for their entertainment value, people watching the game—especially the hard-to-reach males between 18 and 40—tend to also watch the commercials rather than zapping them. The audience for the game wants to see which commercials are outstanding, and having a commercial that is successful is an important plus for advertisers and the agencies that make the commercials. A highly successful commercial helps "make" a brand by attracting the attention and entertaining members of the Super Bowl audience. Commercials on the Super Bowl can help companies that are relatively unknown make a name for themselves.

One company, Budweiser, is the only beer company that advertises on the Super Bowl. It purchased five minutes of ad time in 2006 for its various brands—more than any other advertiser for the game. Budweiser prepares for the broadcast by having advertising agencies create something like fifty different spots that might be used in the game. It then pares the list down to the final ones it will use just before the game. It is in a battle with other advertisers such as Burger King and Pepsi to create memorable commercials. A number of these commercials will be humorous, some will have celebrities, and others will feature animals; and all of them will attempt to become the subject of positive commentary by those who watched the game.

Super Bowl commercials that "bomb" and that fall flat, for one reason or another, are a disaster. Not only do they turn off members of the audience, they are likely to be ridiculed in media reports on the Super Bowl commercials. So the stakes are very high and there is a great deal of competition among the advertising agencies who make the commercials shown during Super Bowl to create "winning" commercials.

The only major competitor to the Super Bowl in building brands is the Winter Olympics, which last for seventeen days and give advertisers more opportunity over the course of the games to reach viewers. For a little more than the $2.5 million a Super Bowl commercial costs, an advertiser can have four spots on the Winter Olympics. The Super Bowl only lasts a few hours, though with the pre-game and post-game shows, it can drag on for much longer than that. Thirty-second spots during the Olympics only cost some $700,000 and over the course of the games, NBC expects to make around $900 million dollars.

One of the reasons the Super Bowl is such an important site for commercials is that the media world is so fragmented. Advertisers know that a large number of Americans, especially males who are often hard to reach, will be watching the game, so it is an extremely useful way for companies to get their messages across to audiences they target.

CONCLUSION

Let me offer here a summary of the main points I have made and a summary of the conclusions I draw from these points.

First, advertising is a huge industry that plays an important role in the socialization of people, young and old, in American society. It provides what might be called "product knowledge," and research evidence suggests that even young children, at 5 or 6 years of age, know a great deal about many of the products advertised on television (and are often able to sing the jingles from commercials).

Second, corporations advertise because it is effective in a number of different ways. Advertising campaigns often have as their primary goal, we are told, holding market share, but it is reasonable to suggest that these campaigns also attract new users. People who are exposed to commercial campaigns may not be able to recall the commercials they have seen or provide evidence that their opinions and attitudes have been affected, but advertising campaigns leave a certain kind of feeling with people, generate a certain kind of sensibility.

In addition, I have suggested that television commercials, in particular, are extremely complicated and powerful texts (or artworks) that work a number of different ways. I list, later in the book, some of the factors to be considered in analyzing commercials. This complexity, the fact that works of art affect people in strange and complicated ways, makes it difficult to measure their effects. But the fact that corporations continue to advertise, and often increase their advertising budgets each year, leads us to conclude that advertising does work. We have only to look around us and observe the way people behave (in supermarkets, at work, at parties) to see the power of advertising.

Finally, I have suggested that commercials are part of what I call "teleculture," which is now probably the most important enculturating and socializing force operating in society. It is naive to think of television (or any of the mass media) as simply an entertainment that does not have a profound impact upon the people who watch it. For one thing, we know that the average person watches television more than three and one-half hours per day. If television does generate "culture," as I've argued, that is a tremendous amount of time for it to enculturate people.

Television has usurped the place that used to be occupied by parents, the clergy, teachers, and other institutions as socializers of the young. We learn from all of our experiences, a phenomenon called incidental learning (though we may not be conscious of the fact that we are learning), and since television is such a large part of our experience, it must play an important role in "teaching" us about life. And commercials are the most ubiquitous genre on television and quite probably the most powerful one.

In this book you will not only learn how to analyze print advertisements and television commercials but will also learn about the impact of the advertising industry on you, on the political order, and on American society and culture. I also offer some examples of analyses I've made of interesting print advertisements and television commercials.

I hope that as a result of reading this book you will be better able to resist "saluting" when some advertising agency creates an advertisement or a radio or television commercial and "runs it up a flagpole."

Advertising transfers its breadth of experience and calculation to its target groups. It treats its human targets like commodities, to whom it offers the solution to their problem of realization. Clothes are advertised like packaging as a means of sales promotion. This is one of the many ways in which commodity aesthetics takes possession of people.

The two central areas in which advertising offers, by means of commodities, to solve the problems of "scoring hits" and sales are, on the one hand, following a career of the labour market and, on the other, gaining the respect of and attracting others. "How is it that clever and competent people don't make it in their careers?" was the question put by a wool advertisement in 1968. "Don't call it bad luck if it is only a matter of 'packaging.' You can sell yourself better in a new suit! And that is often what counts in life." A woman whose romance has failed and who is looking for a new partner was recommended by Teen magazine in 1969, as "step 9" in its advice, to "become overwhelmingly pretty. . . . Why not try what you've never tried before? If you want to scour the market, you've got to show yourself in your best packaging." Where love succeeds, brought about by this fashionable packaging, and leads to encounters which under existing conditions appear in the form of a commodity-cash nexus, the cost of clothes can be interpreted as "capital investment."

—W. F. Haug, *Critique of Commodity Aesthetics: Appearance, Sexuality, and Advertising in Capitalist Society*

2

CONSUMER CULTURES

Students who take courses in critical thinking learn about a major fallacy in thinking called the *post hoc, ergo propter hoc* fallacy. This Latin phrase, discussed earlier, means, roughly speaking, "after something, therefore because of it." Just because someone sees a commercial for some product, such as a Norelco electric razor, and then purchases a Norelco razor, doesn't mean that the commercial necessarily was the prime factor or the only factor leading to the purchase decision. There could have been any number of other factors, or combinations of factors, such as the person's old razor breaking down, a terrific sale on Norelco razors, word of mouth from a friend who has one, and so on.

It is important that we don't oversimplify matters in dealing with advertising. But we also must not underestimate or neglect advertising's influence upon us as individuals and its influence upon our society and culture. Advertising now permeates American culture and has affected, in profound ways, everything from our food preferences and our body shapes to our politics.

A CULTURAL CRITIQUE OF ADVERTISING

The discussion of the impact of advertising on American personality, culture, and society that follows is best understood as an example of cultural criticism. Cultural criticism makes use of psychoanalytic theory, literary theory, Marxist theory, sociological theory, semiotic theory, and various other theories, methodologies, and disciplines that can be used as means of interpreting texts and understanding social and cultural behavior. What I offer here is my interpretation of the impact of advertising on a number of important aspects of American culture and society. My analysis will also draw upon critiques and interpretations of advertising made by other scholars in America and elsewhere. Although my focus is on advertising in the United States, the concepts I use and techniques I explain can also be used to analyze advertising in other countries.

29

Advertising has been of interest to scholars in many disciplines because these scholars see advertising as one of the central institutions in American society. Americans, we must keep in mind, are exposed to more advertising than people in any other society. This is because of the amount of television we watch and the amount of time we spend listening to the radio and because our media tend to be privately owned and financed by advertising. Our media institutions are mostly private, for-profit ones; public television and public radio attract relatively small (though generally highly influential) audiences in America.

David Potter, in his classic work *People of Plenty*, points out that advertising not only has economic consequences, but it also shapes our values. As he writes:

The most important effects of this powerful institution are not upon the economics of our distributive system; they are upon the values of our society. If the economic effect is to make the purchaser like what he buys, the social effect is, in a parallel but broader sense, to make the individual like what he gets—to enforce already existing attitudes, to diminish the range and variety of choices, and in terms of abundance, to exalt the materialistic virtues of consumption. (1954:188)

Potter makes an important point. Advertising, as an industry, is often quite avant-garde and bold in the techniques it uses but, ironically, its impact tends to be a conservative one—to maintain, as much as possible, the status quo. One of the main things companies that advertise try to do is maintain their market share; if they can increase it, all the better. But they don't want to lose share at any cost. And advertising must be examined not only in terms of its economic impact but also in terms of its influence on American beliefs and values.

In this chapter and the ones that follow I discuss topics such as consumer cultures and consumer "lust," the use of sexuality to sell products and services, political advertising, and related matters.

CONSUMER CULTURES DEFINED

Consumer cultures, as I understand them, are those in which there has been a great expansion (some might say a veritable explosion) of commodity production, leading to societies full of consumer goods and services and places where these consumer goods and services can be purchased. In consumer cultures, the "game" people play is "get as much as you can." Success is defined as being the person "who has the most toys." This leads to a lust for consuming products—and conspicuously displaying them—as a means of demonstrating that one is a success and, ultimately, that one is worthy. And the very act of consumption has now also become aestheticized and sexualized and is itself the source of a great deal of pleasure.

In *Consumer Culture and Postmodernism*, Mike Featherstone explains the importance of "lifestyle" in contemporary consumer societies. He writes:

Rather than unreflexively adopting a lifestyle, through tradition or habit, the new heroes of consumer culture make lifestyle a life project and display their individuality and sense of style in the particularity of the assemblage of goods, clothes, practices, experiences, appearance and bodily dispositions they design together into a lifestyle. The modern individual within consumer culture is made conscious that he speaks not only with his clothes, but also with his home, furnishings, decoration, car and other activities which are to be read and classified in terms of the presence and absence of taste. The preoccupation with customizing a lifestyle and a stylistic self-consciousness are not just to be found among the young and the affluent; consumer culture publicity [advertising] suggests that we all have room for self-improvement and self-expression whatever our age or class origins. (1991:86)

And, of course, it is advertising that "teaches" us about the world of consumer goods—what is fashionable and "hot" or, maybe even better for some people, "cool." Semioticians tell us that everything we do is read as a "message" and that we are always sending these messages to other people— just as they are always sending messages to us. These messages are sent by our lifestyle decisions—our clothes, hairstyles, cars, homes, and other material goods—as well as our bodies, facial expressions, and body language. For example, serving the right brand of wine shows that we are sophisticated and have good taste. The advertisements for expensive wine must also be elegant and reflect a sense of refinement (figure 2.1).

Figure 2.1. Beringer Wine Estates

Along with the growth of the supply of material objects, there is also a growth of leisure—which must be filled with the right kind of activities, depending upon one's social class and status. Thus, *upscale* (those with high incomes and an appreciation of elite culture) people also consume high-art cultural products—operas, plays, works of sculpture, paintings, and so on, while those in a lower class tend to consume more ordinary products—inexpensive clothes, drive-to vacations, and fast food, for example.

It doesn't always work exactly that way; some people with limited incomes love opera and ballet, but generally speaking, there is a connection between socioeconomic status and taste level. More elite elements in society (socioeconomically speaking, that is) take expensive vacations, drive expensive cars, and go to trendy and generally expensive restaurants, for example.

TASTE CULTURES AND ADVERTISING

Sociologist Herbert Gans suggested that there are a number of what he called "taste cultures" in the United States. As he writes in his book *Popular Culture and High Culture: An Evaluation of Taste* (1974:x):

> I suggest that America is actually made up of a number of taste cultures, each with its own art, literature, music, and so forth, which differ mainly in that they express different aesthetic standards. . . . The underlying assumption of this analysis is that all taste cultures are of equal worth. . . . Because taste cultures reflect the class and particularly education attributes of their publics, low culture is as valid for poorly educated Americans as high culture is for well-educated ones, even if the higher cultures are, in the abstract, better or more comprehensive than the lower cultures.

These five taste cultures are: high culture, upper-middle culture, lower-middle culture, low culture, and quasi-folk culture. This classification system is similar, in many respects, to the six socioeconomic classes that W. Lloyd Warner found when he analyzed American society.

If Gans is correct and there are these five different taste cultures, this poses a problem: It means advertising agencies have to figure out how to direct messages that will resonate with the various taste cultures. One way that advertising agencies have addressed this problem is by targeting different audiences. That is, advertising agencies look for ways of reach specific audiences for particular products and services, which means, for example, they have to determine who will most likely be watching a certain television program. The larger the audience, the more difficult it is to find ways of reaching all the different taste cultures in print ads and radio and television commercials.

Gans offers some comments about advertising in his book that are worth thinking about. (1974: 35-36):

> Unknown numbers of children and adults are . . . taken in by the puffery and exaggeration of advertising, and ought to be protected against it; but part of the attractiveness of the ads is that people want the offered goods and it is not at all certain that the ads themselves initiate the wants. Nor it is wrong that people should want things that are useful or provide pleasure. Moreover, studies of advertising impact and the complaints of advertising executives suggest that most people retain little of the ad content they see and misinterpret much of the message. Successful ads produce sharp increases in sales curves, but often these reflect the behavior of only a few hundred thousand people and no one yet knows the relative impact of ad and product on buying decisions.

These comments reflect notions about advertising that were rather common some thirty years ago, when it was generally held that the impact of the media was weak. Nowadays, there is less ambivalence about the power of the media and of advertising.

THE POSTMODERN PERSPECTIVE

We often see the term "postmodern" in newspapers and magazines, generally referring to buildings that blend a number of different styles together. For example, Philip Johnson's AT&T building has Roman colonnades at the street level and a Chippendale pediment at the top. But postmodernism is broader than architecture, and has been used by some philosophers and cultural theorists to characterize contemporary societies in which pastiche and a mixing of styles is dominant. The term means, literally, coming after or moving beyond modernism—the period covering (approximately) from 1900 to 1960, which was characterized by a sense that we could know reality and that there were valid rules that governed politics and society.

An influential postmodernist theoretician, Jean-François Lyotard, described postmodernism as "incredulity toward meta-narratives," by which he meant a lack of acceptance of the great philosophical systems that had ordered our lives in the past. He writes:

Eclecticism is the degree zero of contemporary general culture: one listens to reggae, watches a Western, eats McDonald's food for lunch and
local cuisine for dinner, wears Paris perfume in Tokyo and "retro"
clothes in Hong Kong; knowledge is a matter for TV games. It is easy to
find a public for eclectic works. By becoming kitsch, art panders to the
confusion which reigns in the "taste" of the patrons. Artists, gallery owners, critics, and public wallow together in the "anything goes," and the
epoch is one of slackening. But this realism of the "anything goes" is in
fact that of money; in the absence of aesthetic criteria, it remains possible and useful to assess the value of works of art according to the profits they yield. (1984:76)

What Lyotard is describing is the world in which we live, in which—
without any rules that everyone accepts—we all create and change our
lifestyles and identities whenever we feel like doing so. Postmodernism
also doesn't accept that there are significant differences between elite
forms of art and popular or mass-mediated forms and isn't concerned
about narratives having the traditional beginning, middle, and end, in
which everything is resolved. In the postmodern world, simulations are
dominant and everyone is playing games with everyone else. In the postmodernist world, remember, anything goes.

One important theorist of postmodernism, Fredric Jameson, has argued that what we call postmodernism is, in reality, the form that capitalism takes in advanced capitalist societies. The most widespread and eclectic
art form in our day, I would suggest, is the advertisement, which helps us
decide upon what to consume to create our "eclectic" lifestyles. Madison
Avenue and the advertising world have been quick to adopt the postmodern sensibility, and now we see television commercials that don't seem to
make any sense. Things happen but they don't seem to mean anything.

What's important in these commercials is their "look." Jack Solomon
describes a postmodern television commercial for a perfume. He writes in
The Signs of Our Time:

> Traditional commercials often set up a narrative situation of some sort,
> which, though trivial, has a beginning, middle, and an end—as when
> Mrs. Olson saves her young neighbors' marriage by introducing them to
> Folger's Coffee. But in Calvin Klein's postmodern campaign for Obses-
> sion perfume, it's virtually impossible to tell just what is going on. A tor-
> mented woman seems to be torn between a young boy and an older
> man—or does the young boy represent a flashback to the older man's
> youth? Maybe it's her kid brother? Her son? She touches his face for an

instant but he refuses to be touched and glides away. Tears run down her
glacial Art Deco face, but it isn't clear what she's crying about. (1990:229)

It may very well be the confusion created by this commercial that is part of
the sell, but it also may be wrong to look for logic and rationality in a postmodern television commercial. The assumption has to be made that people
with a postmodern sensibility will "get" whatever message the Obsession
commercial is delivering to them.

One essential attribute of postmodernism, as it relates to advertising,
involves what has been described as "de-differentiation." In their book *Consumer Behaviour: A European Perspective,* Gary Barmossy, Soren Askegaard,
and Michael Solomon describe this phenomenon (2002:560):

> Postmodernists are interested in the blurring of distinctions between hi-
> erarchies such as "high and low culture," or politics and show business.
> Examples would be the use of artistic works in advertising and the cele-
> bration of advertising in artistic works. Companies such as Coca-Cola,
> Nike and Guinness have their own museums. Another clear example is
> TV programmes featuring advertising for themselves (in order to increase
> viewer ratings) and TV commercials [that] look like "real" programming,
> as the ongoing soap opera with a couple spun around the coffee brand
> Gold Blend. The blurring of gender categories also refers to this aspect
> of postmodernism.

The authors add fragmentation, by which they mean the ever-growing
brand extensions and categories of products, and hyperreality, involving
simulations and a loss of an ability to distinguish between the authentic and
simulations, as other important aspects of postmodernism.

In postmodern societies, where there are no all-encompassing and
dominating philosophical and ethical belief systems, the notion of a coherent identity is not valued and people are constantly changing their identities
and "looks," and these changes all are tied to purchasing the right products.
Postmodern societies are consumption societies in which people are always
looking for the next craze—whether it is iPods or a new brand of sneaker.

If the postmodern theorists are correct postmodernism represents an
important change in our culture, a "cultural mutation" that has taken place,
which explains why American culture is the way it is and why our young
people behave the way they do. Some critics of postmodernism argue that
it was a passing fad and that we now live in what they describe as a post-
postmodern era. The debate about postmodernism and its influence upon
American culture and society continues in our universities.

CONSUMER CULTURE AND PRIVATISM

One of the most important critiques scholars and social critics make of
the consumer culture is that it is privatistic; the focus is upon personal consumption, not social investment for the public good. Governments spend
also, but if a governmental agency helps build up the infrastructure in some
city, that spending yields jobs and increased productivity and is really a form
of investment. Personal consumption, on the other hand, is based on private desires and the satisfaction of individual wishes. It may have a marginal
benefit to society because the money spent on personal consumption "drips
down" to other people, but economists generally find the amount of
money dripping down to be quite minimal.

A number of years ago, a company that manufactured eyedrops suggested that using its product was the solution to smog and polluted air.
Rather than fix the quality of air for everyone, this company suggested
everyone use its eyedrops instead. When you push the argument to its most
extreme end, society is an abstraction and there are only individuals inhab-
iting the same territory, each of whom pursues (and should pursue) his or
her private destiny. From this perspective, the worse things are, the more
opportunities there are to sell products to people, so the market economy
may have an implicit stake in social disorganization and the neglect of the
public sphere.

Advertising, since it is paid for by private entities, does not generally
have a social-investment message to it but instead focuses upon individuals
pursuing their private passions. "The hell with everyone else" is the subtext
of many of these messages. And as American society becomes more and
more split into two classes, one that is increasingly wealthy and one that is
increasingly poor, the social tensions and possibilities for serious class conflict become stronger. People can retreat to gated communities to avoid
crime, but they end up prisoners of those communities. My point, then, is
that advertising often distracts us from paying attention to the need for social investments, from a concern for the public sphere, and thus, by its very
nature, tends to be politically conservative.

NEIMAN MARCUS AND "COUTHIFICATION"

There is a great deal of pressure upon people to show taste and discrimination, suitable to their place in the great chain of being (that is, to
their socioeconomic status), in the products and services they consume.

Neiman Marcus, for example, was useful to oil millionaires who had plenty of money but no sense of style adequate to their financial resources. What Neiman Marcus did was what I would describe as "couthification." The salespeople at Neiman Marcus made sure that nouveau riche oil millionaires purchased the right clothes for themselves and their families and bought the right home furnishings. (Stanley Marcus provided this insight to me when we appeared on a radio program together.)

The famous Neiman Marcus catalogs, with their absurdly expensive "his" and "hers" gifts, generated a great deal of publicity for the store and also generated a halo effect for items purchased at Neiman Marcus. Anything bought there was, Neiman Marcus suggested, by definition stylish and in good taste. For people with no taste, Neiman Marcus—and the legion of other stores like it—provided an escape from the anxiety of showing poor taste. Neiman Marcus was expensive, but it was worth it.

On the radio program we were on, I suggested to Stanley Marcus that department stores, such as Neiman Marcus, reminded me of medieval cathedrals. One can find interesting parallels between the two. These similarities are reflected in table 2.1.

We can see from the parallels between department stores and cathedrals that there is something holy, something of the sacred, connected to purchasing objects—the things we buy are signs, it can be surmised, that we have been blessed. And so we consume, often with religious fervor—even though we may not recognize the sacred dimension of our activities.

In his book *The Waning of the Middle Ages*, the historian Johan Huizinga explains how the two realms—the sacred and the secular—merged into one another. He writes:

Table 2.1. Department Stores as Functional Alternatives to Cathedrals

Department Store	Cathedral
Modern	Medieval
Paradisical: Heaven on Earth Now	Paradisical: Heaven in the Future
Merchandising	Passion: Salvation
Sales: Save Money	Prayer: Save Souls
Sacred Texts: Catalogs	Sacred Texts: Bible, Prayer Books
Clerks	Clergy
Sell: Products	Sell: God
Possessions as Signs of Spiritual Election	Holiness as a Sign of Spiritual Election
Big Sales	Religious Holidays
Sale of an Expensive Product	Conversion of a Sinner
Buy Incredible Gifts	Experience Miracles
Pay Taxes	Pay Tithe
Muzac	Religious Music
Lighting to Sell	Lighting to Inspire Reverence
Bad Credit	Penance
Advertising	Proselytizing
Cash Register	Offering Plate
Brand Loyalty	Devotion

> All life was saturated with religion to such an extent that the people were in constant danger of losing sight of the distinction between things spiritual and things temporal. If, on the one hand, all the details of ordinary life may be raised to a sacred level, on the other hand, all that is holy sinks to the commonplace, by the fact of being blended with everyday life. (1924:156)

Our lives, in contemporary consumer cultures, are saturated with commercials and other forms of advertising. And beneath these advertisements and fueling our desire to consume more and more products is, I would suggest, a sense that our actions have an unconscious and ultimately religious dimension to them; they are a means of showing our "election" (a good Puritan term) and that we are the worthy beneficiaries of God's grace.

NEEDS ARE FINITE, DESIRES ARE INFINITE

In America, as the quintessential consumer culture (not that many Western European, Asian, or Latin American countries are far behind us), what you can afford becomes the means of determining who you are . . . or who people think you are. In earlier days, consumption was more or less

limited to a small percentage of fabulously wealthy industrialists and entre-
preneurs. America's great genius has been to spread consumer lust to the
middle classes, and for some items, to the lower classes.

One problem with consumer cultures is that people become too caught
up in consuming things as a means of validating themselves and proving
their worth (there is a religious dimension to this, ultimately, as my discussion of department stores and cathedrals suggests). In consumer cultures, all
too often people don't think about what they have but only concern themselves with what they don't have. And that is, in part, because advertising
constantly reminds them of what they don't have. Needs are finite but desires are infinite, and thus, as soon as our needs have been taken care of, we
become obsessed with what we don't have but want. Or, more precisely,
one might suggest, with what advertising tells us we should want.

What advertising does, among other things, is manufacture desire and
shape it, and thus create people who are insatiable and who have been conditioned to continually lust for more things. And the more we have the
more we want. Because the things we buy—the sports utility vehicles, the
expensive vacations, the trophy wives and husbands—are evidence that we
believe of our intelligence, industry, potency, and ultimately, our worth (in
man's and God's eyes).

Paco Underhill, a "retail anthropologist" who studies shoppers for a
living, has noticed this in his work:

> At that exalted level, shopping is a transforming experience, a method of
> becoming a newer, perhaps even slightly improved person. The products
> you buy turn you into that other, idealized version of yourself. That dress
> makes you beautiful, this lipstick makes you kissable, that lamp turns your
> house into an elegant showplace. (2000:116–17)

In his influential book *Ways of Seeing* (also a British Broadcasting
Company television series), the British critic and novelist John Berger of-
fers what is, in essence, a Marxist critique of advertising or "publicity."
He writes:

> It proposes to each of us that we transform ourselves, or our lives, by
> buying something more.
> This more, it proposes, will make us in some way richer—even though
> we will be poorer for having spent our money.
> Publicity persuades us of such a transformation by showing us people
> who have apparently been transformed and are, as a result, enviable. The
> state of being envied is what constitutes glamour. And publicity is the

process of manufacturing glamour. . . . Publicity is never a celebration of pleasure-in-itself. Publicity is always about the future buyer. It offers him an image of himself made glamorous by the product or opportunity it is trying to sell. The image then makes him envious of himself as he might be. Yet what makes this self-which-he-might-be enviable? The envy of others. Publicity is about social relations, not objects. (1972:131, 132)

This is an important point. What Berger suggests is that advertising takes advantage of the desire we have for a better life for ourselves and our loved ones and uses our envy of others and of ourselves—as we might be if we purchase the right things—against us.

MIMETIC DESIRE

The French literary theorist René Girard has a fascinating theory about why we consume things, which he explains in his book *A Theater of Envy: William Shakespeare*. According to Girard, what we desire is what others desire; and "mimetic desire" means we imitate their desire—whether it be for material possessions or marriage partners. Girard argues that mimetic desire explains the behavior of Shakespeare's characters who desire people essentially because others desire them.

As Girard explains:

When we think of those phenomena in which mimicry is likely to play a role, we enumerate such things as dress, mannerisms, facial expressions, speech, stage acting, artistic creation, and so forth. Consequently, we see imitation in social life as a force for gregariousness and bland conformity through the mass reproduction of a few social models.

If imitation also plays a role in desire, if it contaminates our urge to acquire and possess, this conventional view, while not entirely false, misses the main point. Imitation does not merely draw people together, it pulls them apart. Paradoxically, it can do these two things simultaneously. Individuals who desire the same thing are united by something so powerful that, as long as they can share whatever they desire, they remain the best of friends; as soon as they cannot, they become the worst of enemies. (1991:3)

Girard sees mimetic desire and rivalry as a fundamental source of human conflict and suggests that Shakespeare understood the role mimetic desire plays in our behavior. He continually made use of it as a motivating force for characters in his dramas.

Girard offers an example: Helen of Troy and the Trojan War. As he explains, perhaps oversimplifying a bit to make his point (1991:123): "The only reason the Greeks want her back is because the Trojans want to keep her. The only reason the Trojans want to keep her is because the Greeks want her back." What Girard shows, here, is the awesome power of this generally unrecognized force, mimetic desire.

It is also, I believe, a motivating force in our behavior as consumers. It is mimetic desire that helps explain our consumer lust; we desire what others have desired and have purchased, especially those we look up to—such as celebrities, movie stars, and sports heroes. Our desire imitates their desire, which takes the form of our purchasing various products that they have desired and purchased . . . or that they tell us they desire by appearing in advertisements and commercials for these products.

The point here is not only that we identify with and want to imitate these celebrities who advertise products or whose lifestyles we admire. By imitating their lifestyles and product choices, we are caught by a much stronger force, which we do not recognize—our imitating their desires.

ARE THERE FOUR CONSUMER CULTURES, NOT JUST ONE?

When we talk about consumer cultures, we use the term to describe the fact that the private consumption of objects and services is a cultural dominant in many different modern societies. But it may be a simplification to say that there is just one consumer culture. It can be argued that there are actually four different consumer cultures found in democratic societies, based on certain beliefs and values (tied to the strength or weakness of group affiliations and adherence to few or many rules by people in these groups that members hold in common).

This analysis draws on the cultural theories of a political scientist, Aaron Wildavsky, and a social anthropologist, Mary Douglas. Wildavsky suggested

---

Insights from Advertising Agencies

Bianca Jagger would be a good person to associate with the wine we're trying to advertise, since she's one of the new artistocracy or celibritocracy. They are the opinion leaders and style setters thrown up by the world of pop culture, who set trends and influence a number of "hip" people.

that cultural theory tries to help people answer two basic questions—the question of *identity:Who am I?* and the question of *action:What should I do?* Wildavsky writes, in his chapter "A Cultural Theory of Preference Formation":

> The question of identity may be answered by saying the individuals belong to a strong group, a collective that makes decisions binding on all members, or that their ties to others are weak in that their choices bind only themselves. The question of action is answered by responding that the individual is subject to many or few prescriptions, a free spirit or tightly constrained. The strength or weakness of group boundaries and the numerous or few, varied or similar, prescriptions binding or freeing individuals are the components of their culture. (1989:25)

We find, then, that there are four political cultures—and, by extension, so Douglas argues, consumer cultures—that arise from this situation. Wildavsky calls his four political cultures hierarchical or elitist, individualist, egalitarian, and fatalist. These cultures are created by the strength and weakness of group boundaries and the numbers and kinds of rules and prescriptions. Social scientists Michael Thompson, Richard Ellis, and Aaron Wildavsky point out, in their book *Cultural Theory,* how the four cultures are derived:

> Strong group boundaries coupled with minimal prescriptions produce social relations that are egalitarian. . . . When an individual's social environment is characterized by strong group boundaries and binding prescriptions, the resulting social relations are hierarchical [sometimes known as elitist]. . . . Individuals who are bounded by neither group incorporation nor prescribed roles inhabit an individualistic social context. In such an environment all boundaries are provisional and subject to negotiation. . . . People who find themselves subject to binding prescriptions and are excluded from group membership exemplify the fatalistic way of life. Fatalists are controlled from without. (1990:6-7)

The basic characteristics of these four political and consumer cultures are described below.

Hierarchical/Elitists

Hierarchical/Elitists believe in the need for hierarchy in societies, but feel a sense of obligation to those below them.

Individualists

Individualists feel that individuals are basic and that the role of government should be minimal—protecting against crime and invasions and maximizing possibilities for individuals in the business world. They have little sense of obligation to others, since we're all responsible for ourselves.

Egalitarians

Egalitarians believe that everyone has certain needs that have to be looked after by government. They're critics of the status quo and elitists and individualists. They stress the importance of voluntary consent.

Fatalists

Fatalists are at the bottom of the totem pole and have little economic, purchasing, or decision-making power. They depend on luck to escape from fatalist status.

Over the course of time Wildavsky changed the names of some of his cultures, I should add, in attempt to clarify things.

We can use these four political/consumer cultures to understand why people consume the things they do. Some examples follow.

Category	Elitist	Individualist	Egalitarian	Fatalist
Songs	"God Save the Queen"	"My Way"	"We Are the World"	"Anarchy in the UK"
Fashion	Uniforms	Suit	Blue jeans	Thrift Shop
Books	The Prince	Looking Out for Number One	I'm OK— You're OK	1984
Restaurants	French	Cafeteria	McDonald's	Food Kitchen
Automobiles	Rolls Royce	BMW	Civic	Yugo

This chart can be extended and can deal with many other categories of purchases, and it's an interesting project to consider how people in the four political/consumer cultures make the choices they make.

Wildavsky adds an important point—there are only four political cultures possible in any democratic society and individuals make political decisions on the basis of their allegiance to whichever political culture they find themselves in and not on the basis of self-interest, since people generally don't often know what is in their self-interest. Below I list the four consumer cultures and their relation to groups, boundaries, and prescriptions. Members of these four political cultures or consumer cultures don't recognize that they are members of one of these groups; that is, they probably aren't even aware of their existence. But they have certain values and belief systems connected to group affiliation and rule acceptance that Wildavsky and Douglas have identified as placing them in one of the political cultures.

Culture	Group Boundaries	Numbers of Prescriptions
Hierarchists	strong	numerous and varied
Egalitarians	strong	few and weak
Individualists	weak	few and weak
Fatalists	weak	numerous and varied

Mary Douglas, who collaborated with Wildavsky on a number of projects, argues that these four political cultures can also be seen as consumer cultures—which for her purposes she also describes as lifestyles. She substitutes the term "isolates" for "fatalists" and "enclavists" for "egalitarians" and explains that it's membership in one of the four consumer cultures or lifestyles—each of which is antagonistic toward or in conflict with the three others—that best explains people's consumer choices. As she writes in her essay "In Defence of Shopping":

> None of these four lifestyles (individualist, hierarchical, enclavist [egalitarian], isolated [fatalist]) is new to students of consumer behavior. What may be new and unacceptable is the point [that] these are the only four distinctive lifestyles to be taken into account, and the other point, that each is set up in competition with the others. Mutual hostility is the force that accounts for their stability. These four distinct lifestyles persist because they rest on incompatible organizational principles. Each culture is a way of organizing; each is predatory on the others for time and space and resources. It is hard for them to co-exist peacefully, and yet they must, for the survival of each is the guarantee of the survival of the others. Hostility keeps them going. (1997:19)

Douglas offers her theory of the four consumer cultures to counter the theories of consumption that come from a framework based on individualist psychology. She argues that "cultural alignment is the strongest predictor of preferences in a wide variety of fields" (1997:23).

Her theory argues, then, that there is an inherent logic behind the shopping that people do and, furthermore it is shoppers, or consumers, who ultimately dictate what will be sold. We can see this is the case if we examine the households of people from different consumer cultures. Members of the different consumer cultures may have similar incomes (except for the fatalists/isolates, who are at the bottom of the income ladder, generally speaking) but their patterns of consumption and the way they organize their households are affected by their membership in one of the four groups.

Douglas concludes that it is *cultural bias and membership in one of the four consumer cultures that is critical to understanding consumption*. The notion that shopping is essentially the expression of individual wants is incorrect, then. As she writes in the concluding section of her essay:

> The idea of consumer sovereignty in economic theory will be honoured in market research because it will be abundantly clear that the shopper sets the trends, and that new technology and new prices are adjuncts to achieving the shopper's goal. The shopper is not expecting to develop a personal identity by choice of commodities; that would be too difficult. Shopping is agonistic, a struggle to define not what one is but what one is not. When we include not one cultural bias, but four, and when we allow that each is bringing critiques against the others, and when we see that the shopper is adopting postures of cultural defiance, then it all makes sense. (1997:30)

If Douglas is right, there are, in fact, four distinct and mutually antagonistic lifestyles or consumer cultures, even though people who are in each of them may not be aware of the matter. This would mean that it wouldn't be socioeconomic class and discretionary income that is basic in consumption decisions, but lifestyles or membership in one of the four mutually antagonistic consumer cultures.

The comment by Douglas that shopping is "a struggle to define not what one is but what one is not" is similar in nature to Ferdinand de Saussure's writings about how language shapes the way we find meaning in life. In his classic work, *Course in General Linguistics,* Saussure wrote (1966:120) "in language there are only differences" and when it comes to concepts (1966:117) he added:

> It is understood that concepts are purely differential and defined not by their positive content but negatively by their relations with the other terms of the system. Their most precise characteristic is in being what the others are not.

What Saussure is suggesting is that nothing has meaning in itself; it is the relationships in language that are basic and the most important relationship among words and concepts involves opposition.

When we purchase things, Douglas argues, we do so to show what we are by showing what we are not. To simplify matters greatly, what we mean by "poor" is "not rich," and by "happy" is "not sad." That is why she argues that shopping is "agonistic." We want to demonstrate, she says, that we are not a member of the three other consumer cultures and are not guided by their aesthetic standards. From Saussure's perspective, everything has meaning by being opposite of something else.

Douglas moves consumption decisions from psychology to membership in a consumer culture. Modern societies may be characterized as being consumer societies and "consumer cultures" but, if Douglas is correct, there are really four consumer subcultures and they are of major importance when it comes to such things as individuals making decisions about what to buy or, to the extent that voting is a kind of consumption, whom to elect to public office.

There is the question, of course, of whether Douglas is correct and whether her four consumer cultures typology is the best way to understand patterns of consumption. It is certainly worth keeping in mind when we consider the way advertising attempts to persuade people to buy various products and services. Later in the book we will see that marketers have devised many different ways of breaking down American society into different target audiences.

What we have to wonder about is whether these many different target audiences can each be subsumed under one of the four consumer cultures Douglas writes about or whether her theory is, while intellectually elegant, too narrow. For example, marketers have focused a good deal of attention on how to reach children and make use of their notorious "pester power." (I'll deal with this subject in more detail at the end of this book.) How does Douglas's theory take into account the influence of children on the consumption patterns of their parents?

CLASSIFIED ADVERTISING

One of the curious ironies about advertising is that generally the most banal and trivial aspects of life are advertised at great expense and with great care, while important matters, such as finding jobs, selling houses, and looking for relationships, are relegated to the bland monotony of the classified advertising pages in newspapers. A remarkable amount of talent and money are used to sell aspirins, cold remedies, soaps, soups, detergents, and other such products. These products are quite inconsequential in terms of our everyday lives, though when you add everything up, the amount of money we spend on these items is enormous.

On the other hand, the most important and personal aspects of our lives are generally dealt with in the most mundane and impersonal of formats, the classified advertising sections of newspapers. In these classified advertisement sections we find advertisements for jobs, houses, and lovers that are printed in small typefaces and, to save money (since we pay for each word), make use of all kinds of shorthand devices to communicate information, such as: SWM seeks SWF (single white male seeks single white female).

These classified advertisements reflect with compelling power, it can be argued, the anonymity and alienation that pervade our culture. The fact that we have elaborate advertising campaigns about sandwich wraps or snacks only serves to heighten the sense of pettiness that many of us feel about ourselves. For we are reduced to the cheapest and least expressive kinds of advertising for the most important aspects of our lives. Inadvertently advertising may be reflecting a basic question that has troubled us for much of our history—which is more important, people or property (things)? As far as advertising is concerned, the contrast between the advertisements involving human relationships and important matters like jobs, housing, and the elaborate advertisements for products suggest that it is things that are of most concern to us. As Emerson put it many years ago in his "Ode to W. H. Channing," "Things are in the saddle, and ride mankind."

Most of the products we buy are designed to help people do things they consider useful and to gain various kinds of satisfactions—such as avoiding smelly armpits or having beautiful, lustrous hair—but the distinction between the kind of advertising for products and services of commercial organizations and classified advertisements is quite compelling. It is in the classified "want-ads" that the "little people" speak—telling the world of an old refrigerator for sale or a house or a "proven" blackjack system or trying to find a lost calico cat.

The pages of the classified ads are generally gray—except for advertisements for certain jobs or car ads—messages reduced to the lowest possible number of words, using certain abbreviations and stacked one on top of another for page after page. Does the monotonous and tedious nature of these little advertisements reflect anything on the part of the people who place these ads or read them? Does the "art form" of the classified advertisement reflect anything about the personality of the writers of these ads? We find in the classified ad sections of newspapers a world of errors made in purchases, of useless or no longer wanted objects, and an almost staggering number of services, notices, statements, and announcements. It is a study in chaos—a chaos above which, by virtue of its general categories, there seems to be a semblance of order. It is the chaos of the lives of the "little people" who read little boxes or write little advertisements about everything from trivial matters to the most important things in their lives— jobs, housing, and love.

In some of the "relationships" classified advertisements we find humor and imagination, but most classified advertisements are telegraphic in nature and communicate at the most elemental levels. These classified advertisements offer an alternative picture of American culture and society—and are characterized by a gritty realism that counters the rosy and celebratory optimism of traditional newspaper, magazine, and television advertising.

For the semiotician, the contradictory nature of the American myth of equality is nowhere written so clearly as in the signs that American advertisers use to manipulate us into buying their wares. "Manipulate" is the word here, not "persuade"; for advertising campaigns are not sources of product information, they are exercises in behavior modification. Appealing to our subconscious emotions rather than to our conscious intellects, advertisements are designed to exploit the discontentment fostered by the American dream, the constant desire for social success and the material rewards that accompany it. America's consumer economy runs on desire, and advertising stokes the engines by transforming common objects—from peanut butter to political candidates—into signs of all the things that Americans covet most.

—Jack Solomon, *The Signs of Our Times:*
The Secret Meanings of Everyday Life

Any analysis of the system *of* objects must ultimately imply an analysis of discourse *about* objects—that is to say, an analysis of promotional "messages" (comprising image and discourse). For advertising is not simply an adjunct to the system of objects; it cannot be detached therefrom, nor can it be restricted to its "proper" function (there is no such thing as advertising strictly confined to the supplying of information). Indeed, advertising is now an irremovable aspect of the system of objects precisely because of its disproportionateness. This lack of proportion is the "functional" apotheosis of the system. Advertising in its entirety constitutes a useless and unnecessary universe. It is pure connotation. It contributes nothing to production or to the direct practical application of things, yet it plays an integral part in the system of objects not merely because it relates to consumption but also because it itself becomes an object to be consumed.

—Jean Baudrillard, *The System of Objects*

3

ADVERTISING AND THE COMMUNICATION PROCESS

It is useful, at this point, to place advertising in the communication process—so we can better understand how print advertisements and radio and television commercials (and other forms of advertising in other media) function. To do this I offer a brief overview of communication theory, focusing on one of the most famous statements, the famous Lasswell formula, and an amplification of this formula that I've made. There are, of course, numerous models for understanding the communication process, just as there are many different ways of analyzing and interpreting advertisements and commercials and the role they play in our lives.

THE LASSWELL FORMULA

Harold Lasswell—an influential political scientist—said, in a 1948 article, that to understand the communication process we should ask the following questions:

Who?
Says what?
In which channel?
To whom?
With what effect?

I have offered an overview of the communication process that is somewhat similar to the Lasswell formula. I deal with four focal points in the study of communication and with their relation to media. These focal points are: (1) the work of art, (2) the artist, (3) the audience, and (4) America (or the society in which the work of art is created or disseminated by the media).

FOCAL POINTS AND THE STUDY OF MEDIA

We can see the relationships that exist among these focal points in figure 3.1. The arrows connect each focal point to every other focal point, either directly (for example, art and audience or art and artist) or indirectly (art/medium/America or artist/medium/audience).

The work of **art** (or "text" in the jargon of communication scholars) is, in terms of our interests, a print advertisement or a radio or television commercial. It is important that we realize that print and electronic advertisements are works of art—even though their purpose is a commercial one—to convince people to use some product or service. Thus, we have to consider, among other things, aesthetic matters when dealing with advertising.

All advertising is directed toward a target **audience**—the people who are the most likely purchasers of the product or service being advertised. Copywriters and artists work hard to create advertisements and commercials that will interest and appeal to members of their target audience. Advertisers talk about upscale audiences, who have a considerable amount of money to spend (on things such as expensive cars and vacations), and downscale audiences, who are targeted for low-cost products. Research companies have elaborated various schemes and categories of purchasers, based on zip codes, racial and ethnic characteristics, values and lifestyles, and so on. A number of these matters are discussed later in the book.

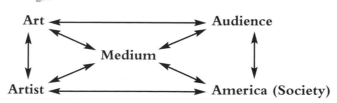

Figure 3.1. Focal Points in the Study of Communication

Insights from Advertising Agencies

A great ad is one that connects people to what you're selling and isn't too subtle. If it's too subtle people will see it but not remember it. But if it's too gimmicky, people will get bored with it once they've seen it. We conduct wear-out analyses to see how long an ad will last. Sometimes we put them on the shelf and then bring them back after a while.

Advertising is a collaborative medium. So when we talk about **artists** in my chart of focal points, we really are talking about teams of copywriters, artists, directors, musicians, filmmakers, and numerous other creative artists, in addition to researchers and others involved in the complicated process of making advertisements. Television commercials are the most complex form of advertising, since they involve script writers, actors, musicians, cinematographers, and others.

The fourth focal point is **America** or the society in which advertisements are disseminated—either via print or via electronic media, such as radio, television, or the Internet. The term "society" is probably too broad, since advertisements are traditionally targeted and directed to certain segments of the general population—based a good deal of the time on demographic factors such as age, gender, sexual orientation, or socioeconomic standing.

Finally, there is the **medium** that is used to disseminate the advertisements. The medium used has a major impact on the creation of texts. Each medium—print (newspapers, magazines), radio, or television—has certain strengths and weaknesses. So although the medium may not be the message (the late Marshall McLuhan, a famous communication theorist, argued that "the medium is the message"), it has a lot of impact upon the message.

In figure 3. 1, there are arrows pointing in all directions, which signifies that all of the focal points are connected to one another. We can focus our attention on the following:

1. one focal point: the work of art (the advertisement), the artist, the audience, America, or the medium
2. the relationship that exists between any two:
   A. the advertisement and the artists who create it
   B. the advertisement and the audience to whom it is directed
   C. the advertisement and the society in which it is found
   D. the advertisement and the medium in which it is transmitted

3. any three
4. any four
5. all five

The more focal points we consider, the more complicated the analysis becomes, which leads me to suggest that it is generally more productive to focus on fewer focal points.

THE LASSWELL FORMULA AND FOCAL POINTS

I developed my model of the focal points by extending one used by literary theorist M. H. Abrams. When I elaborated this model (discussed in considerable detail in my book *Essentials of Mass Communication Theory*), I did not realize that my focal points were similar to the different elements found in the Lasswell formula, described by some researchers as probably the most famous phrase ever uttered in communication research.

The similarities between the Lasswell formula and my focal points are shown in table 3. 1. The major difference between the two, aside from the fact that I've used alliteration as a mnemonic device, is that my focal point America (or society) doesn't concern itself as directly with effects.

A PROBLEM WITH THE LASSWELL FORMULA

Some researchers have faulted Lasswell, suggesting that he overemphasizes the effects of communication. As Denis McQuail and Sven Windahl write in *Communication Models: For the Study of Mass Communication*:

> The Lasswell Formula shows a typical trait of early communication models. It more or less takes for granted that the communicator has some intention of influencing the receiver and, hence, that communication

Table 3.1. Comparison of the Lasswell Formula and Focal Points

Lasswell	Berger
Who?	Artists, copywriters, etc.
Says what?	Artwork (advertisements)
In which channel?	Medium
To whom?	Audience
With what effect?	America (society)

should be treated mainly as a persuasive process. It is also assumed that messages always have effects. Models such as this have surely contributed to the tendency to exaggerate the effects of, especially, mass communication. (1993:14)

McQuail and Windahl make a good point. Some communication is not necessarily meant to persuade. But some is—especially the kind of communication I am dealing with in this book, advertising. In some cases, of course, advertisements have unintended consequences.

Another well-known model of the communication process is similar, in certain ways, to the models discussed above, but adds some new factors to understanding the communication process. The famous linguist Roman Jakobson elaborated a communication model (figure 3.2) that is useful for us because it uses many of the terms currently popular with communication theorists. In this model someone, a sender, sends a message to someone else, a receiver, using a code such as the English language. The context helps us interpret the message better.

The Jakobson model was explained in part by Robert Scholes, a literature professor, in *Structuralism in Literature: An Introduction*. As Scholes writes:

> Whether we are considering ordinary conversation, a public speech, a letter, or a poem, we always find a *message* which proceeds from a sender to a receiver. These are the most obvious aspects of communication. But a successful communication depends on three other aspects of the event as well: the message must be delivered through a *contact*, physical and/or psychological; it must be framed in a *code*; and it must refer to a *context*. In the area of context, we find what a message is about. But to get there we must understand the code in which the message is framed— as in the present case, my messages reach you through the medium of an academic/literary subcode of the English language. And even if we have the code, we understand nothing until we make contact with the

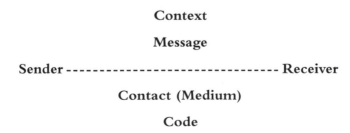

Figure 3.2. The Jakobson Model of Communication

utterance; in the present case, until you see the printed words on this page (or hear them read aloud) they do not exist as a message for you. The message itself, uniting sender and receiver, in the quintessentially human act of communication, is simply a verbal form, which depends on all the other elements of a speech event to convey its meaning. *The message is not the meaning.* Meaning lies at the end of the speech event, which gives the verbal formula its life and color. (1974:24)

One of the problems those who make advertisements and commercials face comes from the fact that audiences or receivers "aberrantly decode" the messages (advertisements and commercials) they are sent. In part this is because communication is such a complicated process, but also this problem stems in a general sense from differences in education, socioeconomic class, and cultural level between the senders of the messages and the receivers of the messages.

The Jakobson model uses different (and now common) terms from the Lasswell model and my focal points model, but there are also a number of similarities, as table 3.2 shows. What the Lasswell model doesn't deal with are codes and the importance of context in interpreting (decoding) messages. And the Jakobson model doesn't concern itself with effects, as the Lasswell model does. The Berger model indirectly involves context, in that American society provides a background that helps people decode messages. With these models we have a good understanding of the communication process and can understand how print advertisements and commercials function from a theoretical point of view.

In this book, I use various aspects of communication theory such as different focal points, codes, receivers and senders, and so on, from time to time as it suits my purpose, in my discussion of specific print advertisements or television commercials and advertising in general. Consider, for example, all those television commercials we watch. They all want to persuade us to do something—whatever the maker of the product or provider of the service being advertised (the advertiser) and the advertising agency that made the commercial want us to do.

Table 3.2. Comparison of Models of Communication

Lasswell	Jakobson	Berger
Who?	Sender	Artist
Says what?	Message	Artwork (Text)
In which channel?	Contact (medium)	Medium
To whom?	Receiver	Audience
With what effect?		America

The phrase "run it up a flagpole to see if anyone salutes" actually is, in its own way, similar to the Lasswell formula. We can see this by comparing the flagpole phrase and the Lasswell formula:

Lasswell Formula	**Run It Up a Flagpole**
Who?	(Let us) run
Says what?	It (the advertisement or commercial)
In which channel?	Up a flagpole (print or electronic medium)
To whom?	To see if anyone (some audience)
With what effect?	Salutes (is affected by it)

In both the Lasswell formula and the flagpole phrase, most of the elements in the communication process are taken into consideration, though the advertising phrase is much more colloquial and doesn't seem to be concerned with the communication process, except in a rather vague manner.

But how do they do this? How do they manipulate us? How do they manufacture desire in us? How do they (when they do, that is) engineer our consent? One way is by wearing us down under a constant barrage of advertisements and commercials. One way we resist—not on purpose, of course—is by decoding these advertisements and commercials aberrantly; that is, not the way those who created them expect us to or want us to.

METAPHOR AND METONYMY

There are two rhetorical devices, metaphor and metonymy, that are used by copywriters and artists to communicate with people. Jakobson argues that metaphor and metonymy are the two essential ways that people communicate meaning. Metaphor is a technique that uses analogy to create its effects. It explains or interprets one thing in terms of something else. "My love is a rose" is a metaphor. There is a weaker form of metaphor known as simile, which uses a "like" or "as." "My love is like a rose" is a simile.

Metaphor, it turns out, is a very important matter. As George Lakoff and Mark Johnson point out in their book *Metaphors We Live By*:

> Most people think they can get along perfectly well without metaphor. We have found, on the contrary, that metaphor is pervasive in everyday life, not just in language but in thought and action. Our ordinary

conceptual system, in terms of which we both think and act, is funda-
mentally metaphoric in nature.

The concepts that govern our thought are not just matters of the in-
tellect. They also govern our everyday functioning down to the most
mundane details. Our concepts structure what we perceive, how we get
around in the world, and how we relate to other people. Our conceptual system thus plays a central role in defining our everyday realities.
(1980:3)

So metaphor is a crucial element in our lives, because it shapes our thinking and our communicating—even if we don't recognize it as such or assume that metaphor is just a literary device.

Metonymy uses associations to communicate information and attitudes
that we all learn as we grow up. Thus, if we see a Rolls Royce in an advertisement we know that the person who owns the car is very wealthy and
can afford "the best." The person who drives a Rolls Royce is different
from the person who drives a Ferrari, and they are both different from people who drive Honda Civics. Copywriters and art directors can use this information we all have (i.e., certain associations or metonymies) to communicate, rather quickly, notions they want us to have. There is a form of
metonymy in which a part stands for a whole, or vice versa, that is known
as synecdoche.

For example, when people say "The Pentagon" we interpret this to
stand for the United States military services. When we see a Mercedes-Benz
symbol, we know it stands for a car.

Metaphor, it turns out, is one of the basic ways human beings make
sense of things, so metaphor and metonymy—which are often mixed
together—turn out to be very powerful tools that advertisers use to provide information to us and to generate desired emotional responses in us.
Table 3.3 compares the two devices.

Table 3.3. Metaphor and Metonymy

Metaphor	*Metonymy*
analogy	association
meta = to transfer; phor = bear	meta = to transfer; onoma = name
"My love is a rose"	Rolls Royce associated with great wealth
simile analogy with "like" or "as"	*synecdoche* part stands for whole or vice versa
"My love is like a rose"	"The crown" stands for royalty
Spider-Man's costume	Royal seal on British marmalade jars
"Drive = Love"	Derby suggests English society

Insights from Advertising Agencies

"Bad taste" is anything that keeps a person comfortable in his situation and reactions, anything that soothes rather than stimulates, anything dated rather than trendy, anything sentimental rather than sophisticated. This is the taste of more than 70 percent of the public, and it is this taste that dictates to advertisers. Advertising does not *lead*, it only *follows*. It's a service of communication, of selling, of a dialogue with consumers that is supposed to argue, cajole, or coax them into learning about goods for sale. It depends not on orders from manufacturers or retailers or providers of goods and services, but on *dictation* from the public. By a dictation from the public's instincts or habits of mind or mindlessness, too strongly *entrenched* for mere word-spinners and picture-makers to do *anything* about.

We can see from this table that there are both verbal and graphic forms of metaphor and metonymy and they are used to great effect in all kinds of advertising. For example, an image of a snake in an advertisement can be construed metaphorically as a phallic symbol and metonymically as alluding to the snake in the Garden of Eden. Later in the book I will analyze an advertisement that uses a snake prominently and we will see that it is a complicated symbol.

In the second half of the twentieth century in Europe, or at any rate in France, there is *nothing*—whether object, individual, or social group—that is *valued* apart from its double, the image that advertises and sanctifies it. This image *duplicates* not only an object's material, perceptible existence but desire and pleasure that it makes into fictions situating them in the land of make-believe, promising "happiness"—the happiness of being a consumer. Thus publicity [advertising] that was intended to promote consumption is the first of consumer goods; it creates myths—or since it can create nothing—it borrows existing myths, canalizing signifiers to a dual purpose: to offer them as such for general consumption and to stimulate the consumption of a specific object.

—Henri Lefebvre, *Everyday Life in the Modern World*

The knowingness and scepticism of advertising audiences are now taken for granted by advertising professionals and media studies analysts. . . . The knowledge of the audience, and their indifference, pose problems both for the advertisers and for analysts of advertising. For the advertisers, the problem is getting around the scepticism, the knowingness, and the boredom, and still having an effect, or even using these responses for their own purposes. For the analysts, the scepticism and knowingness undermine simplistic critiques of advertising effects, in which people do what ads tell them, accept the roles offered in ads as representations of the world, and take up the positions offered by advertising texts. But if they know how advertising works, does this protect them against its effects? Or is their knowingness limited and ultimately deceptive?

—Greg Myers, *Ad Worlds: Brands/Media/Audiences*

4

RUNNING IT UP A FLAGPOLE
TO SEE IF ANYONE SALUTES

L et me start by offering a somewhat exaggerated account of a typical morning of a typical college student. The heroine of this story is Lisa Greatgal, but I could also use Johnny Q. Public or any number of other male or female figures of varying ages, ethnicities, racial groups, socioeconomic groups, subcultures, and so on.

LISA'S MORNING: A FICTION

Lisa Greatgal got up at 8:30 A.M. and got ready to go to the college, where she was a sophomore. She had a 9:10 class. She shared an apartment near the campus with another girl, Melanie Valleygirl, and a junior at her school, Johnny Q. Public. Lisa put on a Maidenform bra and panties from Nordstroms, a yellow Nike T-shirt with a green swoosh, a pair of faded Polo jeans by Ralph Lauren with torn knees, white Nike anklet socks, and a pair of thick-soled black Doc Martens boots that had become popular in England a few years earlier. She scrubbed her face using Dove soap, brushed her teeth with Colgate Total toothpaste and a Colgate Reach toothbrush. She rinsed her mouth with Listerine mouthwash. She dabbed a bit of Fidji perfume on her neck. Her hair was dyed blond with Loreal Preference haircolor. Her eyeglass frames were by Guess?

For breakfast she had a glass of Ocean Spray Ruby Red and Mango juice (which Martina Hingis says she loves), a bowl of Post Shredded Wheat cereal with Lucerne 1 percent milk, and a cup of Yuban coffee with Carnation evaporated skim milk. She made some toast with Wonderbread and spread Brummel & Brown margarine, made with yogurt, on it. She hastily dumped some textbooks in an L.L. Bean knapsack and rushed off to class, arriving only ten minutes late.

That afternoon, after she had a Boston Carver lunch—a double-sided meat loaf, corn bread, and salad—she got a telephone call from a marketing-survey company. She was asked whether she felt she was influenced by advertising.

"I'm *aware* of advertising," she replied, "but I'm not influenced by it."

LISA GREATGAL'S AND JOHNNY Q. PUBLIC'S DAILY MEDIA DIET

Lisa Greatgal and Johnny Q. Public are both students, but let's assume their media diet is typical of the American public. According to the 2005 Kaiser Family Foundation study, "Generation M: Media in the Lives of 8–18 Year Olds" (www.kff.org) we find the following for media usage per day:

HOURS	ACTIVITY
3:04	watching television
0.55	listening to the radio
0.49	listening to CDs, Tapes, MP3s
0.48	going online★
0.32	playing console video games
0.25	watching a movie
0.26	reading books
0.17	playing hand-held video games
0.14	watching pre-recorded television
0.14	reading magazines
0.6	reading a newspaper

★In 2006 teens spent more than three hours a day online (www.ITfact.biz/index.php?id=07670).

According to the Kaiser Foundation media usage survey, children and teenagers lead "media saturated" lives, spending an average of 6.5 hours a day with the media.

Maybe, since they're students, Lisa and Johnny spend a bit more time than forty minutes a day reading, though on the basis of teaching for almost forty years, I wonder how much time students actually spend reading books, especially in this era of ever-changing technology. Many students now work, and school is something they have to fit into their busy schedules, and nowadays students and the general population alike read articles online.

In addition, the Kaiser Family Foundation provided data on what new media devices eight-to-eighteen-year-olds own and how they use them:

64% have downloaded music from the Internet
48% have streamed a radio station through the Internet
66% use instant messaging
39% have a cell phone
34% have a DVR such as a TiVo in their homes
35% have created a personal web site or web page
18% have an MP3 player
13% have a hand-held device that connects to the Internet

We see, then, that children and teenagers spend an enormous amount of time involved in the media of all kinds. It's important to keep in mind that if children watch something like twenty hours of television per week, they are exposed to an enormous number of television commercials. It has been estimated that children are exposed to 20,000 thirty-second television commercials a year.

TELEVISION VIEWING AND EXPOSURE TO COMMERCIALS

A United States Census report on projected media usage for the *general* population for 2005 offers the following statistics:

MEDIUM	HOURS PER YEAR
Television	1679
Radio	998
Recorded Music	243
Daily Newspaper	144
Consumer Magazines	100
Home Videos	81
Video Games	115
Consumer Internet	194★
TOTAL	3649 Hours

★Teens spent 1400 hours per year in 2006.

We can see, then, that media dominate our lives. If we work forty hours a week for fifty weeks, we work for 2000 hours. So you can see how large the 3649 hours figure is. In some cases, people multi-task and consume several kinds of media at the same time, so the figures may be a bit inflated, but however you figure things, we can see that, to a great extent, our lives are saturated by the media.

Let me quote from a book, published twenty-odd years ago, about what our constant exposure to television means. In *Spots: The Popular Art of American Television Commercials* (Arts Communications) Bruce Kurtz writes:

> The National Association of Broadcasters' Television Code limits the number of commercials permitted on television to 9.5 minutes an hour during prime time and 16 minutes an hour during other times, except during children's programming, which is more limited. Since the currently preferred length of a single TV spot is 30 seconds, the number of spots per hour averages from 19 to 32. The largest percentage of television viewing occurs during prime time, but if we average 19 and 32, we arrive at a figure of 25.5 spots per hour. On the average, each American sees 156 spots a day, or 1,092 spots a week. One hour and 18 minutes of the average American's daily television viewing consists of television spots, or about nine hours and six minutes a week. There may be no other single form of visual imagery which occupies that much of Americans' time, or of which Americans see such a quantity. (1977:7)

Kurtz's figures are more than twenty years old; in recent years, fifteen-second and ten-second television commercials have become popular, which means we're exposed to even more commercials than before. Kurtz's figures suggest that we spend 486 hours a year watching television commercials—that's the equivalent of working more than twelve weeks a year, at forty hours per week, just watching television commercials.

Thus, roughly speaking, more than a quarter of the time we spend watching television (and the same applies to listening to the radio) is devoted to commercials. In situation comedies, for example, the scripts generally take up twenty-two minutes and leave eight minutes for commercials and station promotions.

Advertisers have also begun to emphasize product placement and are paying to have performers in films and other media use their products in shows. And there is talk of putting advertisements, in one form or another, onto screens in cell phones. This move to bring advertising to cell phones was described by Gary Ruskin, executive director of a nonprofit consumer group, Commercial Alert, as "This is part of the creep of advertising into every nook and cranny of our lives. This is advertising right in your face."

(*New York Times,* Jan. 16, 2006, page C1).

The chart that follows shows how much we *spend* on advertising in the United States by media. These figures were taken from the *Advertising Age* 2005 FactPack and are for 2003.

MEDIUM	AMOUNT SPENT (billions)
Direct Mail	$48.37
Broadcast Television	$44.84
Radio	$19.10
Cable Television	$18.81
Yellow Pages	$13.90
Consumer Magazines	$11.44
Internet	$5.65
Out of Home	$5.44
Business Publications	$4.00
All Other	$31.99
TOTAL	$254.48

The figure for Internet advertising has increased greatly since 2003, with the explosion of advertising on Google and Yahoo and other Internet sites. Advertising executives expect something like 10 percent of all advertising dollars to be spent on online advertising in 2004, according to a report on MediaLiteracy.com (9/19/2005).

Television commercials, we must realize, often cost five to ten times as much per minute to make (not counting the cost of purchasing time on television shows to broadcast the commercials) than the programs during which they are aired. This means we are exposed to the work of some of the most sophisticated artists, writers, directors, musicians, and performers—whose sole purpose is to manipulate our behavior and get us to do what they want us to do, use the product or service being advertised.

It used to be a rule of thumb, a few years ago, that the average thirty-second television spot cost around $350,000 to make. If it costs, say, $500,000 now to make a thirty-second commercial, this means that a thirty-minute program, if it cost as much per second as a television commercial, would cost $15 million—which is more than the price of making a low-budget movie.

L-CONSUMING PASSION FOR CONSUMING

ᴦ pamphlet, "All-Consuming Passion: Waking up from the American Dream" (New Road Map Foundation, 1993), offers the following statistics about television commercials and their impact:

1. **360,000**
   Number of television commercials American teenagers are typically exposed to by the time they graduate from high school. (I've seen other estimates that put this figure closer to 500,000 commercials by graduation time.)
2. **One entire year of his or her life**
   Amount of time the average American will spend watching TV commercials.
3. **93 percent**
   Percentage of teenage girls who report store-hopping as their favorite activity. (Do you agree or disagree with this statistic?)
4. **$230 a year**
   The average amount of pocket money for American children. (This figure represents more than the total annual income of the world's half-billion poorest people.)

THE PRICE WE PAY FOR "FREE" TELEVISION

The price we pay for "free" television is being exposed to countless commercials. The impact of these commercials is not to be measured only in terms of the pressure they put on us to purchase things; commercials (and advertising in general) have a much more profound impact than we imagine upon our consciousness, our identities, our belief systems, our private lives, and our societies and culture in general. It is to these subjects that I now turn in this chapter on what might be generally described as the cultural consequences of the commercial and of the advertising industry in general.

THE ILLUSION OF CONTROL

In May 1998 I received a telephone call from a reporter from the *New York Daily News*. She asked me to comment on a survey that found that many young men and women reported that they were aware of print advertise-

Insights from Advertising Agencies

When I'm having a hard time thinking something up, I run through the seven deadly sins—sloth, envy, and so on—to look for ideas.

ments and radio and television commercials, but felt they weren't influenced by them. Since the average person watches almost four hours of television per day (it's a bit less for teenagers) and listens to the radio for an hour or so, it's impossible to be unaware of advertisements and commercials.

But is it possible to be immune to their influence? That's the question. And is it not likely that the illusion many young people have—that they aren't affected by advertising—contributes to their seduction by the advertisements and commercials to which they are exposed?

We must keep in mind the insight provided to us by Carl Jung, the great Swiss psychologist. Jung wrote in *Man and His Symbols* (1968:22), "Many people mistakenly overestimate the role of willpower and think that nothing can happen to their minds that they do not decide or intend. But we must learn carefully to discriminate between intentional and unintentional contents of the mind." Freudians would make the same point. Sigmund Freud argued that there were three levels to the human psyche. One level is consciousness, in which we are aware of what is in our minds. Just below consciousness is a level Freud called preconsciousness, a level we generally don't think about but one we can access if we put our minds to it. And below this level, at the deepest level and one which is not accessible to us, is what Freud called the unconscious.

Freud explained his notions about the unconscious in his pioneering essay "Psychoanalysis" (1963):

> It was a triumph of the interpretive art of psychoanalysis when it succeeded in demonstrating that certain common mental acts of normal people, for which no one had hitherto attempted to put forward a psychological explanation, were to be regarded in the same light as the symptoms of neurotics: that is to say, they had a *meaning,* which was unknown to the subject but which could easily be discovered by analytic means. . . . A class of material was brought to light which is calculated better than any other to stimulate a belief in the existence of unconscious mental acts even in people to whom the hypothesis of something at once mental and unconscious seems strange and even absurd. (pp.235-236).

According to Freud, we are not aware of everything that goes on in our minds and, in fact, only a small percentage of our mental activity is accessible to us.

Ernest Dichter, who did important work on motivation research, points out in his book *The Strategy of Desire* that "many of our daily decisions are governed by motivations over which we have no control and of which we are often quite unaware" (p.12). It is our unconscious desires and urges, Dichter suggests, that shape our behavior in many different areas, including, of course, purchasing products and services.

This hypothesis can be best visualized by imagining an iceberg floating in the water. We know that the part of the iceberg floating above the water is only a relatively small part of the iceberg. This part of the iceberg represents our consciousness. We can also dimly make out part of the iceberg that is five or ten feet below the water. It is accessible to us with a bit of work. That area represents our preconscious. And the rest of the iceberg, most of the iceberg, that exists in the black depths of the ocean, which we cannot see, represents our unconscious. It is not accessible to us, unless we have the help of a psychologist or psychiatrist.

If Freud is correct, something can be in our minds without our being aware of it. We can make a preconscious thought conscious by paying attention to it and, conversely, something we are conscious of is no longer so when we stop paying any attention to it. The important thing about the unconscious is that it determines many of our actions, even though we are unaware that it is doing so. We have repressed much of the material in our unconscious and thus find ourselves doing things at the "command," so to speak, of forces in our unconscious.

Wilson Bryan Key expands upon this point in his controversial book *Subliminal Seduction*. Key takes Freud's notions about sexuality and the unconscious and pushes them, some have argued, to ridiculous extremes. Whatever the case, it is interesting to see how Key explains the power of advertising. He writes:

> The basis of modern media effectiveness is a language within a language— one that communicates to each of us at a level beneath our conscious awareness, one that reaches into the uncharted mechanism of the human unconscious. This is a language based upon the human ability to *subliminally* or *subconsciously* or *unconsciously* perceive information. This is a language that today has actually produced the profit base for North American mass communication media. It is virtually impossible to pick up a newspaper or magazine, turn on a radio or television set, read a promotional pamphlet or the telephone book, or shop through a supermarket without having your subconscious purposely massaged by some monstrously clever artist, photographer, writer, or technician. As a culture, North America might well be described as one enormous, magnificent, self-service, subliminal massage parlor. (1973:11)

Key's thesis, that advertising agencies are using subliminal means—means that we are not conscious of—to persuade us to buy the products and services they are peddling, has never been proved. That is, the notion that certain symbols or phrases are hidden in many print advertisements and commercials (or even products like crackers) is highly questionable. But Key's point about our being susceptible to influences beyond our consciousness is an important one, especially since advertising is so ubiquitous and plays so big a role in our entertainment and our lives.

This notion is not only held by psychoanalytically oriented scholars. Those with a more behavioral orientation make the same point. This is made

---

Insights from Advertising Agencies

You can think of me as an architect. I help translate the desires of the person who wants to have a house built into a plan for the house. Sometimes, of course, our clients don't know what they want. We have a number of groups of people involved in dealing with clients. The brand planner thinks "my consumer." The creative people think "my ad or commercial." The client of the agency thinks "my brand."

clear by an article in the *Wall Street Journal* which suggests that Ivan Pavlov, rather than Freud, may be the real founder of modern advertising techniques.

> Do television commercials make people behave like Pavlov's dogs? Coca-Cola Co. says the answer is yes. In recent years the Atlanta soft-drink company has been refining an ad-testing procedure based on the behavioral principles developed by the Russian physiologist. So far, Coke says, its new testing system has worked remarkably well.
>
> In his classic experiment, Ivan Pavlov discovered he could get dogs to salivate at the ring of a bell by gradually substituting the sound for a spray of meat powder. Coca-Cola says that, just as Pavlov's dogs began to associate a new meaning with the bell, advertising is supposed to provide some new image or meaning for a product.
>
> Although the specifics of Coke's test are a secret, the company says it attempts to evaluate how well a commercial "conditions" a viewer to accept a positive image that can be transferred to the product. During the past three years, Coca-Cola says, ads that scored well in its tests almost always resulted in higher sales of soft drinks.
>
> "We nominate Pavlov as the father of modern advertising," says Joel S. Dubrow, communications research manager at Coke. "Pavlov took a neutral object and, by associating it with a meaningful object, made it a symbol of something else; he imbued it with imagery, he gave it added value." That, says Mr. Dubrow, "is what we try to do with modern advertising." ("Coca-Cola Turns to Pavlov," *Wall Street Journal,* January 19, 1984, p. 34)

So whether we buy something because of deep, hidden unconscious forces of the kind Freud and his followers discussed or because we've been "conditioned" like one of Pavlov's dogs to buy it, one fact remains all-important—we've bought something, as a result of some process affecting our minds, that an advertiser wanted us to buy.

BEING A "BRANDED" INDIVIDUAL

Lisa Greatgal might be a caricature of a "branded" individual—someone who has been led to purchase only brand-name products, and certain brand-name products, at that—but she's probably much more representative of what goes on in American households than her opposite, someone who buys only store brands and consults *Consumer Reports* before purchasing most products and services. And, to make matters worse, many people delude themselves into thinking that they don't buy brand-name products, but they actually do. These brand-name products are used to help create an image of one-self for others and to reinforce this assumed identity. We can use clothes, eye-glasses, and other props to create identities for ourselves and to change these identities when we tire of them.

The following comes from an article, "The Case of the Closet Tar-get," by Martin Solow, who is a copywriter. (It was published in *Madison Avenue* magazine originally.) He describes being invited to a party in Long Island's Nassau County. When his hostess hears that he's in the advertising business, the following takes place:

> "I'm sorry," [the hostess] says, "I never watch TV commercials, I can't stand advertising . . . any advertising." Chimes of approval and assent from the small group around us. I throw up a few defenses, because I know the syndrome: "How do you buy the products you buy?" I want to know. I get a patronizing smile. She buys what she considers best; what *Consumer Reports* tells her; what **knows** (and **how** does she know, I murmur to myself) to be the best. I excuse myself and ask, since it is a large house, for a roadmap to the bathroom. Once in the large bathroom, the door safely locked, I open the medicine cabinet and survey the contents: Col-gate toothpaste, L'Oreal hairspray; Trac II shaving cream and the new Gillette Trac II razor; Ban Roll-On Deodorant (for him, I guess) and Arid Extra Dry (for her—or maybe vice-versa); Bayer aspirins. . . . (1988)

Solow goes on, at considerable length, listing the numerous name-brand products he found in the medicine cabinet. Bayer aspirin is significant be-cause, according to *Consumer Reports*, all aspirin is the same, so people who use Bayer aspirin are paying two or three times as much for their aspirin as they would if they bought Rite-Aid aspirin; that is, they really are paying for Bayer's advertising.

It's the same story all the time, he says, which leads him to offer "Solow's First Law: Those who claim they don't watch TV are much more vulnerable to commercials than those who unashamedly do." And when he asks people who use brand-name products why they do, they invariably, as he puts it, "play back the message"—that is, repeat the claim, sometimes verbatim, made by the advertiser in the commercial. Many young children, who watch a great deal of television each day, can sing the lyrics of jingles found in countless commercials. Isn't that cute? we think. Is it possible that we have a subtle form of brainwashing going on here? Or is it that I'm tak-ing something that's actually rather trivial too seriously?

In an unpublished paper, "Suspension of Disbelief as a Bridge between Media and Consumption," social scientist Norbert Wiley of the University of Illinois offers an interesting insight into the relationship between advertising and consumption. The term "the willing suspension of disbelief" was first used by the writer Samuel Taylor Coleridge to describe the way people attending theater productions (and by extension films, videos, and other similar kinds of productions) identify with the characters in these works. What happens is that we forget that we are watching a show and become involved in the drama as if we were actually part of it.

Wiley's thesis is that "the suspension of disbelief places customers in a relaxed and unguarded state, such that it is easier to sell them products." (undated: p. 1). He suggests that that the owners of stores and the manufacturers of the products in these stores have to infuse products with the suspension of disbelief. He writes:

> They have to get the aesthetic suspension of disbelief somehow *into the products,* so that people find themselves caught up in fantasy and identified with the things on the shelf. Once that is done, access to the wallet or pocketbook is almost automatic.
>
> A clue to how this might be done is what the shopper might do, or think they might do, with the product. Needs are pretty physical and body-based. We die, or at least languish, without needs. Wants are another matter. They get to be wants, not through elementary body drives, but through the action of the mind. That darling toy, or powerful fishing rod or adorable outfit became a want by thought and fantasy. The advertisers may have dinned us with temptation and suggestion, but at some point we give in to their blandishment. We begin to let the image enter the play of our minds.

Thus, the item we purchase becomes part of our fantasy life and we suspend disbelief and, in most cases, the strictures of the ego and superego, when we buy things.

As we've seen, Freud posited that our psyches have three components that are in constant conflict at the unconscious level:

our ids, which represent desire and lust;
our egos, which represent knowledge of reality;
our superegos, which represent conscience and guilt

It is the task of the ego to mediate between our ids and superegos, between our desires, on the one hand, and our sense of guilt, on the other hand. Our ids provide energy and our superegos provide restraint. When people have a balance between the id and superego, all is well. When either the id or superego is too dominant, then we have problems. Much advertising seeks to evade the strictures of our superegos and the reasonableness of our egos and appeal directly to our ids. These contending forces represent those found in the dramas that Wiley talks about.

As Wiley concludes, "fantasying ourselves with the object was the performance and buying is the catharsis," the resolution of the drama with attendant emotional rewards. Aristotle argued that theatrical performances led to a catharsis, an outpouring of emotion, in the audiences of these works. We need these commodities, Wiley argues, to complete the dramatic performances in which we are caught up.

Many sociologists have used theatre as a metaphor to explain various aspects of social life, and Wiley's notion that advertising helps us "suspend disbelief" and enter into fantasies in which we use the commodities we purchase for various satisfactions is an excellent example of how the theatrical metaphor can help explain consumer behavior and how people become "branded" and attached to certain products and services.

Advertising agencies stress the importance of "branding," which means developing an emotional tie between some product or service and individuals. More precisely, it involves an emotional tie between individuals and images they have of the product.

In his book, *Provocateur: Images of Women and Minorities in Advertising*, Anthony J. Cortese offers a good description of branding. He writes (2004:4):

> *Branding*—the process of differentiation—is at the core of advertising. What distinguishes similar products is not ingredients but packaging and brand names. Most major shampoos, for example, are made by two or three manufacturers. . . . The major thrust of advertising is to remind shoppers to seek out and purchase a particular brand. Branding seeks to nullify or compensate for the fact that products are otherwise fundamentally interchangeable. Tests have shown that consumers cannot distinguish between their own brand of soap, beer, cigarette, water, cola, shampoo, gasoline from others. In a sense, advertising is like holding up two identical photographs and persuading you that they are different—in fact, that one is better than the other.

One of the reasons that we become attached to certain brands is that they help us form an identity. We use brands to differentiate ourselves from other people and to generate images of ourselves to others that we think are positive. We become, so to speak, the sum of our brands. It is the symbolic value of brands, not the functions of the products, that become most important.

Figure 4.1

And once established, it is relatively easy for brands to extend themselves. For example, the Mont Blanc pen company, which has a reputation for making outstanding fountain pens, now sells expensive watches (figure 4.1).

There is what might be called a "halo effect" that transfers from the Mont Blanc fountain pens to their watches. Once a brand becomes very popular, it is often the case that we find brand extension, and the brand is used to sell other products. At the core of branding is a sense of confidence people develop that the brands they use are good and reflect positively upon them. Branding, we may say, sells the sizzle not the steak.

SELLING ONESELF

In a marketing society like the United States, we learn to market ourselves, and using brand names gives anxiety-ridden people a sense of security that they believe will enhance the job of selling themselves that they feel they must do. Personality is the product, so to speak. The term *personality* has its root in the Latin word *persona*, which means "mask."

So our personalities are *masks* we wear to sell ourselves to others—to become popular, to market ourselves, to find a job, a mate, whatever. The matter is complicated because almost everyone we meet is in the same bind—we are always (with few exceptions) marketing ourselves to others, and they are marketing themselves to us. And much of this marketing—

another term might be "manipulation"—is done by using products that announce to others our sense of who we are, and by implication, what our socioeconomic level is and what kind of taste we have.

I knew someone who wanted to work in advertising. He wore Robert Hall cheapie suits in a world where, at the time, rather expensive Brooks Brothers and J. Press suits were what advertising people wore. The people in the advertising agencies took one took at him in his Robert Hall suit and thought, "Not one of us!"

But the products we use keep changing, which means our personas, to the extent that they are intimately connected to the products we use, keep changing also. And our sense of ourselves—whether we are "successes or failures"—is tied, we are taught by advertising, to what we can afford. Of course, there are people who are frauds—who drive cars and wear clothes that really are too expensive for them; they are putting on a front. And there is the reverse—wealthy people who drive and dress poor; at least in public, that is.

Our personalities, then, are to a considerable degree, products based on the material culture that we make part of our lives. And so we are doomed to constant change. This is part of our postmodern world, in which we sample different styles and identities to suit our whims. The problem is that identity suggests some kind of coherence, and a constantly changing identity is a contradiction in terms.

THE PROBLEM OF SELF-ALIENATION

What happens, ultimately, is that we become alienated from ourselves; we learn to see ourselves as infinitely malleable "material" that we can mold whenever we have the whim to do so to suit our purposes. But the cost of all of this is a kind of estrangement from any true self that we might have been able to fashion. We become so absorbed in manipulating others that we don't recognize that we have also manipulated our own sense of self and our own identity—or is it identities?

In modern capitalist societies, there is—to give the Devil his due—a kind of dynamism and excitement that is not found in some traditional societies, where people have worn the same costume, handed down by tradition, for hundreds of years if not longer. These traditional societies are, let me suggest, a polar opposite of the postmodern societies of modern industrialized nations. There is a kind of stagnation on one extreme and a kind of restless, mind-numbing change at the other extreme. What we must do is find some kind of middle ground that allows for change but does not lead to alienation and estrangement.

I see advertising as one of the central institutions in modern societies, and thus it is important we learn to understand better how advertisements and radio and television commercials work and how they help shape our consciousness. We have to realize that fashion, style, lifestyle—all of these concerns—are forms of collective behavior. An individual—Lisa Greatgal—reaches out her hand at a supermarket and chooses this or that item. But behind this seemingly free choice, there are all kinds of forces at work that have led to that choice. Lisa, I argue, and all those like Lisa, has been manipulated by the advertising industry, but is unaware that this has happened. All she knows is that this skirt or pair of shoes or jeans or hairstyle that was "hot" last year suddenly looks dull and isn't fashionable anymore.

And Lisa's sense of style and fashion, her desire to be "with it," to have the "hot" things, profoundly affects her choices of friends, mates, restaurants, pets, cars, homes, jobs, clothes, foods, colleges, vacations and tourism destinations, and almost everything else one can think of. The term "affects" is crucial here, for there are often other factors involved in the choices we make in life.

The question of how much autonomy we have and how free we are to make choices leads to a step back in history and the ideas of one of America's most powerful thinkers, Jonathan Edwards.

WE CAN CHOOSE AS WE PLEASE,
BUT CAN WE PLEASE AS WE PLEASE?

In the 1740s, the Puritan minister Jonathan Edwards, one of the greatest minds America has produced, tried to reconcile his belief in man's free will with God's omnipotence. He asked, How can man be free if God is all-powerful? His answer was ingenious and quite relevant to our interest in advertising. Edwards argued that there were two realms to be considered: the realm of action and the realm of choice.

Men and women are free to act as they wish, suggesting that we have free will. That is, we can act as we please. But in the realm of choice, God is all-powerful and all determining. Though we can act as we please, we can't please as we please; God determines what will please us. This means, in effect, that we only have the *illusion* of freedom. For though we can do anything we want to do, God has already determined what it is that we will want to do.

In an introduction to Edwards's *Freedom of Will* (1754), Norman Foerster explains Edwards's ideas as follows:

> Edwards argues that all acts of will, like events in physical nature, are subject to the law of causation. Since an act of will has its cause in a previous act of will, and this in turn in an earlier one, we must eventually arrive at a first act, which was necessarily caused by the agent's inborn disposition. Having traced the whole series backward to the start, we come to realize that the will has no independent activity but is merely passive and mechanical. Man does have freedom, to be sure, in the sense that he feels no compulsion or restraint but can "do as he pleases." Yet his will cannot determine *what* he pleases to do. He is free to *act* as he chooses, but has no *freedom of choice.* (1957:86–7)

Thus, because our choices are determined for us, though we can act as we wish, we only have the illusion of freedom. For Edwards, it was an all-powerful God who determined what our choices would be; in contemporary mass-mediated societies, God has been replaced, let me suggest, by advertising agencies and marketing consultants.

We can make an argument similar to Edwards's about the role of advertising and our free choice, except that advertising is not all-powerful—just very powerful, and part of its power stems from the fact that we don't recognize how advertising shapes our consciousness and helps determine how we act. Table 4.1 shows these relationships more graphically.

Table 4.1. Freedom and Determinism Compared

Freedom	Determinism
Individuals	God (now advertising agencies)
Realm of action	Realm of choice
We act as we please	God (now advertising agencies) determines what pleases us
John buys Colgate	Advertising agencies have helped make John want to buy
Total toothpaste	Colgate Total toothpaste

There is a fascinating image that brings this matter of freedom and determinism into sharp relief. We find it on the cover of Wolfgang Haug's book, *Critique of Commodity Aesthetics*. It is a photograph of pigeons in St. Mark's Square in Venice who have been lured there to eat corn and who form the word Coca-Cola. Workers scattered birdseed that spelled out Coca-Cola and the pigeons gathered to eat the birdseed.

The pigeons were free to do whatever they wanted to do, in theory, but we know that when pigeons find birdseed available, they will fly to wherever it is and eat it. As Haug explains (1986:118):

> The pigeons did not gather with the intention of forming the trademark but to satisfy their hunger. But equally the seed was not scattered to feed the pigeons but to employ them on its tracks as extras. The arrangement is totally alien and external to pigeons. While they are consuming their feed, capital is subsuming, and consuming, them. This picture, a triumph of capitalist advertising technique, symbolizes a fundamental aspect of capitalism.

The moral we can take away from this photo is that while we are pursuing our private interests, without our being aware of it, we are often being motivated and manipulated by forces of which we are unaware, in their interest. Of course people are not pigeons and are much more complicated, but we can, in certain situations, be motivated to do things that are not always based on rational thought about what's in our best interest.

I am exaggerating and simplifying things, of course. But this little scenario—and ones like it—is acted out countless times in a given day by millions of people who "choose" this brand or that brand of some product and who don't recognize the extent to which their actions have been shaped or, to use a stronger term, manipulated by the numerous print advertisements and commercials they've seen. Many of these advertisements and commercials are brilliant works that involve glamour, sex, drama, humor, and various aesthetic and rhetorical devices to attract our attention and stimulate our desire.

Advertisements and commercials obviously aren't 100 percent effective. If they were, we'd probably buy whichever product we saw advertised last. But companies don't spend hundreds of millions of dollars advertising their products and services for the fun of it. They expect that when they run their product or service "up the flagpole," that is, when they advertise it, people will salute—by purchasing the product. And if people (not just anyone, of course, the right people) don't salute, or don't salute enough, the companies get a different advertising agency—one that promises that it can achieve the desired results, that is, that it can *make* people salute.

THE AGONY OF CHOICE

A psychologist, Barry Schwartz, discussed what might be described as "the agony of choice" in his book *The Paradox of Choice.* He had an experience going into a store and asking for a pair of jeans that led him to think about the problems consumers face when they decide to purchase certain products. In his article "When It's All Too Much," he writes about what happened when he went into a Gap store to buy a pair of jeans. He writes (Schwartz, 2004:4):

> One day I went into the Gap to buy a pair of jeans. A salesperson asked if she could help. "I want a pair of jeans—32-28," I said. "Do you want them slim fit, relaxed fit, baggy or extra baggy?" she replied. "Do you want them stone-washed, acid-washed, or distressed? Do you want them button fly or zipper-fly? Do you want them faded or regular?

This experience alerted him to how many different decisions must be made to purchase certain products, since there are so many different versions that are available. These increased choices have not made us happier but, it turns out, decreased our sense of well being.

He concluded that there are two kinds of consumers, what he called "maximizers" and "satisfizers." The basic characteristics of these two groups are shown below:

Maximizers	Satisfizers
Must have the best	Good enough is acceptable
Very high expectations	Modest or low expectations
Anxiety	Ease

The problem the maximizers have is that no matter how good a deal they got on some purchase, they always are troubled by the notion that they could have done better if they looked around more. Searching for the "best deal" led to the maximizers becoming very stressed and anxiety-ridden. He suggests that people would do well to avoid trying to maximize and settle for good enough.

What his theory suggests is that advertising may lead a person to desire a certain product or service, but that due to personality characteristics of certain people, the implementation of that desire by purchasing that product or service can be very stressful. Implicit in Schwartz's theory is the notion that most people are maximizers.

His ideas may explain why our fantasies about our purchases tend to fade very quickly when we face the reality of buying them, and even faster once we have bought them—especially in those cases in which people suffer "buyer's remorse." In such cases, we decide that we made a mistake in purchasing whatever it is we bought, but we blame ourselves and not the advertisements and commercials that persuaded us to buy the product.

NON-ADVERTISING FORMS OF ADVERTISING

As a result of the development of new technologies such as TiVo (which enables people to record television programs on a hard disk and eliminate all commercials), advertisers have had to find new ways to get television viewers to purchase products and services. One of the most insidious developments has been the spread of "product placements." Advertising agencies pay film companies to have scriptwriters include products they want to push in films and in other media. Thus, the product is integrated into the action of a film and advertisers get the "halo" effect of having a famous actor or actress actually use a product. For example, advertisers put Pepto-Bismol into *Law and Order* and Bud Light into *Survivor*. There are many other examples that could be given. One added benefit of product placements is that they serve as the equivalent of a testimonial for the product or service by the performer.

One of the most notorious cases of product placement involves what was called a "literasement." Bulgari, a maker of very expensive jewelry, hired well-known novelist Fay Weldon to write a story featuring Bulgari jewels in it. She came up with a thriller called *The Bulgari Connection*. Ellen Goodman wrote a column on this book, lamenting the development of what she called "literatisement" or "litads." Weldon, Goodman notes, was attacked for being the first well-known author to "erase the line between literature and advertising." By this she meant serious literature; advertising can be seen, I would suggest, as a form of literature and can be analyzed by the same methods used to interpret higher forms of literature.

There is yet another form of advertising that is not recognized as such—reviews of films, television shows, plays, restaurants, vacation resorts, and anything else that involves people paying for goods and services. These reviews, whether they are positive or not, call reader's attention to whatever is being reviewed. Over the course of time, many people come to regard certain reviewers as being accurate and having "good taste," so their reviews function, for these readers, as the equivalent of a word-of-mouth endorsement.

Google and other search engines have made billions of dollars when they recognized that people who were searching for information could be looked upon as target audiences. These search engines scan messages and provide sites where people using the search engine can find products related to their interests, as reflected in the topic they are investigating. This kind of advertising is very effective since it zeros in, very directly, on the interests of the person doing the searching.

Another important change from tradition mass-mediated advertising involves the development of what is described as "in-store" advertising. An article by Emily Nelson and Sarah Ellison on the first page of the September 21, 2005 *Wall Street Journal* describes the phenomenon under the title "In a Shift, Marketers Beef Up Ad Spending Inside Store." As the reporters note:

> Procter & Gamble Co. believes shoppers make up their mind about a product in about the time it takes to read this paragraph.
>
> The "first moment of truth," as P&G calls it, is the three to seven seconds when someone notices an item on a store shelf. Despite spending billions on traditional advertising, the consumer products giant thinks this instant is one of its most important marketing opportunities. It created a position 18 months ago, Director of First Moment of Truth, or Director of FMOT, (pronounced "EFF-mott") to produce sharper, flashier in-store displays. . . . P&G's insight is helping to power a shift in the advertising business: the grown and increasing sophistication of in-store marketing. . . . Now, in response to the fragmentation of television and print ads, it wants to tout its brands directly to consumers where they're most likely to be influenced: the store.

This phenomenon was described by the German media scholar Wolfgang Fritz Haug some twenty years ago, in his book *Commodity Aesthetics, Ideology & Culture,* when he discussed what might be described as the "aesthetization," beautification, and sexualization of stores and the buying experience.

We can see, then, that as print media, radio, and television—traditional venues for advertising—decline, advertising agencies and the corporations they work for have been finding new ways of getting their messages across, using devices such as product placement, Internet advertising (including studying Blogs to see how people feel about certain products and services), and developing in-store advertising.

ITEM: **Daring Campaign**: Models wearing only body paint with strategically placed oranges are part of a new campaign from Campari, an Italian aperitif. The brand import by Diageo's UDV of Fort Lee, N.J., has an initial bitter taste. The pitch suggests drinking Campari with orange juice, in hopes of accelerating sales growth in the U.S., as happened in international markets. The ads were created by Mullen Advertising.

—*Wall Street Journal*

Advertisers have an enormous financial stake in a narrow ideal of femininity that they promote, especially in beauty product ads. . . . The image of the beautiful woman . . . may perhaps be captured with the concept of the *perfect provocateur* (an ideal image that arouses a feeling or reaction). The exemplary female prototype in advertising, regardless of product or service, displays youth (no lines or wrinkles), good looks, sexual seductiveness . . . and perfection (no scars, blemishes, or even pores). . . . The perfect provocateur is not human; rather, she is a form or hollow shell representing a female figure. Accepted attractiveness is her only attribute. She is slender, typically tall and long-legged. Women are constantly held to this unrealistic standard of beauty. If they fail to attain it, they are led to feel guilty and ashamed. Cultural ideology tells women that they will not be desirable to, or loved by, men unless they are physically perfect.

—Anthony J. Cortese, *Provocateur: Images of Women
and Minorities in Advertising*

5

SEXUALITY AND ADVERTISING

The exploitation of the female body—and more recently the male body—for advertising is a common critique of the advertising industry. Women, and now men, are made into sex objects, used to sell everything from automobiles to toothpaste, though women are exploited much more than men in advertising. One problem with advertising is that it has the uncanny ability to resist being affected by critiques of it. Attacking advertising is like throwing thumbtacks in the path of a herd of stampeding elephants. As Judith Williamson points out in *Decoding Advertisements: Ideology and Meaning in Advertising* (1978:167), "Advertisements [ideologies] can incorporate anything, even re-absorb criticisms of themselves, because they refer to it, devoid of content. The whole system of advertising is a great recuperator: it will work on any material at all, it will bounce back uninjured from both advertising restriction laws and criticisms of its basic functions." It is helpful, nevertheless, to examine one of the most important and most often criticized aspects of advertising—its sexism.

In the article "Primping or Pimping" (Tuesday, September 26, 2000, *San Francisco Chronicle*) Valli Herman-Cohen discusses some "raunchy" sexually explicit fashion ads:

> Fashion's plunge into soft porn didn't happen overnight. In the 1960s, the late French photographer Guy Bourdin brought sex and violence to French fashion magazines, while his American counterpart, photographer Helmut Newton, added a fetishistic element beginning in the 1970s. Now lesbian sex and sadomasochism have been added to the lineup.
>
> Tongues wagged over this year's taboo-touting campaigns for French designers Emmanuel Ungaro and Christian Dior. For Ungaro's spring ads, a model offered suggestive interpretations of "petting" as she caressed her male pooch. This fall, Ungaro used the same model, who intimately embraced a nude classical statue. For Dior's spring 2000 and new fall ads, two women tumbled in designers togs like lovers experimenting in a clothes dryer.

Figure 5.1

These ads seem to have struck a responsive chord, for when asked about his advertisements, Ungaro said that his "sales have gone through the roof." A look at a magazine such as the October 2002 issue of *Harper's Bazaar*, and it is only typical of many such magazines, shows any number of fashion ads that are best described as soft porn. Many of the models have their blouses wide open, revealing most of their breasts, and there is an atmosphere of sexual obsession and decadence that pervades the advertising. Notice in figure 5.1 how the pointed white area leads the eye directly to the model's breasts, which are lighted to give them maximum impact.

SEX IN ADVERTISING

John Berger's *Ways of Seeing* explores human sexuality as one of the most potent tools of advertising. Berger points out that advertising makes greater and greater use of sexuality to sell products and services. As he explains:

> . . . this sexuality is never free in itself, it is a symbol for something presumed to be larger than it: the good life in which you can buy whatever you want. To be able to buy is the same thing as being sexually desirable. (1972:144)

The implicit message in advertising is, Berger adds, that if you can buy a given product, you'll be lovable and if you can't, you'll be less lovable. This means that purchasing products and services is always charged with fantasies and dreams of sexual desirability and power, even though we may not be conscious that such is the case.

Berger's theory explains, for example, why we often see beautiful young women in ads for automobiles, beer, fashions, and so on, ad infinitum. Though this process works in our unconscious, we make a connection between buying a product and becoming desirable to (or emulating) these women. For other products, handsome men are used in the same way. The subtext of many advertisements, then, involves the matter of sexuality and desirability, which explains why the act of buying things is so important to people and yields such great anticipated pleasures. The foundation of modern consumer societies, then, is human sexuality.

It is generally assumed in the advertising industry that there is some kind of a transfer of desire from male lust for sexually attractive women to the products that are being sold. Since it is women who are generally exploited for their sexuality, I will focus on them, but let me point out that there is also a growing use of male sexuality and homoerotic images and scenarios in selling products.

In theory, seeing a beautiful woman in a print advertisement or commercial with a certain amount of cleavage showing and revealing other parts of her body "excites" men and women who are exposed to the image. In television commercials, the woman can gaze at and directly address viewers, adding the power of the voice to the seduction of the viewer. In many commercials, the sexuality of the women is enhanced by lighting, by camera angles, by cutting and all the other techniques available to editors. Some advertising agencies have been attacking the stereotypes of women in commercials by using women who are not tall and slender but more normal—in come cases, even "pleasingly plump" or heavy.

In his book, *Visual Persuasion: The Role of Images in Advertising*, Paul Messaris offers an interesting insight into the use of very slender models in fashion advertising. He discusses studies of male preferences of physical attractiveness in women that give higher ratings to heavy women with narrow waists than slender women with narrow hips. He writes (1997:49):

> Superficially, this preference for thin models among fashion executives may seem to be a perverse, and persistent, miscalculation. But of course, that is not the case. The fashion industry's predilection for thinness does not stem from a misreading of real-world sex cues; rather, it represents a

deliberate suppression of those sex cues to heighten the sense of the human body as pure status display. In other words, this situation could be described as a conflict between sexual and social status cues, with the latter coming out on top.

What Messaris reveals is that there is often a sociological and class aspect to the images of women found in advertisements and that the sexual characteristics of the women found in advertisements is not the whole story.

These aspects in fashion advertising, and other kinds of advertising as well, are shown by other things than body shape and involve such matters as the context where the woman is shown, her props, the kind of clothes she is wearing (or almost wearing in some cases), her hairstyle and her facial characteristics. It could be argued, in fact, that many of the models in fashion advertisements are reflecting their unavailability and sense of separateness and alienation from ordinary concerns and everyday life. Fashion advertising, more than any other kind, I would suggest, generate stereotypes of what women are supposed to look like—and act like. The effects of these stereotypes, which involve being beautiful and yet, as you can see from many of the poses, submissive, are very pernicious. The mixture of sex and sociological and cultural matters means that there is often a great deal more to sexually exciting and erotically stimulating advertising than we might imagine.

SEXPLOITATION AND ANXIETY

Sexuality, sexual desire, sexual lust, and even intimations of sexual intercourse are ubiquitous in contemporary advertising. As Germaine Greer points out in *The Female Eunuch*:

> Because she is the emblem of spending ability and the chief spender, she is also the most effective seller of this world's goods. Every survey has shown that the image of an attractive woman is the most effective advertising gimmick. She may sit astride the mudguard of a new car, or step into it ablaze with jewels; she may lie at a man's feet stroking his new socks; she may hold the petrol pump in a challenging pose, or dance through the woodland glades in slow motion in all the glory of a new shampoo; whatever she does her image sells. (1971:51–2)

We use beautiful women, in various stages of dress and undress, to sell everything from automobiles to new technological gizmos, as the Palm Pilot advertisement (figure 5.2) demonstrates.

Figure 5.2

One of the problems this sexploitation of the female body causes is a sense of inadequacy on the part of many women, who don't have the lean and boyish or, in some cases, anorexic bodies that so many supermodels do—who aren't twenty years old, who aren't six feet tall, who don't weigh ninety-five pounds, who don't wear size three dresses, who aren't made up to kill, and who aren't dressed in expensive fashions.

These supermodels, "it" girls, and movie stars also cause problems for many men, who see these women and become dissatisfied with their sexual partners. As Raphael Patai explains in *Myth and Modern Man*:

> The movies, television, magazine and newspaper ads, posters, store-window mannequins, life-size, smaller than life, bigger than life, in colors or in black-and-white, in partial or total undress, in all kinds of alluring and enticing positions with the most express indications of availability, willingness, readiness to welcome you into their arms . . . have the combined and cumulative effect of making many men dissatisfied with whatever sexual activity is available to them. (1972:286)

What Patai suggests, then, is that not only women but also men are affected—and to a considerable degree disturbed—by the endless number of sexually provocative advertisements and commercials to which they are exposed. *Men can satisfy their sexual hunger with their wives and girlfriends, but not their erotic fantasies.* (The same applies to women as well, no doubt—since they are continually exposed to virile, rugged, handsome men in advertisements and commercials.)

Let me quote a number of passages relating to gender in advertising found in Erving Goffman's "Gender Advertisements." The general thrust of his argument is that by various means, such as bent knees, smiles, and being shown smaller than men, women are placed in positions of subordination and weakness. See figure 5.3, in which the woman in the Nautica advertisement is in a subservient position to the man.

1. One way in which social weight—power, authority, rank, office, renown—is echoed expressively in social situations is through relative size, especially height.
2. Women, more than men, are pictured using their fingers and hands to trace the outlines of an object or to cradle it or caress its surface.
3. In our society when a man and a woman collaborate face-to-face in an undertaking, the man—it would seem—is likely to perform the executive role.
4. Smiles . . . often function as ritualistic modifiers, signaling that nothing antagonistic is intended or invited, meaning that the other's act has been understood and found acceptable. (1976)

Figure 5.3

I am, of course, stating things in a rather extreme way. But the models used in a significant number of commercials and fashion advertisements—for expensive, upscale products, that is—are frequently unusual physical specimens. Advertisements for cosmetics often play upon the anxiety women feel as they start getting older about no longer being young and no longer being beautiful. It may even be more extreme than that: no longer young, therefore no longer beautiful.

THE PEACH THAT BECAME A PRUNE: A CAUTIONARY FABLE

In this respect, consider the copy for a moisturizer that follows. There is a large headline followed by copy that reads:

**There is
a fountain of youth.
It's called water.**

> Nature has been telling us this forever. Water keeps a rose fresh and beautiful. A peach juicy. All living things, living. Including your skin. The millions of cells in your skin contain water. This water pillows and cushions your skin, making it soft and young-looking. But, for a lot of reasons, cells become unable to hold water. And the water escapes your skin. (If you'll forgive us, think of a prune drying up and you'll know the whole story.)

This copy was in an advertisement for Living Proof Cream Hydracel by Geminesse, a moisturizer that promises to do two things. First, it promises to help women develop younger-looking skin, and second, it promises to help women avoid drying up and looking, if you'll forgive the harsh analogy, like prunes.

There is a question that now must be considered. What is this overwhelming need women have to be "moist"? At first glance, and I use the phrase purposefully, it seems to involve looking younger by having soft, peachlike, skin. And it also has something to do with being roselike (see Lancôme's recent ad in figure 5.4), whatever that might mean. But underneath it all, I think the fear of losing moisture really has to do with anxieties women have—generated by the advertisement or, at least, exploited by the advertisement—about their loss of fertility, about changing from being a "garden" (where things can grow) to being a "desert" (barren, lifeless, and sterile).

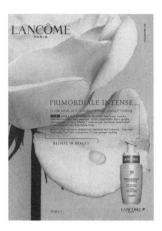

Figure 5.4

This is symbolized in the ad by the two fruits mentioned—the juicy (young) peach and the dried-up (old) prune. And if you aren't one, the bipolar logic of the advertisement suggests, you must be the other. It is this drying-up that women must avoid at all costs, this loss of youth and fertility symbolized by having soft, moist skin. And that is where moisturizers come in—especially moisturizers like Hydracel (and Lancôme's "Primordiale Intense" in figure 5.4). They preserve the illusion women have that they are still young, the illusion of generativity by merging pseudoscience and magic. These products succeed by terrorizing women—who live in constant fear of water gushing out of their cells, flooding out of their bodies, until the magic no longer works or is no longer needed.

As the Living Proof Cream Hydracel by Geminesse advertisement adds, discussing "the truth about moisturizers":

> Most people think a moisturizer literally puts moisture into your skin. Not true. (Your skin has all the water it needs. Holding it there is the problem.) An average moisturizer holds the water in by blocking its escape. But, unfortunately, this does not affect your cell's ability to retain water. This is where we come in. . . . The name Hydracel tells you what we're all about: water and cell. Cream Hydracel actually helps the cellular tissues retain water. We let nature do the work, not heavy creams. And this can make all the difference. Your skin will breathe and start to recover its water-holding power. And your face will feel softer and look younger, naturally. . . . Nature gave you a fountain of youth. Cream Hydracel keeps it flowing.

This is only one example of the campaign of terror waged by cosmetic companies and all the industries involved with feminine sexuality through such matters as hair, clothes, eyeglasses, jewelry, watches, shoes, stockings— you name it. Women are put in a no-win situation. Beauty is associated with youth, and women are made to feel that when they lose their youth, they will lose their beauty. The passage from ripe, juicy "peach" to dried-up old "prune" whose fountain of youth no longer flows is inevitable—though one can, through the magic of cosmetics, so the advertisements and commercials imply, hold off the ravages of getting older. Advertising creates the problem and then provides the solution—some product or service that will help women become beautiful and stay beautiful, which means keeping them looking young and juicy, like a peach.

THE PSEUDO-POETIC APPEAL TO THE ILLITERATI

A good deal of the writing found in advertisements for perfumes and other cosmetics has what might be described as a pseudo-poetic character to it. One of the best descriptions of this phenomenon was written by the anthropologist Jules Henry in his book *Culture Against Man*. He writes:

> Consider the advertisement for *Pango Peach*, a new color introduced by Revlon in 1960. A young woman leans against the upper rungs of a ladder leading to a palm-thatched bamboo tree-house. *Pango Peach* are her *sari*, her blouse, her toe and finger nails, and the cape she holds. A sky of South Pacific blue is behind her, and the cape, as it flutters in the winds, stains the heavens *Pango Peach*. "From east of the sun—west of the moon where each tomorrow dawns . . ." beckons the ad, in corny pecuniary lingo. But when you are trying to sell nail polish to a filing clerk with two years of high school you don't quote Dylan Thomas! The idea of this ad is to make a woman think she is reading real poetry when she is not, and at the same time to evoke in her the specific fantasy that will sell the product. Millions will respond to poetry as a value and feel good when they think they are responding to it, and this process of getting people to respond to pseudo-values as if they were responding to real ones is called here *pecuniary distortion of values*. (1963:59)

Henry quotes some other phrases from the advertisement—Pango Peach is described as "a many splendoured coral . . . pink with pleasure . . . a volcano of color," and it adds, "It's full ripe peach with a world of difference

. . . born to be worn in big juicy slices. Succulent on your lips. Sizzling on your fingertips. . . . Go Pango Peach . . . your adventure in paradise."

He then discusses the significance of the language used in the Pango Peach advertisement. He writes:

> Each word in the advertisement is carefully chosen to tap a particular yearning and hunger in the American woman. "Many splendoured," for example, is a reference to the novel and movie *Love Is a Many Splendoured Thing*, a tale of passion in an Oriental setting. "Volcano" is meant to arouse the latent wish to be a volcanic lover and be loved by one. The mouthful of oral stimuli—"ripe," "succulent," "juicy"—puts sales resistance in double jeopardy because mouths are even more for kissing than eating. "Sizzling" can refer only to *l'amour à la folie*. (1963:59)

We can see then that what seems to be a simple advertisement for a new color contains any number of oral stimuli and references to a culture that will, it is hoped, persuade the readers of the advertisement to purchase Pango Peach lipstick and other products and put themselves, like the model, in the South Pacific where "volcanic" love awaits. Notice, also, that this advertisement—like the Hydracel moisturizer advertisement—makes use of peaches as symbols of youth, beauty, and sexual allure. I return to this subject in chapter 8 in my analysis of an advertisement for Fidji perfume. The ad in figure 5.5 suggests that teenagers are an important marketing category and that certain kinds of appeals can be made to them and can be effective. We will see shortly how cigarette advertisers used a symbolic cartoon figure, Joe Camel, to induce teenagers and preteens to start smoking.

Insights from Advertising Agencies

The sentimentality and warmth appeal is being dropped for a campy sex-and-youth appeal, and they aren't trying to sell people on the idea of cognac but on their particular brand. There was much talk about the Smirnoff Vodka campaign, which was a great success and which was based on sexploitation and the double entendre. The problem they faced involved thinking up an advertisement that would command attention, that was original, and that worked. There was some talk about thinking up some kind of a catchy phrase that would become part of public currency, that comedians might repeat, and that might strike the public's fancy.

Wise Up to Teens

Insights into Marketing and Advertising to Teenagers

By Peter Zollo
Here at last is the expert analysis that will help you capture your share of the nearly $100 billion that teenagers spend. This book explains where teens get their money, how and why they spend it, and what they think about themselves and the world around them. It presents five rules that will make your advertising appealing to teens. Learn about brands teens think are cool, words to use in advertising to teens, which media and promotions teens prefer, and how much influence teens have over what their parents buy. This is a fascinating look into the world of teens—a market whose income is almost all discretionary.
—Advertisement for a book on marketing to teens in the November 1995 *Marketing Power: The Marketer's Reference Library*

Figure 5.5

SEX SELLS CIGARETTES

I have suggested earlier in this book that we cannot always make a connection between a person's exposure to a commercial or print advertisement for a product and his or her subsequent use of that product. But we can see that collectively, large numbers of people may be influenced by their exposure to advertising. While we cannot make a connection between one person seeing an advertisement for a product (or many advertisements for the product) and buying it, statistically we can note that advertising campaigns do have effects on large numbers of people.

THE CASE OF JOE CAMEL

According to an American Medical Association study, Joe Camel, the cartoon figure of a camel shown smoking a cigarette, is "twice as familiar" to 3- to 6-year-olds "as a box of Cheerios" and is "as well-known to 6-year-olds as Mickey Mouse." Joe Camel ads have played an important role in making Camels "the brand of choice among male children, 12 to 17 years old."

Majorie Garber explains the power of the Joe Camel drawing in her article "Joe Camel, an X-Rated Smoke" (*New York Times*, March 20, 1992).

As she writes: "His long straight snout bulges from above two pouchy folds as he stares insouciantly out at the viewer, a lighted cigarette hanging from his lips. Look again. Any schoolchild can recognize this ribald caricature; only adults need to have it pointed out." What we have, Garber points out, is a phallic symbol—an example of what Freud described as "displacement upward," a translation in dreams and fantasies of a taboo part of our bodies from below the waist—where its significance would be easily seen—to above the waist, frequently to the head or to the face, where its significance is not so apparent.

In this respect Garber discusses noses and cigars as some of the most commonly used phallic symbols. Freud said that "sometimes a cigar is only a cigar." True. But the obverse of his statement, which we must keep in mind, is that sometimes a cigar *isn't only* a cigar. It is the unconscious appeal to sexual potency that is behind the acceptance by puerile young males of Joe Camel's inducements to choose Camel cigarettes.

Cigarette smoking, to a rather alarming extent, is also found in many recent films. Directors use cigarettes because they help define characters, they give characters something to do with their hands, and because there are aesthetic dimensions to capturing cigarette smoke as it drifts upwards and disperses. And recently cigars, an even more potent phallic symbol than cigarettes, have become popular—with men and to a limited extent with women. Young men and women learn from watching films that smoking is glamorous and "cool." (In some cases, certain brands of cigarettes are "placed" in films—the tobacco companies pay to have their cigarettes used in them; the same applies to other products as well.) And since teens have a good deal of discretionary income, many of them use it to buy cigarettes. Placing products in films is a kind of advertising that is not recognized as such and thus is even more insidious than regular advertising, especially since young people often identify with and strive to imitate famous actors.

Many young girls smoke because, among other things, they believe smoking will enable them to stay slim and look like the supermodels they see in fashion magazines (figure 5.6). Ironically, obesity has now reached epidemic proportions among the American public. Young people don't get enough exercise nowadays, and older populations also eat too much and exercise too little. One of the things we do when we watch television is eat snacks, and one of the things we are bombarded with when we watch television is commercials for foods. And, of course, many of these commercials are for diet products—so the foods we eat won't make us fat. So advertising, let me suggest, plays a role in shaping our bodies as well as affecting our choices of all kinds of products—from foods to cigarettes.

Figure 5.6

Because of the numerous protests by parents' groups and other organizations against the Joe Camel advertisements, they have been discontinued. The recognition that sexuality has been used to induce teenagers (and preteens) to smoke has now led to a counterattack using sexuality—and the fear of sexual impotence and lack of function—to convince young boys and girls not to smoke. In one commercial, a young teenager sees an attractive girl and as he looks at her, the cigarette dangling from his mouth goes limp. It is an excellent example of fighting fire with fire.

SEX AND THE PROBLEM OF CLUTTER

One reason for using sexuality to sell products is explained by Jack Solomon in his book *The Signs of Our Times*. His thesis is that sexuality enables advertising agencies to avoid the clutter of competing ads and commercials. As he writes:

> The sexual explicitness of contemporary advertising is a sign not so much of American sexual fantasies as of the lengths to which advertisers will go to get attention. Sex never fails as an attention-getter, and in a particularly competitive and expansive era for American marketing, advertisers like to bet on a sure thing. Ad people refer to the proliferation of TV, radio, newspaper, magazine, and billboard ads as "clutter," and nothing cuts through clutter like sex.

By showing the flesh, advertisers work on the deepest, most coercive human emotions of all. Much sexual coercion in advertising, however, is a sign of a desperate need to make certain that clients are getting their money's worth. (1990:69)

On the other hand, if advertising agencies compete with one another by using sexuality to sell, they just raise clutter to a different or higher level, creating what might be called "sexual clutter."

And I think this is, to a considerable degree, what has happened. Sexuality is all-pervasive in American media, and as it becomes more and more commonplace, advertisers have to develop new and more daring, and in some cases more explicit, ways of having their sexual commercials and print advertisements stand out or attain some degree of differentiation. As the Pierre Cardin advertisement (figure 5.7) shows, companies do whatever they can to differentiate themselves from their competitors and catch a reader's attention.

There is also the law of diminishing returns to consider. For as the American media becomes oversaturated with sexual images, in programming as well as in advertising, the law of diminishing returns starts operating and the power of any particular sexual image to attract attention and stimulate demands weakens. This leads to the crisis that advertising now faces as companies and their agencies engage in what has been called "sign wars" to attract the attention of the American public. Sexual imagery is so all-pervasive that the commercials of one company may be neutralizing the commercials of its competitors and leading, ultimately, to a kind of "turn-

Figure 5.7

Figure 5.8

ing off" by the general public as it becomes overwhelmed by sexuality in advertisements and commercials.

In her "Primping or Pimping" article, Valli Herman-Cohen quotes an editor who makes this kind of an argument:

> "Everybody is reaching, and I no longer know what they are reaching for," said Edie Locke, former editor-in-chief of *Mademoiselle*. "If every image now is centered around sex, or almost-rape, or lesbian chic, the difference between the ads is no longer perceptible." (2000)

As I've argued, sex is used to sell everything from video games to milk (figure 5.8). So there is a problem fashion and other advertisers face—their advertisements get lost in the sexual advertising clutter, and no matter how far they are willing to go, it seems that some other advertiser is willing to go further.

We must never underestimate the power of sexual images to affect us in mysterious and profound ways. But the incessant clutter of sexual images may weaken the power of any one advertisement or commercial to sell us some product or service and may even be having an impact upon our sexual lives. There is so much vicarious sex in our lives that the "real thing" may be losing its appeal for a goodly number of people.

The effect of advertiser-driven campaigning has been felt in more than just the professionalization of electoral propaganda, though the slickly produced political advertisement is certainly its most visible product. Promotion has been drawn into the heart of the process. Through the 1970s and 1980s it has become normal practice for the managers of campaign advertising to be recruited directly from the highest ranks of the advertising industry. Their role, moreover, sometimes in collusion with the official party machine, has been not just to supervise the specifics of advertising, but to map out entire campaigns. The scope for involvement is endless. Every public statement or gesture by campaigners, whether intentional or not, can be considered part of the campaign, and is therefore susceptible to promotional orchestration.

—Andrew Wernick, *Promotional Culture: Advertising, Ideology and Symbolic Expression*

Under the heading of deceptive editing of "documentary" material, we might also want to consider a notorious political ad used in Richard Nixon's 1968 presidential campaign. Aired only once, the ad juxtaposed images of Nixon's Democratic opponent, Hubert Humphrey, with scenes of warfare in Vietnam, protests in the streets of Chicago, and poverty in Appalachia. Because Humphrey was smiling in some of the shots, these juxtapositions created the impression that he was indifferent to the suffering and disturbances in the other images.

—Paul Messaris, *Visual Persuasion: The Role of Images in Advertising*

6

POLITICAL ADVERTISING

In recent decades, political advertising has assumed greater and greater importance in campaigns for offices at all levels. There is a reason for this. As political scientists Stephen Ansolabehere and Shanto Iyengar write in their book *Going Negative: How Political Advertisements Shrink and Polarize the Electorate*:

> Unlike most channels of communication, advertising allows candidates to reach uninterested and unmotivated citizens—those who ordinarily pay little attention to news reports, debates, and other campaign events. After all, the "audience" for political advertising is primarily inadvertent— people who happen to be watching their preferred television programs. Of course, viewers can choose to tune out or channel-surf during advertising breaks, but the fact remains that the reach of advertising extends beyond relatively attentive and engaged voters. (1995:52)

Thus, advertising is a tool that enables politicians to send their messages to a large number of people who tend to be apolitical, who are not particularly interested in political campaigns. What is important to recognize is that these people are often profoundly affected by the political advertisements to which they are exposed.

What follows is an introduction to an important and very controversial subject—how advertising has become a major instrument of campaigning for and winning political office. I have chosen to discuss political advertising because, although many people do not think about it, our decisions about who we vote for play a crucial role in determining what laws will be passed and how we will lead our lives. From my perspective, political advertising can be seen as the most important genre of advertising. I would hope the information presented in this book will help readers learn to "read" or "decode" political advertisements better by offering insights

into the methods used by political advertisers and thus make more informed and more intelligent decisions when they vote.

We must recognize that all political advertisements are not the same. In her book *30-Second Politics: Political Advertising in the Eighties*, Montague Kern, a social scientist, suggests there are four kinds of political advertisements. We tend to lump all political advertising together, but if you examine political ads over the course of a typical campaign, you discover there really are a number of different *kinds* of political advertisements, which are used at different *times* in a typical campaign.

There are some theorists, I should point out, who consider *all* advertising to be political in that advertising suggests a political order that produces all the products and services being advertised. Hans Magnus Enzensberger ties advertising to the need political orders have for acceptance by the public. He writes in his essay "The Industrialization of the Mind":

> Consciousness, both individual and social, has become a political issue only from the moment when the conviction arose in people's minds that everyone should have a say in his own destiny as well as in that of society at large. From the same moment any authority had to justify itself in the eyes of those it would govern; coercion alone would no longer do the trick; he who ruled must persuade, must lay claim to the people's minds and change them, in an industrial age, by every industrial means at hand. (*The Consciousness Industry*, 1974:8)

This leads to the development of what Enzensberger calls the "mind industry," whose basic concern is to convince people that the existing order should be perpetuated. The mind industry's main task—and advertising is a major element of the mind industry—is "to perpetuate the prevailing pattern of man's domination by man, no matter who runs the society and by what means. Its main task is to expand and train our consciousness—in order to exploit it" (1974:10).

With this insight in mind, it is worth examining in some detail Kern's insights into the kinds of political advertisements and how political advertising works.

KINDS OF POLITICAL ADVERTISEMENTS

Kern discusses political advertisements and points out some changes that have taken place in them in recent years:

> If recent research indicates that contemporary political advertising has an impact that includes but is much broader than that of informing the public about candidate positions on the issues, content research based on ads supplied by campaigns also suggests that the purpose of advertising has changed since 1972. It is concerned as much with conveying impressions about candidate character as with providing information about issues. Richard Joselyn has argued that there are four types of ads, with issue statements that are largely sloganistic relating to only two of them: *prospective* and *retrospective* policy satisfaction appeals, as opposed to *election as ritual* and his largest category, *benevolent leader* appeals. (1989:6)

The most significant development in political advertising in recent decades, of course, is just the opposite of the benevolent leader appeal. Much political advertising is now negative, and it attacks political figures for their policies and often for their character and behavior as well. This leads to counterattacks, so that negative advertising becomes a dominant method in many campaigns. These attack ads are used, as Kern explains, generally only at certain times in campaigns.

She discusses different kinds of commercials one finds at different stages in a typical campaign for political office. It isn't just a matter of developing name awareness in voters anymore. As she explains:

> Further, now-classic theory of media use argues that there are four types of ads associated with four stages in a campaign: first, *name identification*

spots, which are shown early in the campaign; second, *argument* spots, which present candidate positions on issues; third, *attack* spots, which focus on the opponent; and fourth, *positive* visionary appeals, which are used at the end of a campaign to give voters a reason to vote for the candidate. (1989:6)

We see then that political advertising has developed over the years and television spots have different purposes at different times in a typical campaign.

Political advertising in electoral campaigns is, ultimately, aimed at persuading voters to do what the person paying for the advertisements wants them to do—that is, to vote *for* a particular candidate, which means not voting for any other candidates. Or, in the case of political propositions, to vote the way the advertiser wants them to vote.

We must remember that when advertisers pay to have something "run up a flagpole," they always expect large numbers of people to "salute." Or to use a different metaphor, it may always be the case that "he who pays the piper calls the tune," but it doesn't always work out that the tune is one people like or one that convinces them to sing along. In the case of political advertising, "saluting" or "singing along" means voting for a particular candidate or in a certain way on propositions.

Table 6.1 lists the four stages in a typical political campaign and describes the kinds of political advertisements found at each stage in the campaign. I've also suggested what the specific function of each kind of advertisement is, using words beginning with *I* as a mnemonic device to facilitate remembering them.

Early in the campaign the politician wants to gain name recognition or persuade voters to associate him or her with the position he or she is running for. Then the campaign moves into issues the politicians believe in or don't believe in. Later the politicians use attack ads or what we commonly call "negative ads" to put opponents on the defensive. Finally, politicians offer "visionary" ads to give voters reasons to vote for them on the basis of their character.

Table 6.1. Stages and Kinds of Advertisements in Political Campaigns

Time in Campaign	Kind of Advertisement	Function
Early	Name Identification Ads	Identity
Later	Argument Ads	Ideology
Later Still	Attack Ads (Negative Ads)	Insult
End of Campaign	Positive Visionary Ads	Image

THE 1998 CALIFORNIA PRIMARY:
A "VIRTUAL" CAMPAIGN FOR GOVERNOR

The 1998 California campaign for governor has achieved a rather legendary status. In the campaign there were three Democratic candidates. The least-known one, at the beginning of the campaign, was Al Checchi, a multimillionaire former airline executive who spent $40 million (his own money) seeking the nomination. When Dianne Feinstein, a Democratic U.S. senator from San Francisco, decided not to enter the race, Jane Harman, a two-term U.S. congresswoman, entered. She spent $15 million (her own money) seeking the nomination. Checchi's $40 million is the most any nonpresidential candidate has ever spent on a primary campaign.

The underdog was Gray Davis, the lieutenant governor of the state, and a person with more than twenty years of experience in state government. He spent $9 million (not his own money) on the race and won the primary. The slogan for his campaign was brilliant:

EXPERIENCE MONEY CAN'T BUY

This slogan did two things. First, it pointed out that Davis was a person who had a lot of experience in government. Al Checchi, it turned out, hadn't even voted in a number of elections and was a political novice. And though his $40 million bought him name recognition, when he started running negative advertisements about Jane Harman, he neutralized her as a political force and he alienated many voters. Thus, one unintended consequence of Checchi's campaign was to weaken Harman so Davis had an easier time getting the nomination.

Davis's slogan also played on a feeling people in California have that wealthy people shouldn't be able to buy an election. And they shouldn't be able to start at the top. These notions seem to be, in part, an outgrowth of a particularly vicious and expensive self-financed campaign run by Michael Huffington, a wealthy Republican in California's 1996 U.S. Senate race, which Feinstein barely won.

California is an enormous state with a population of more than thirty million people. The only way to get one's message out to the people in the state, aside from whatever news coverage a candidate may get, is through advertising—and chiefly through commercials on radio and, more importantly, on television. There were several debates in the campaign, with the Republican nominee Dan Lungren participating, but for all practical purposes, all that most voters in California saw in the primary were commercials—which is why the campaign was dubbed a "virtual" campaign.

QUESTIONS RAISED BY THE "VIRTUAL" CAMPAIGN

The 1998 primary raises some interesting questions about the relationship between political advertising and voting.

1. *Are people no longer affected by negative campaigns?*
People always say, in polls, they don't like negative campaigns but voting records seem to indicate that they are affected or influenced by them. Numerous case studies of elections show that negative campaigns, full of attack commercials, are effective. One theory is that negative campaigns turn many viewers off (dissuade them from voting at all) and thus play into the hands of politicians, generally conservative Republican ones, who rely on the minority of conservative Republicans who *do* vote (in contrast to the majority of generally liberal Democrats, who don't vote).

It may also be that California voters are somewhat different from voters in other states, or that California voters have established a new trend.

2. *Is it the number or the quality of the advertisements that counts?*
The primary showed, at different times, each of the candidates in the lead. First Checchi, with his advertising blitz, took the lead. Then when Harman entered, she took the lead—until Checchi's negative ads hurt her. Then when he started advertising late in the race, Gray Davis's advertising campaign put him in the lead, and he stayed there and captured the nomination by a large margin.

Davis's $9 million was a considerable amount of money, but it paled in comparison with Checchi's $40 million and Harman's $15 million. Statewide campaigns in California, especially for important and high-profile positions such as governor, are very expensive—due in large measure to the enormous size of the state and its huge population.

3. *Is it the advertising or the record of the candidate that is crucial?*
This matter is particularly significant. Do people vote for someone because of advertising per se or because the advertising points to a person's record or stand on important issues (and attacks opponents' positions)? In the 1998 California primary, the experience of the winning candidate seemed to be crucial. If so, that would suggest Californians have rejected the notion that experience in government is bad and that the less experience a politician has, the better—a position made popular by Ronald Reagan and by many conservative Republicans.

It is estimated that by a ratio of something like four to one, Americans get their information about the positions of candidates from advertising rather than the news. Much of the news in political campaigns tends to focus on the horse race aspect of the campaign—who's ahead rather than differences on issues. And curiously, what the news programs on television decide to cover is often shaped by the candidates' political advertisements. The advertisements set the agenda for the newspapers and radio and television news programs.

Kathleen Hall Jamieson explores the relationship between news and advertising in her book *Dirty Politics: Deception, Distraction and Democracy*. She writes:

> News reporting can provide a frame through which viewers understand ads. Conventional campaign wisdom holds that news sets the context for ads. If the news accounts are inconsistent with the ad, the power of the ad is diminished. When the two are consistent, the power of both is magnified. But news can only reframe ads if reporters question the legitimacy of their claims, point out the false inferences that they invite, and so on. Without such reframing by reporters, campaign ads have the potential to shape the visual and verbal language of news, and in recent campaigns they have become increasingly successful. (1992:124)

This failure of news reporters to deal with misleading statements and matters of that nature is due, in part, to the obsession newspeople have with who is winning a campaign rather than the truth or falsity of advertisements. In addition, written critiques of political commercials in newspapers generally cannot undo the damage done by them, since the impact of television commercials is so great.

Political advertisements about issues can be divided into two categories. There are so-called platform ads, which are full of broad generalities, and slogan ads, which contain some slogan related to an action the candidate promises to take or gives an important insight into the candidate's character. When Dwight David Eisenhower said "I will go to Korea" in 1952, he was offering a slogan ad. And Gray Davis's "Experience money can't buy" was another slogan ad that took his primary campaign and reduced it to one slogan that people could remember.

THE 2002 CALIFORNIA CAMPAIGN FOR GOVERNOR

Governor Gray Davis had very high popularity ratings for the first two years in which he was in office. He spent a great deal of money on education and was riding high when, in 2000, California was hit by an energy crisis—manufactured by Enron and other companies, which used illegal tactics to gouge California for electricity. Davis didn't handle this crisis to the satisfaction of most Californians and his popularity plummeted.

Compounding his problems was his rather aloof and somewhat authoritarian manner, leading to difficulties with members of his own party. With the demise of the dot-com boom and the flat economy, California suddenly found itself with a gigantic budget deficit, just when the 2002 elections came around. From the moment he became governor, Davis started gathering a huge amount of money for his campaign chest—estimated at around $60 million—because he was afraid that some rich California Republican might decide to run for governor, which is exactly what happened.

In the Republican primary, a wealthy Republican, Bill Simon, ran against the former mayor of Los Angeles, Richard Riordan. Riordan is a moderate Republican and polls suggested he had a very good chance of defeating Gray Davis. So, in a brilliant move, Davis spent $10 million attacking Riordan and ensured that Simon, a bumbling, doltish and very conservative candidate, won the Republican nomination for governor. Even though Simon ran what some Republicans described as the worst campaign in the country, he only lost to Davis by six percentage points. Lyn Nofziger, a Republican campaign expert, called Simon "too dumb to win."

Simon made one disastrous mistake after another, but still came close. In part, this was because many Californians, though they didn't like Davis very much, didn't like Simon at all. In truth, most Californians said they didn't like either candidate and picked the lesser of two evils. Many people felt that Davis had spent too much time getting money for his campaign and that he had looked after companies that had given large donations to his campaign. Simon called him a "pay to play" governor. Davis ran essentially a negative campaign, filling the airwaves with attacks on Simon. Toward the end of the campaign, Davis ran some positive commercials about his achievements.

Dan Walters, a reporter from California, wrote an article, "A State of Gray," that appeared in the *Wall Street Journal* on October 24, 2002. In it he quotes from the endorsement that the *Los Angeles Times* gave Davis:

> Davis's obsessive pursuit of every last campaign dollar from special interests is unseemly, and the governor has been slow to grasp the lead on critical issues. . . . Davis is aloof. He agonizes over minor decisions most governors would leave to aides. He is robotic and largely humorless. He is often at war with the Legislature.

This, remember, is from a newspaper that endorsed Davis.

Davis had predicted he would win by double digits and mentioned, a number of times, when he was giving his victory speech on November 5, how he found politics to be "humbling" (by that he meant his humiliating victory over Simon). He did pass some very forward-looking social legislation in the weeks before the election, which shows—as one commentator put it—that if pressed, Davis does "the right thing." Being the governor of a large state like California is often a stepping-stone to the presidency, and Davis was, for a while, thought to have a very good chance of securing the Democratic nomination for the presidency. In a remarkable turn of events, California held a special election in the fall of 2003 and Davis was voted out of office. His replacement, Republican and actor Arnold Schwarzenegger, served out his term and was reelected in 2006 by a landslide.

THE CODE OF THE COMMERCIAL
(AND OTHER POLITICAL ADVERTISING)

The television commercial, because it is the most powerful form of advertising, is the most interesting and most complex kind of political advertisement. In these commercials, a set of emotional values is established

Table 6.2. Positive Appeals and Their Negations

Positive	Negative
hope (for the future)	despair
compassion (for those in need)	coldness, aloofness
ambition (to do what's needed)	lethargy
trust	deviousness
nostalgia (for the mythic past)	unconcern for the past
intimacy	distance
reassurance	gloominess
local pride	local shame
national pride	national shame

around common themes, values, or beliefs. Table 6.2 shows these values by offering a set of opposites and listing the negative notions that most Americans find repellent.

Political advertisements use symbols, as best they can, that generate the positive appeals listed in table 6.2. These appeals lead to positive feelings about a candidate, which then translate into votes for the candidate.

We want candidates who reassure us, who give us hope, who are compassionate toward the poor and disadvantaged, who make us feel proud about where we live and about America. We like to feel that our candidates are like us and aware of people like us, even though they may be quite far removed—in distance and socioeconomic status—from us.

One of the most important things candidates do is to use visual symbols to get their messages across directly and viscerally. Thus we see them appropriating important American symbols: the flag, the hard hat (identification with the blue-collar worker), a "visionary" look over the horizon, the all-American family, and so on, to generate the emotional responses that lead to instant and powerful identification with the candidate and hopefully, as a consequence, votes for the candidate. Not that language is unimportant, but in commercials a great deal of the communication burden is carried by physical symbols.

And that is why politics has become, to such an important degree, dominated by advertising—just like so many other areas of American life. Presidents (and other politicians) are just one more product to be sold to the American public, and while advertising isn't the only determining factor, it does play a major role in political campaigns and, by implication, in the governmental process.

The Internet advertisement for George W. Bush's 2000 campaign (figure 6.1) offered a slogan that helped define him and associated him with prosperity. Bush redefined himself a number of times with different slo-

Figure 6.1

gans, and voters may have gotten confused trying to decide whether Bush was a "compassionate conservative" or a "reformer with results."

THE EMOTIONAL BASIS OF PARTISAN POLITICS

A psychologist at Emory University, Dr. Drew Westen, did some research using M.R.I. scanners that revealed something very interesting about political choices. What he discovered, by scanning the brains of partisan Democrats and Republicans, when they were given information that either attacked their beliefs or reinforced them, was that most of the decisions people make are unconscious. Political scientists have suggested that unconscious emotional forces shape our political decision making, and Westen's research proves it, by showing that certain regions of the brain have increased activity when people are shown material that leads to dissonance—that is, material that conflicts with strongly held beliefs.

When material that was unwelcome to the participants in his experiment was shown to them, certain areas of their brains flared with activity due to their unconscious rejection of this material. The experiment also found that people who unconsciously rejected certain information that was contrary to their beliefs had spikes in areas of their brain that are associated with feeling relieved or being rewarded.

What this suggests is that our political decision making is primarily guided by unconscious forces and that the arguments we make to support our positions can be seen as, to a large degree, rationalizations to justify our views. At least this is the case with people with strong commitments to one or another political party. What these findings imply is that political commercials are most effective when they strike hidden chords in our psyches that resonate with their beliefs, when they "touch" us in ways whose importance we cannot, generally speaking, fathom. In essence, we believe what we want to believe, for reasons we cannot fathom.

Westen said that it is possible, in theory, to overcome our unconscious beliefs and biases but it is very difficult to do so. As Freud pointed out, the unconscious is not accessible to people under ordinary circumstances, so to the degree that our political behavior is shaped by unconscious forces, generally speaking we are unable to recognize the extent to which this has occurred and do anything about it. Freud said that where there is id (that is, unconscious emotional desires that shape our behavior), there should be ego (by which he meant logical and rational behavior), but in life and in politics, it isn't very easy to do this.

We should also keep in mind how Grid-Group theory relates to political decision making. Political scientist Aaron Wildavsky argued that the four lifestyles or consumer cultures, discussed earlier, also have relevance to politics and that these cultures affect our politics and voting. He argued that people cannot know what their interests are so they must have other ways of deciding how to vote and what guides them is their membership in one of the four political cultures—even though they may not recognize that they belong to one of these political cultures. What voters do recognize is that they don't accept the ideas and beliefs of members of the other political cultures and so they vote accordingly. What Westen's research shows is that this process of determining how to vote, based on one's membership in a political culture, is largely an emotional one, shaped by unconscious imperatives.

THE DEATH OF THE TOBACCO BILL

I've been discussing political advertising and campaigns for elected office to this point. But there is another kind of political advertising that is worth considering—advertising done by interest groups to support their goals and affect decision making in the Congress. One of the most significant recent examples of a successful campaign is the one run by the cigarette companies to defeat the tobacco bill by Senator John McCain (Republican from Arizona) in the U.S. Senate.

Tobacco companies spent $40 million on advertising in a national campaign waged mostly on television and radio to defeat the McCain bill. The money was spent to turn around public opinion in America and thus give cover to those senators who wished to defeat the bill, which was intended to curb teenage smoking.

What the campaign did was redefine the nature of the McCain bill and change the terms of the matter being debated. The cigarette makers argued that the McCain bill was not really an attempt to curb teenage smoking *but a new tax on working-class Americans* advocated by a number of tax-and-spend members of Congress.

Since McCain is a Republican, the advertisers couldn't claim it was a liberal Democratic tax bill, but the advertisements and commercials suggested that was the case. The commercials didn't say that those paying the tax would be the people who smoked (and then ran up enormous medical bills to treat the diseases caused by smoking), not the general public. The McCain bill was described as an attack on "the American way of life."

To quote from one tobacco advertisement: "Washington has gone haywire, proposing the same old tax and spend. Half a trillion dollars in new taxes . . . 17 new government bureaucracies. Cigarettes up to $5 a pack. . . . Huge job losses among farmers, retailers and small businesses." Attacking Washington—that is, the government—is a standard technique used by interest groups. These are the same groups, let me point out, that spend enormous amounts of money on lobbyists to influence the government.

Ironically, the person who designed the campaign, Carter Escew, is an advertising executive who has been associated with the Democratic party over the years. Escew also added a "scare" issue to the campaign against the tobacco bill—some advertising by the tobacco industry intimated that the McCain bill would inevitably lead to a huge black market in cigarettes and thus would not be effective.

Escew explained his tactics as follows (quoted in an article by Howard Kurtz, *Washington Post*, "How an Adman Helped Kill Tobacco Bill"): "The message is bounced off the satellite—the satellite being the American people—and comes back to the members [of the Senate]." Escew did this by advertising heavily in the markets where there were wavering senators—and it was the senators who were his ultimate audience.

We see then that advertising is used not only to sell politicians to the voting public during elections, it also can be used to help shape public policy. Forty million dollars for an advertising campaign is a small amount to pay if you think that by spending that money you'll save billions.

In Japan, firms suffering severe competition have devised a course of instruction which aims to instill the fanaticism of selling for its own sake. The pressure of competition faced by these companies is heightened by the structure of each sector: they specialize too little, and thus too many firms crowd into the market. In particular, the virtual absence of specialization makes additional demands on the sellers. The programme developed under these conditions is called *Moretsu* (or "feverishly active"). It involves "breeding," the goal of which is the fanatical seller whose drives and energy are subordinated to their selling activity. "The aim is to breed a sales genius, with an elbow of cast-iron, brain like a computer and the constitution of a horse." In short, "they want to breed the sales robot." The breeding programme starts its day with an hour of strenuous exercise. After breakfast it is time to practice "self-forgetting." "They achieve this by hitting the furniture with clubs and yelling war-cries." This is succeeded by detailed discussion of the company's sales figures. Whoever is criticized by the instructor must literally wallow in the dust while accusing themselves of worthlessness. "After a time the conviction grows inside the participants on the course that the sales plan must be fulfilled at any cost."

—W. F. Haug, *Critique of Commodity Aesthetics:*
Appearance, Sexuality, and Advertising in Capitalist Society

If we were to sum up the total number of product advertisements we are exposed to on TV, radio, newspapers and magazines, the number could be as high as 400 per day. . . . If we were to add up *all* promotional messages—including logos on products, program promos and ads on billboards (two media that carry nothing but advertisements)—this number could reach 16,000. . . . Jacobson and Mazur . . . argue that typical Americans will spend almost 3 whole years of their lives just watching commercials on television. The United States, in fact, is ad burdened. This country accounts for 57% of the world's advertising spending, yet the U.S. population makes up less than 10% of the world's population.

—Matthew P. McAllister, *The Commercialization of American Culture:*
New Advertising, Control, and Democracy

7

THE MARKETING SOCIETY

L et me start with some statistics that reflect the extent to which American society is saturated with advertisements and commercials.

STATISTICS ON ADVERTISING

An article on advertising written a couple decades ago calculated that "the average U.S. adult is bombarded by 255 advertisements every day—100 on TV, 70 in magazines, 60 on the radio and 45 in newspapers" (Jamie Beckett, "Ad Pitches Popping Up in Unusual Places," *San Francisco Chronicle*, July 17, 1989).

These figures are very low and gravely understate the situation. I've quoted statistics in other chapters to the effect that we see more than 150 television commercials a day and more than 1,000 in a typical week. Whether it is 100 or 150 television commercials per day, the average American is exposed to an enormous number of television commercials, radio commercials, print advertisements, billboards, and so on. Some estimate we are exposed to 15,000 commercial messages each day. Think, for example, how many advertisements we see when we read a typical newspaper.

In the years since Beckett's article was written, the problem has only grown worse, since television commercials are now frequently much shorter—often only ten seconds long. The thrust of Beckett's article is that advertising is now found in other places, such as videos, shopping carts in supermarkets, luggage carts in airports, walls of sports arenas, sides of buses, and numerous other places.

In previous chapters, I also quoted statistics for the total amount spent on advertisements in 2003, almost $260 billion. Another estimate puts spending on all forms of advertising in 2005 in the United States at around $280 billion. This figure comes from Robert J. Coen of Universal McCann, who is the most often cited expert on advertising spending. His estimate for global advertising is $521 billion. If you consider the number of people who are the target of this advertising you get the following:

United States	The Rest of the World
$280 billion	$241 billion
300 million people	6 billion people

You can see from these statistics that people in the United States are subjected to something like twenty times as much advertising as people in other countries, in very rough terms. This means advertisers spend more than $800 per person in the United States and approximately $40 per person in all other foreign countries. (Note: These statistics were cited in an article in Stuart Elliott's "The Media Business: Advertising" in the December 7, 2004 issue of *The New York Times*.) This world average is a bit misleading because people living in many First World countries also are subjected to a great deal of advertising while people in some Third World countries, where television isn't as ubiquitous as it is in the First World, see relatively fewer commercials.

MORE COMMENTS ON THE ILLUSION OF FREEDOM

Hans Magnus Enzensberger, a poet and cultural critic, argues in his book *The Consciousness Industry*:

All of us, no matter how irresolute we are, like to think that we reign supreme in our own consciousness, that we are masters of what our minds accept or reject. Since the Soul is not much mentioned any more, except by priests, poets, and pop musicians, the last refuge a man can take from the catastrophic world at large seems be his own mind. Where else can he expect to withstand the daily siege, if not within himself? Even under the conditions of totalitarian rule, where no one can fancy anymore that his home is his castle, the mind of the individual is considered a kind of last citadel and hotly defended, though this imaginary fortress may have been long since taken over by an ingenious enemy.

No illusion is more stubbornly upheld than the sovereignty of the mind. It is a good example of the impact of philosophy on people who ignore it; for the idea that men can "make up their minds" individually and by themselves is essentially derived from the tenets of bourgeois philosophy. (1974:3)

THE GLOBAL NATURE OF ADVERTISING AGENCIES

Over the last twenty years there has been a great deal of consolidation in the advertising industry and now there are just a small number of dominant advertising holding-company super-agencies or mega-agencies such as Omnicom, Interpublic (USA), WPP (UK), and Publicis (France). Each of these mega-agencies owns many smaller agencies that are located all over the world. For example, it is estimated that Omnicom owns around 1500 agencies.

The relationship that exists between individual or "subsidiary" agencies and their holding companies is often a source of considerable friction and the movement towards gigantic multi-agency mega-advertising agencies has been countered by the development of small, so-called "boutique" agencies that are independent and in many cases are freer to create more imaginative advertising.

It is important for companies with global campaigns to take into consideration the different belief systems and cultural values of the countries where advertisements and commercials will be shown. That is why holding-company advertising agencies, with branches in various countries, are useful to advertisers planning global campaigns. The advertising has to fit with the cultural values and beliefs of people in the countries who will be exposed to the advertisements, and branches in each country can help advertisers avoid making mistakes. The infamous Chevrolet campaign for its Nova automobile in Latin America was a disaster, since the word "Nova" sounds like "no va" in Spanish, which means, roughly speaking, "doesn't go."

The growth of the Internet has had an enormous impact on the way the advertising industry is organized and online advertising is forcing advertising agencies everywhere to reconsider how they operate. New kinds of advertising agencies that specialize in the Internet and in so-called "interactive" advertising are now an important force to be reckoned with. The growth of advertising on the Internet has been considerable, as anyone who uses Google or any other search engine can see. And now advertising is expanding its reach to mobile phones and other gizmos. So the giant mega-agencies have changed their methods of operation to take advantage of the Internet and other new-tech opportunities for advertising on cellphones, iPods, and other devices.

Figure 7.1

Enzensberger then quotes Karl Marx, who wrote, "What is going on in our minds has always been, and will always be, a product of society" (1974:3).

You don't have to be a Marxist philosopher railing against bourgeois society to recognize that Enzensberger and Marx make a valid point. We are, after all, social animals. The idea of "individualism" is something we learn from growing up in an advanced society, where philosophers and others talk about the idea.

Ernest Dichter, one of the founding fathers of motivation research, makes a similar point in his book *The Strategy of Desire*:

> Whatever your attitude toward modern psychology or psychoanalysis, it has been proved beyond any doubt that many of our daily decisions are governed by motivations over which we have no control and of which we are often quite unaware. (1960:12)

We are all, then, under the illusion that our decisions are all based on logic, rationality, need, and our own notions of what is best for us.

THE MARKETING VIEW

It may be true, as I've pointed out a number of times, that exposure to an advertisement or commercial for a particular brand of blue jeans or beer may not lead to a purchasing decision by a given individual, but when we take a broader look at American society, we discover that large numbers of people do purchase that brand of blue jeans or beer. You might object that many people buy things on the basis of price. The question then is, When two products cost the same price, why does someone purchase one product and not another? Conventionally, a distinction is made between marketing, which deals with selling goods and services in general, and advertising, which involves selling products and services by creating texts (such as print advertisements and commercials) that are paid for by a sponsor of some kind.

Insights from Advertising Agencies

People in advertising agencies are practical individuals who have a mission—selling both themselves and the products they are engaged to advertise—and who must have a grasp of their publics and audiences. It is fascinating on the theoretical level and often tedious on the practical level, and since it attracts people who are frequently highly intelligent, articulate, and sophisticated, it is a trying job.

Marketers have broken American society down into various ~~...~~ what we might think of as target audiences—on the basis of d factors (age, race, religion, gender, geographical region, and zip code) and psychographic factors (values and beliefs). And they've developed *typologies*— essentially classification systems to deal with the various types of consumers in America.

A valid or useful typology or classification system should have several features. First, it must cover the entire population—in this case, adult Americans who have money to purchase products and services. Second, its categories must be (to the extent possible) mutually exclusive. That is, the type of person who fits in one category shouldn't fit in any others. There are many different ways we can classify any group of people—according to race, religion, ethnicity, age, income, educational level, socioeconomic class, gender, or occupation. The important thing, as far as marketers are concerned, is to find some typology that will help get people to buy a given product or service.

We all see ourselves as special and unique individuals—and we are— but marketers see us in broadly demographic terms, for example, as senior citizens or members of Generation X or Generation Y, members of the Asian-American market, or members of the 35-to-59 age group. Marketers have created numerous marketing typologies—categories of consumers— which they use to reach their target audiences.

THE VALS 1 TYPOLOGY

VALS is an acronym that stands for Values and Life Styles, a typology developed by SRI International, a think tank in Menlo Park, California. This typology focuses on people's lifestyles rather than on demographic statistics. The VALS 1 typology is based on theories of psychological development and

argues that there are nine different and distinctive kinds of consumers. This is important, SRI suggests, because advertisers can target their appeals to the specific values of each kind of consumer. My description of the VALS 1 typology uses material from articles by Niles Howard (*Dun's Review*, August 1981) and Laurie Itow (*San Francisco Sunday Examiner and Chronicle*, June 27, 1982).

In her article, Itow explains the VALS system as follows:

> The system, called Value and Lifestyles Program (VALS) draws on behavioral science to categorize consumers, not only by demographics such as age, sex, and the products they use, but according to their state of mind. Marie Spengler, VALS director at SRI, says the program is based on an analysis of cultural trends that can be used to develop products and target markets as well as match employees with jobs and make long-range business decisions such as where to build plants. . . .
>
> VALS, Spengler says, captures "a deep, underlying sense of what motivates the consumer," using data from a 30-question survey. Consumers are questioned about demographics, such as age and sex. But more importantly, they're also asked about their attitudes and values.

This provides SRI with the data needed to create the various categories of consumers found in VALS.

The nine categories of consumers in the VALS typology are as follows:

Need-Driven

These consumers are "money restricted" and have a hard time just affording their basic needs. They are divided into two subcategories:

1. *Survivors*: These people are old, poor, and out of the cultural mainstream.
2. *Sustainers*: They are young, crafty, and on the edge of poverty but want to get ahead in the world.

Need-driven consumers make up approximately 11 percent of the adult population in the United States.

Outer-Directed

These consumers, who often live in Middle America, want others to feel positive about them. There are three subcategories of outer-directed consumers:

3. *Belongers*: They are conservative and conventional in their tastes, nostalgic, sentimental, and not experimental.
4. *Emulators*: These people are upwardly mobile, status conscious, competitive, and distrustful of the establishment. They want to make it big.
5. *Achievers*: They are the leaders of society, who have been successful in the professions, in business, and in the government. They have status, comfort, fame, and materialistic values.

Outer-directed consumers make up about two-thirds of the adult population in America.

Inner-Directed

These consumers tend to purchase products to meet their inner needs rather than thinking about the opinions of other people. There are three subcategories of inner-directed consumers:

6. *I-Am-Me's*: They are young, narcissistic, exhibitionist, inventive, impulsive, and strongly individualistic.
7. *Experientials*: This group is in essence an older version of the I-Am-Me's and is concerned with inner growth and naturalism.
8. *Societally Conscious Individuals*: They believe in simple living and smallness of scale, and support causes such as environmentalism, consumerism (not the same thing as consumption), and conservation. This group made up around 28 percent of the adult population in the United States in 1990 and has, perhaps, grown considerably since then.

Integrateds

9. *Integrateds:* This is the last subcategory, one that is characterized by psychological maturity, tolerance, assuredness, and a self-actualizing philosophy. These people tend to ignore advertising, and relatively few advertisements are made to appeal to them. Integrateds make up only around 2 percent of the adult American population, but they are very influential and are disproportionately found among corporate and national leaders. While integrateds may not be as susceptible to advertising as other groups, their taste in lifestyle products may be highly influential and they may function as what might be described as "taste opinion leaders."

USING THE VALS 1 TYPOLOGY: A CASE STUDY

As an example of the usefulness of the VALS typology, Itow explains why Merrill Lynch switched its ad campaign from "Bullish on America" (illustrated with a herd of bulls) to "A Breed Apart" (illustrated with a lone bull). The "Bullish on America" appealed to belongers—the essentially middle-class conservative members of the mass market who want to fit in. Belongers were not as good a market for Merrill Lynch as achievers—who liked the "Breed Apart" advertisements much better than the "Bullish on America" ads and who had more money to invest.

ltow discusses the developmental structure of the VALS typology:

> It's based on the theory that as people grow they fill certain needs for survival and security and then seek a sense of belonging. Next, they strive for self-esteem and then move upward to "self-actualization," developing their inner self and realizing their full potential. (1982)

Thus, using the VALS 1 typology, advertisers are able to make appeals that will resonate most directly with the deep-seated beliefs, values, and lifestyles of different segments of the American population. The VALS 1 typology is a logical one—but it has certain problems. So, in 1989, SRI revised the VALS typology.

VALS 2: A REVISION OF THE VALS 1 TYPOLOGY

The VALS typology was revised because it was thought that it did not adequately connect consumer motivations with economic status and the ability to purchase goods and services being advertised. VALS 2 was an attempt to remedy this deficiency by doing a better job of matching consumers with products they could afford.

Wanting to buy something is only one step; consumers have to be able to afford what they want. So VALS 2 came up with a set of categories that took into account such matters as income, education (the two are often correlated), health, and the strength of a consumer's desire to purchase something. This led to a modification of the original VALS typology—one that focused upon matters involved in consumer decision making. The VALS 2 categories are described below.

1. *Actualizers:* They are successful individuals with a great deal of money. They are concerned with their image as a reflection of their taste and their character, not as a reflection of their power or socioeconomic status. They are interested in social issues and amenable to change.
2. *Fulfilleds:* They are practical and value functionality and durability in products they purchase. They tend to be mature, financially comfortable, and satisfied with their lives and situations, but also open to social change.
3. *Achievers:* Achievers are career-oriented and value stability and structure, self-discovery, and intimacy. They purchase products to gain an image reflecting their success.
4. *Experiencers:* They love to spend money and tend to be young, impulsive, and enthusiastic. They are willing to try the offbeat and the new and are risk takers.
5. *Believers:* They are highly principled conservative consumers who purchase well-known brands. They are similar to fulfilleds but have less money.
6. *Strivers:* They are like achievers, except they aren't as well off. They are concerned about the opinions of others and greatly desire their approval.
7. *Makers:* People in this category are like experiencers and are active, with much of their energy going into various forms of self-sufficiency such as fixing a car or canning vegetables.
8. *Strugglers:* These people are at the bottom of the economic totem pole and have to struggle to make ends meet.

It's interesting to compare the two VALS typologies—VALS 1 and VALS 2. In table 7.1 I, to the extent that it is possible, line up the various categories according to similarities, starting with the wealthiest groups and

Table 7.1. Comparison of VALS 1 and VALS 2

VALS 1	VALS 2
Integrateds	Actualizers
Societally Conscious	
Experientials	
I-Am-Me's	Experiencers
Achievers	Achievers
Emulators	Strivers
Belongers	Believers
Sustainers	
Survivors	Strugglers

working my way down to the poorest ones. The two systems are different in that VALS 2 is concerned with income level and the ability of consumers to purchase goods and services they desire. But there are some similarities.

One problem with this system is that it assumes rationality. That is, it assumes, on the one hand, that people won't purchase things they can't afford and, on the other hand, that people won't purchase things that are "beneath" them. Thus, it assumes that rich people won't "dress poor" and poor people won't "dress rich" or "drive rich" or be willing to become "house poor" (that is, spend most of their income on a mortgage and the upkeep for a house). But many a person driving an expensive car has leased it and doesn't have much money in the bank.

There are numerous other ways of understanding consumers and what makes them tick (and buy or not buy), a number of which I will discuss in the material that follows.

ZIP CODES AND KINDS OF CONSUMERS

Market researchers can tell (so they claim) what you eat for breakfast, what newspapers and magazines you read, what you watch on television, what kind of car you drive, and so on—all on the basis of your zip code. According to Michael Weiss, author of *The Clustering of America* (Harper & Row, 1988), people who have the same zip codes tend to be remarkably

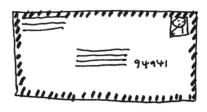

similar. Weiss has developed a typology of forty different lifestyles—each of which is quite different from all the others—with relatively little overlap. His ideas are described in an article by Sam Whiting in the *San Francisco Chronicle* (November 23, 1988, B3).

Weiss gives each zip code a nickname. Some typical nicknames are as follows:

Nickname	Zip Code	Location
"Blue-Blood Estates"	94025	Atherton
"Money and Brains"	94301	Palo Alto (Stanford University)
"Single City Blues"	94704	Berkeley (University of California)
"Hard Scrabble"	94103	Inner Mission (San Francisco)

As Weiss explains things, "We're no longer a country of 50 states but of 40 lifestyle clusters. . . . You can go to sleep in Palo Alto and wake up in Princeton, NJ, and nothing has changed except the trees. The lifestyles are the same. Perrier is in the fridge, and people are playing tennis at three times the national average."

Weiss offers an interesting comparison between two neighborhoods— what he calls the Urban Gold Coast and the Bohemian Mix (table 7.2). We must keep in mind that Weiss's statistics are from 1988 and there have been considerable changes in America since then. Still, his information is quite interesting.

You can see from this comparison that there are considerable differences between Urban Gold Coasters and Bohemians. Both, of course, are relatively small percentages of the U.S. population.

Some of Weiss's other clusters are as follows:

Young Influentials   Black Enterprise
Two More Rungs   Dixie-Style
Pools and Patios   Heavy Industry
New Beginnings   Levittown, USA
Gray Power   Hispanic Mix
Furs and Station Wagons   Public Assistance
New Melting Pot   Small-town
Downtown

Table 7.2. Urban Gold Coast and Bohemian Mix Compared

Urban Gold Coast	*Bohemian Mix*
94111 Embarcadero (SF)	94117 Haight-Ashbury (SF)
10021 Upper East Side (NY)	20036 Dupont Circle (Washington, DC)
10024 Upper West Side (NY)	02139 Cambridge, MA
20037 West End (Washington, DC)	60614 Lincoln Park (Chicago)
60611 Fort Dearborn (Chicago)	15232 Shadyside (Pittsburgh, PA)
0.5 percent of U.S. households	1.1 percent of U.S. households
Age group: 18-24 and 65+	Age group: 18–34
Median household income: $36,838	Median household income: $21,916
Liberal/moderate politics	Liberal politics
High Usage	**High Usage**
Aperitifs, specialty wines	Environmental organizations
Champagne	Irish whiskey
Tennis	Downhill skiing
Pregnancy tests	Country clubs
Passports	Classical records
Magazines and Newspapers	**Magazines and Newspapers**
New York	*Atlantic Monthly*
New York Times	*Harper's*
Metropolitan Home	*Gentlemen's Quarterly*
Atlantic Monthly	*The New Yorker*
Food	**Food**
Rye/pumpernickel bread	Whole wheat bread
Tomato/vegetable juice	Frozen waffles
Butter	Fruit juices and drinks
Fresh chicken	TV dinners

We can guess, just from the descriptive names, what people living in such zip codes might be like.

Weiss explains that eventually marketers may move beyond zip codes to specific mailing addresses. As he points out:

> Right now, Americans are bombarded with 15,000 messages a day. Marketers keep trying to match that little clustering niche that's your lifestyle with whatever they're trying to sell you. People leave a paper trail of warranties and subscriptions. Pretty soon Big Brother will know what's going on in your household. It's only a matter of time until businesses get into the black box of what's in a consumer's head.

Weiss's fears have long been realized. Now shoppers who use Safeway or other supermarket cards or purchase products with credit cards feed computer databases that keep track of their purchases and know what they eat and drink, where they travel, and all kinds of other things about them.

Weiss's book is, it would seem, a popularization of the typology developed by the Claritas Corporation, which uses zip codes to classify 250,000 neighborhoods in the United States into the consumer clusters that Weiss writes about.

THE CLARITAS TYPOLOGY

The Claritas Corporation argues that "birds of a feather flock together," which suggests that people who live in a given zip code tend to have similar socioeconomic levels. Claritas argues that there are, in fact, some sixty-six different categories of consumers in the United States and it has come up with jazzy names for each of them. The complete list of these groups (some of whom were described by Weiss earlier) follows.

01. Upper Crust
02. Blue Blood Estates
03. Movers & Shakers
04. Young Digerati
05. Country Squires
06. Winner's Circle
07. Money & Brains
08. Executive Suites
09. Big Fish, Small Pond
10. Second City Elite
11. God's Country
12. Brite Lites, Li'l City
13. Upward Bound
14. New Empty Nests
15. Pools & Patios
16. Bohemian Mix
17. Beltway Boomers
18. Kids & Cul-de-Sacs
19. Home Sweet Home
20. Fast-Track Families
21. Gray Power
22. Young Influentials
23. Greenbelt Sports
24. Up-and-Comers
25. Country Casuals
26. The Cosmopolitans
27. Middleburg Managers
28. Traditional Times
29. American Dreams
30. Suburban Sprawl
31. Urban Achievers
32. New Homesteaders
33. Big Sky Families
34. White Picket Fences
35. Boomtown Singles
36. Blue-Chip Blues
37. Mayberry-ville
38. Simple Pleasures
39. Domestic Duos
40. Close-in Couples
41. Sunset City Blues
42. Red, White, & Blues
43. Heartlanders
44. New Beginnings
45. Blue Highways
46. Old Glories
47. City Startups
48. Young & Rustic
49. American Classics
50. Kid Country, USA

51. Shotguns & Pickups	59. Urban Elders
52. Suburban Pioneers	60. Park Bench Set
53. Mobility Blues	61. City Roots
54. Multi-Culti Mosaic	62. Hometown Retired
55. Golden Ponds	63. Family Thrifts
56. Crossroads Villagers	64. Bedrock America
57. Old Milltowns	65. Big City Blues
58. Back Country	66. Low-Rise Living

If you go to the Claritas web site, and go to their My Best Segments in its Prism NE Segmentation System, you can check for the clusters in your zip code.

In my zip code, 94941, which is in Marin County, you find a number of clusters at the top of the list. Cluster 03 offers the following information:

03: Movers & Shakers
Group: Elite Suburbs
CY2002 Statistics:
US Households: 1,718,417 (1.59%)
US Population: 4,589, 292 (1.6%)
Median Household Income: $92,163
Lifestyle Traits:
Go scuba diving/snorkeling
Plan travel on the Internet
Read PC Magazine
Listen to adult contemp. Radio
Drive a Porsche.
Demographic Traits:

Ethnic Diversity	White, High Asian
Family Types	Couples
Age Ranges	35–64
Education Levels	College Grad+
Employment Levels	Professional
Housing Types	Homeowners
Urbanicity	Suburban
Income	Wealthy

Claritas provides similar descriptions of each of its sixty-six clusters. It argues that by knowing who you are targeting for your advertising, and what they are like, you can do a better job of reaching them. There are, I should point out, other marketing research organizations that don't believe that "demographics is destiny," but rely on psychological characteristics of targeted consumers and other kinds of information as well.

Another typology that claims to be more accurate than demographic factors or zip codes, based essentially on magazine choice, is also available to marketers.

MAGAZINE CHOICE AS AN INDICATOR OF CONSUMER TASTE

Yankelovich Partners, a well-known marketing and research company located in Westport, Connecticut, conducted a survey in 1992 that led to a very interesting discovery. According to Yankelovich, the publications that consumers read, especially the magazines they like, are a better indicator of consumer behavior than demographic factors such as age, marital status, gender, and residence.

This is because people, so the argument goes, choose magazines based on their editorial content, and this content is generally congruent with (or a reflection of) their interests, beliefs, and values.

The Yankelovich survey divided the American public into five groups, or media communities, based on their media tastes. These groups and the basic magazines read by members of each group are described below. Like many marketing typologies, the names of the groups are jazzy and meant to characterize each group in a clever and memorable manner.

1. *Home Engineers*: Women who read magazines such as *Family Circle, Woman's Day*, and *Good Housekeeping* that contain instructions and are didactic in nature.
2. *Real Guys*: Men who choose magazines based on their hobbies. They read magazines such as *Hot Rod, Popular Mechanics, Mechanix Illustrated,* and *Guns and Ammo*.
3. *Ethnic Pewneps (People Who Need People)*: Readers of magazines such as *Entertainment Weekly, Sporting News,* and *Ebony*, who are interested in celebrities and identify with them, treating these celebrities as if they were involved in their lives. Both men and women can be members of this category.
4. *Information Grazers*: People who think of themselves as intellectuals and read magazines such as *Time, Bon Appetit*, and *People*, to obtain opinions and gain information they can discuss with others. Information grazers are generally male.

5. *Armchair Adventurers*: Older, conservative, more traditional people who experience the world vicariously through magazines such as *Reader's Digest* and *Modern Maturity*. Both men and women are members of this group, and they tend to vote Republican.

The theory behind this typology is that the media choices consumers make are key indicators of their behavior as consumers. This notion suggests there is a logic to people's behavior as consumers, and certain basic interests and beliefs, reflected in magazine choice, shape consumer behavior in general.

This discussion draws upon an article by Stuart Elliott in the January 7, 1993, issue of the *New York Times*. Elliott points out that the Yankelovich survey didn't cover people in their twenties and people with annual household incomes of more than $150,000. The question we must ask about this typology—and all typologies, for that matter—is whether it is the best way of doing justice to the information discovered in the survey or whether, somehow, it is reductionistic.

Marketers are basically interested in consumer behavior, so they always reduce groups of people to various consumer categories. Does the Yankelovich classification system do justice to the survey results? Are there more than five categories that could be elicited from the data? And, most important, is it describing a *correlation* (for our purposes, something that's associated with something else) or discovering *causation* (the "real" reason why people buy this or that product)? It may be, of course, that all we can get from marketing research are correlations between some factor or factors and consumer behavior.

TYPES OF TEENAGE CONSUMERS

There are (1998 figures) almost 30 million teenagers living in America now, and in 1997 these teenagers spent around $4 billion on clothing, cosmetics, and various other kinds of fashion items. Most teenage spending is discretionary and not based on purchasing essentials such as food or housing.

Teen-Age Research Unlimited, a Northbrook, Illinois, market research company that specializes in teenagers—known as "Generation Y" or more recently the "Internet Generation"—has come up with a typology that argues that all teens can be placed in one of four categories: Influencers, Edge Group members, Conformers, and Passives. The characteristics of each group are as follows:

1. *Influencers*: They are quick to embrace fashion trends, spend a good deal of money on fashion trends, and influence spending habits of other teenagers.
2. *The Edge Group*: Members of this group continually change their looks in an attempt to be antifashion and drop their fashion looks when influencers adopt them.
3. *Conformers*: Most teenagers fall into this category. Conformers use popular brands to strengthen their self-esteem.
4. *Passives*: Teenagers in this category aren't particularly interested in using fashion as a statement or a means of fitting in. They buy clothes based on what is available rather than being concerned about being fashionable.

The thing we must remember about these consumers is that not only do they spend $4 billion on fashions, they also have a significant influence on purchases made by their parents.

Teenagers spend a lot of time shopping, in part because it is the only "adult" role they are offered in American society. What does it mean to be an adult in American society—one characterized by some critics as based on "consumer lust"? An adult, so it seems to many teenagers, is someone who buys things and thus in their effort to be adults they become consumers.

A Rand Youth Poll conducted in 1990 found that girls spend $73.95 a week, and a third of this amount, approximately $25.00 a week, is spent on clothes. (That adds up to more than $1,000 a year on clothes.) This $73.95 breaks down as follows, in rounded-off figures, based on a 1989 study by the Rand Youth Poll:

food and snacks	33%
clothing	20% (males and females combined)
savings	17%
entertainment and movies	14%
records	5%
misc.	5%
grooming	4%
hobbies	3%

An article, "The Young Are Getting and Spending, Too," by Trish Hall (*New York Times*, August 23, 1990, B7), quotes Selina Guber, a psychologist (and president of Children's Market Research Inc. in New York), about the similarity between children and adults as far as consuming is concerned: "Throughout the country there is a tremendous emphasis on possessions. [Children] reflect that. Like adults, they face pressure to possess the right brands and the right objects. Their wishes are of increasing interest to marketers because American children 6 to 14 years old are believed to have about $6 billion in discretionary income." Thus, children—as well as adults—are of "consuming" interest to marketers, especially since children have so much discretionary income. This figure, $6 billion, is for 1990; in 2007 it is, no doubt, considerably higher.

As a blurb for *Kids as Customers* (in the November 1995 catalog *Marketing Power: The Marketer's Reference Library*) explains:

> This indispensable handbook describes 4-to-12 year olds as having the greatest sales potential of any age or demographic group. Each year, children spend over $9 billion of their own money; they influence $130 billion of adults' spending; and as future adult customers, they will control even more purchasing dollars tomorrow.

The various citations of billions of dollars differ in various studies because of differences in age groups being dealt with and in when the studies were made. Whatever the case, the amount of money young children and teenagers have to spend, and do spend, is simply astonishing.

BLOGS AND MARKETING

The web logs that people write are now being mined as a source of valuable information about consumer preferences. An article in the June 23, 2005, *Wall Street Journal*, "Marketers Scan Blogs for Brand Insights," points out that marketing organizations are gaining valuable insights into people's attitudes towards various products by searching through chat rooms, message boards, electric forums, and the millions of web logs that are on the Internet. The opinions of the bloggers, which are unsolicited and honest, can be seen as a kind of gigantic focus group. Rick Murray, executive vice president of Edelman, a Chicago public relations firm, says "We look at the blogosphere as a focus group with 15 million people going on 24/7 that you can tap into without going behind a one-way mirror." Some of the insights that scanning blogs revealed are:

Teens	Fear exceeding their cellphone minutes
Children	Love minivans
Teens	Like SUVs
Dieters	Losing interest in Atkins
Drug Makers	Poor trials not necessarily seen as negative

(*Wall Street Journal,* June 23, 2005, Page B1)

Advertising agencies are also using blogs to get their message across. They do this by purchasing space on popular blogs, some of which are read by thousands—even hundreds of thousands—of people. But blog ads have to be done carefully, lest the blog reader be turned off, so most blog ads are not conventional. An article "Bloggers' new brand starts to click with advertisers" in the March 28, 2005 *Financial Times,* mentions an advertising campaign by the United Church of Christ, which spent $15,000 on a blog campaign. Some 74,000 people clicked on the advertisement, which means the cost per viewing of their ad was around twenty cents. (March 28, 2005, p. 14)

A company in Boulder, Colorado—Umbria Communications—has software called "Buzz Report" that data mines millions of blogs to find out what the bloggers are saying about various products and trends. As the article by Bridget Finn in the September 2005 (p. 36) issue of *Business 2.0* reports, "Umbria uses language-processing algorithms that track positive and negative mentions of a brand and predict the age range and gender of every opiner." Now market research firms are deeply involved in studying blogs where people offer private thoughts and opinions in a very public forum that is accessible to everyone. (*Business 2.0* September 2005, p. 36)

A TYPOLOGY FOR EVERYONE IN THE WORLD

The typologies I've been discussing to this point have all been for people in the United States—the country where marketing has reached its highest level of development. People who live in America and are considered "normal" in terms of the amount of television they watch are exposed to many more advertisements and commercials than people in other countries, all things considered.

On the basis of 35,000 interviews with consumers in thirty-five different countries, Roper Starch Worldwide claims it has identified basic values that are universal in nature, values shared by people in all countries (or at least values that cross national borders). People were studied in North America, South America, Europe, and Asia in terms of their bedrock values and the basic motivations that shape their behavior. Roper Starch released a study, "Global Consumer Hot Buttons," that claims there are six basic categories of consumers in all countries. They are listed below, with the traditional catchy names market researchers use.

1. *Strivers*: This is the largest group, with 23 percent of the world's adult population. They tend to be middle-aged and materialistic, and value status, wealth, and power. They tend to be found in developing and developed countries.
2. *Devouts*: They are almost as large as strivers, with 22 percent of the world's adult population. As the term "devout" suggests, they believe in more traditional values such as faith, obedience, duty, and respect for elders. Devouts tend to be found in the Middle East, Africa, and Asia.
3. *Altruists*: Some 18 percent of the world's adult population are altruists. They are, as a rule, well educated, older (median age: 44) and interested in social causes and political issues. They tend to be found in Latin America and Russia.
4. *Intimates*: Only 15 percent of the world's adult population are intimates. They are very similar to a different typology called pewneps—people who need people. That is, intimates are primarily concerned with relationships with spouses, family, friends, colleagues, and significant others. Intimates are primarily found in the United Kingdom, the United States, the Netherlands, and Hungary. They have in common a heavy use of media.
5. *Fun Seekers*: About 12 percent of the adult population falls in this category. They are the youngest group in the typology and

are primarily interested in excitement, pleasure, and adventure. They value looking good and spend a good deal of time in restaurants, bars, and clubs. Fun seekers are an MTV generation.

6. *Creatives*: At 10 percent, creatives are the smallest category in the worldwide typology. Their focus is on technology and knowledge, and they are trendsetters who own and use computers, surf the web, and consume the greatest amount of media—especially print media such as newspapers, magazines, and books, of any category.

Table 7.3 shows the basic characteristics of the six groups so that you can see how they compare with one another.

The question we must ask about these categories is whether they miss any important groups of people—that is, does this typology cover all the adults and are the categories mutually exclusive? Can every adult in the world be put into one, and only one, of these six categories? In some cases, as table 7.3 shows, there was no information (or, more precisely, no information in the article that discussed the report) for some categories. That explains the gaps.

What I wonder is, Are some of the fun seekers also altruists? Or some of the devouts also creatives? We must remember, of course, that this typology, like all of the typologies I've described, focuses on consumer behavior and thus is, by definition, reductionistic. The Roper Starch typology is about consumers and their values and is primarily concerned with the belief systems or "hot buttons" that can be used to understand the minds of consumers.

In 1951, Marshall McLuhan explained in *The Mechanical Bride* what advertising agencies were doing. He compared advertising agencies with Hollywood and wrote, in his chapter "Love-Goddess Assembly Line":

The ad agencies and Hollywood, in their different ways, are always trying to get inside the public mind in order to impose their collective dreams

Table 7.3. International Consumer Values and Beliefs

Strivers	Devouts	Altruists	Intimates	Fun Seekers	Creatives
23%	22%	18%	15%	12%	10%
Wealth	Obedience	Social issues	Relationships	Adventure	Knowledge
Newspapers	Least media use	Like media	Music	MTV	Highest media use
Developed nations	Middle East, Asia, Africa	Latin America, Russia	U.K., U.S., Netherlands		

on that inner stage. And in the pursuit of this goal both Hollywood and the advertising agencies themselves give major exhibitions of unconscious behavior. One dream opens into another until reality and fantasy are made interchangeable. The ad agencies flood the daytime world of conscious purpose and control with erotic imagery from the night world in order to drown, by suggestion, all sales resistance. Hollywood floods the night world with daytime imagery in which synthetic gods and goddesses [stars] appear to assume the roles of our wakeaday existence in order to console us for the failures of our daily lives. The ad agencies hold out for each of us the dream of a spot on Olympus where we can quaff and loll forever amid the well-known brands. The movies reverse this procedure by showing us the stars—who, we are assured, dwell on "beds of amaranth and holly"—descending to our level. (1951:97)

The advertising agencies and marketing experts, with their various typologies, do offer some very interesting information about the human psyche and about what it is that makes us tick. They are continually probing us, trying to get at the G spot of consumer behavior and decision making, doing everything they can to understand us so they can—in starkest terms—manipulate us.

A COMPARISON OF THE DIFFERENT TYPOLOGIES

Now that I've offered a number of different marketing typologies, it's worth looking at them all together to see what they reflect about the way marketing research sees human beings. In table 7.4 I list the various typologies—though, in some cases, not all the subcategories.

Table 7.4 does not compare types and categories horizontally. That is, there is no similarity between survivors, actualizers, and so on. What is interesting is how more than 100 million adult Americans can be classified in the first four typologies, how 30 million teenagers are characterized in the teenager typology, and how around 3 billion adult human beings are characterized in the last typology, the Roper Starch system.

One generalization that emerges from the chart is that certain people are trendsetters or opinion leaders, and others, who form the majorities, imitate and follow the trendsetters. And there are various other subcategories, depending on the typology, of those who fit on various rungs of the ladder below that of the trendsetters, opinion leaders, creatives—what you will. There are some who have opted out of the system and are very hard for marketers to reach, such as the integrateds and others who follow the trendsetters and purchase things to generate an image of success.

Table 7.4. Marketing Typologies Compared

VALS 1	VALS 2	Zip Codes	Yankelovich	Teenagers	Roper Starch
Survivors	Actualizers	Blue Bloods	Home Engineers	Influencers	Strivers
Sustainers	Fulfilleds	Money and Brains	Real Guys	Edge Group	Devouts
Belongers	Achievers	Single City Blues	Ethnic Pewneps	Conformers	Altruists
Emulators	Experiencers	Urban Gold Coast	Information Grazers	Passives	Intimates
Achievers	Believers	Bohemian	Armchair Adventurers		Fun Seekers
I-Am-Me's	Strivers	Young Influentials			Creatives
Experientials	Makers	Two More Rungs			
Societally Conscious	Strugglers	Gray Power			
Integrateds		Pools and Patios			
		Hispanic Mix			

Some of the typologies, such as the Yankelovich one, don't seem to be directly involved with fashion and such, but the magazines people in the various categories read suggest that these people are motivated by the same things as are those people in categories more directly related to marketing.

We can also see various oppositions in these typologies:

Actives	Passives
Leaders	Followers
Creatives	Imitators
Achievers	Strugglers
Influencers	Conformists
Experience Seekers	Safety Seekers

These polarities reflect the way the human mind functions. According to the Swiss linguist Ferdinand de Saussure, concepts are by nature differential—and our minds find meaning by setting up paired oppositions.

A CONCLUSION IN THE FORM OF A QUESTION

The primary goal of advertising and marketing, of course, is to shape our behavior; advertising agencies can be looked at as hired guns, whose main job is to destroy consumer resistance and shape consumer desire and action—whether it be to sell cigarettes, beer, politicians, or, lately, prescription medicines. And in some cases, it is to sell socially positive messages. There is little question that the information marketers have about consumer motivation and the minds of consumers is a source of power. Is this power used ethically and for socially constructive purposes? That is the question.

[Dan] Nichols' McDonald's spots possess the most accelerated time sense of any on television. "Quick Cuts" contains more cuts than can be counted: after repeated views the author had to slow down the tape to count 65 different scenes in 60 seconds. A seven-second segment of this spot contains fourteen separate scenes, or two per second. Incredible as it may seem, it is possible for the viewer to perceive these different scenes even though they go by faster than they can be counted.

The effect on the viewer is a sense of extreme urgency and of the present tense: the action is thrust into the immediate present because it is rendered as more alive and exciting than even the most engaging real-life experience. Nichols taps the "live" associations of television in this way more insistently than any other director. Because of the sense of urgency and of presentness which the spots communicate, the viewer actually experiences the exciting life style which Nichols depicts rather than passively observing events which occur to someone else.

The excitement communicated by way of life the viewer thus experiences is associated with the product even though the product is not the primary subject of the spots. More than promoting a particular product, these spots advertise an appealing way of life associated with the restaurant, causing the viewer to turn to the product for gratification.

—Bruce Kurtz, *Spots: The Popular Art of American Television Commercials*

Beyond attracting the viewer's attention, the image(s) in an ad are typically meant to give rise to some emotional disposition toward the product, politician, social cause, or whatever else the ad is about. The iconicity of visual images serves this process by making it possible for images to draw upon the rich variety of visual stimuli and associated emotions to which we are already attuned through our interactions with our social and natural environments: facial expressions, gestures, postures, personal appearance, physical surroundings, and so on. Moreover . . . visual images are capable of simulating certain aspects of these interactions by means of the variables that control the viewer's perspective: degree of proximity, angle of view, presence of or absence of subjective shots, and so on.

—Paul Messaris, *Visual Persuasion: The Role of Images in Advertising*

8

ANALYZING PRINT ADVERTISEMENTS

or: Six Ways of Looking at a Fidji Perfume Advertisement

The thing we have to realize about radio and television commercials and print advertisements (and all other forms of advertising as well) is that they are, aside from their commercial functions, works of popular art. Or maybe "commercial" art is a more fitting term. In this chapter and the next I focus upon print advertisements and television commercials, the two most interesting—from my point of view—kinds of texts. I will use the term "text" here for both; it is a term conventionally used in criticism nowadays to cover all forms of artworks.

LOTMAN'S CONTRIBUTIONS TO UNDERSTANDING TEXTS

One important thing to remember about these texts is that every aspect of them is significant. This point is made by the Russian semiotician Yuri Lotman in *The Structure of the Artistic Text*. Lotman writes, "The tendency to interpret *everything* in an artistic text as meaningful is so great that we rightfully consider nothing accidental in a work of art" (1977:17). Lotman also explains why texts yield to so many different interpretations:

> Since it can concentrate a tremendous amount of information into the "area" of a very small text . . . an artistic text manifests yet another feature: it transmits different information to different readers in proportion to each one's comprehension; it provides the reader with a language in which each successive portion of information may be assimilated with repeated reading. It behaves as a kind of living organism which has a feedback channel to the reader and thereby instructs him. (1977:23)

Lotman's two points are important for us to keep in mind.

1. *Everything* in a text such as a commercial is important; and
2. The *more you know, the more you can see* in a text.

This is because texts store a tremendous amount of information in themselves and are a great deal more complicated than we might imagine. This
notion that texts are storehouses of information explains, for example, why
we can read novels several times and see films a number of times and still
enjoy the experience. That's because we see new things in the novel each
time we read it and we see new things in the film each time we see it. And
the same, of course, applies to many other kinds of artworks—paintings,
music, sculpture, poems, and so on.

WHAT'S THERE TO ANALYZE
IN AN ADVERTISEMENT?

Let me start with an imaginary print advertisement in which we find a
photograph of a man and a woman and some textual material. Here's a list
of possible topics to consider in analyzing the advertisement.

1. How would you describe the design of the advertisement? Do
    we find axial balance or an asymmetrical relationship among
    the elements in the advertisement?
2. How much copy is there relative to the amount of pictorial
    matter? Is this relationship significant in any respect?
3. Is there a great deal of blank (white) space in the advertisement
    or is it full of graphic and textual material?

4. What angle is the photograph shot at? Do we look up at the people in the advertisement? Do we look down at them from a height? Or do we look at them from a shoulder-level position? What significance does the angle of the shot have?

5. How is the photograph lit? Is there a great deal of light or is there a little light and very dark shadows (chiaroscuro lighting)? What is the mood found in the advertisement?

6. If the photograph is in color, what colors dominate? What significance do these colors have?

7. How would you describe the two figures in the advertisement? Consider such matters as facial expression, hair color, hair length, hair styling, fashions (clothes, shoes, eyeglass design, and jewelry), various props (a cane, an umbrella), body shape, body language, age, gender, race, ethnicity, signs of occupation, signs of educational level, relationships suggested between the male and female, objects in the background, and so on.

8. What is happening in the advertisement? What does the "action" in the photo suggest? Assume that we are seeing one moment in an ongoing narrative. What is this narrative and what does it reveal about the two figures?

9. Are there any signs or symbols in the photograph? If so, what role do they play?

10. In the textual material, how is language used? What arguments are made or implied about the people in the photograph and about the product being advertised? That is, what rhetorical devices are used to attract readers and stimulate desire in them for the product or service? Does the advertisement use associations or analogies or something else to make its point?

11. What typefaces are used in the textual parts of the advertisement? What importance do the various typefaces have? (Why these typefaces and not other ones?)

12. What are the basic "themes" in the advertisement? How do these themes relate to the story implied by the advertisement?

13. What product or service is being advertised? Who is the target audience for this product or service? What role does this product or service play in American culture and society?

14. What values and beliefs are reflected in the advertisement? Sexual jealousy? Patriotism? Motherly love? Brotherhood of man? Success? Power? Good taste?

15. Is there any background information you need to make sense of the advertisement? How does context shape our understanding of the advertisement?

This list of questions will direct your attention to various matters that might be considered when interpreting a typical print advertisement found in a newspaper or magazine.

ANALYZING THE FIDJI AD

The more critics know, the more they can find in commercials or any kind of artistic or literary text. There are a number of standard approaches to interpreting commercial texts—such as semiotic analysis, psychoanalytic criticism, Marxist analysis, and sociological analysis—which I will briefly exemplify in my interpretation of one of the most interesting print advertisements in recent decades—the Fidji "Woman with the Snake" perfume ad (figure 8.1).

1. *Semiotic Analysis*: What signs, symbols, and codes are found in the text? How does the advertisement or commercial generate meaning in people?
2. *Psychoanalytic Theory*: How does the text make use of the basic elements of the human psyche to sell goods and services? What appeals to unconscious elements, id/ego/superego aspects of the psyche, sexuality, anxiety, and so on, are found in the text?
3. *Sociological Analysis*: What does the text contain that is relevant to such matters as socioeconomic class, gender, race, status, and role? What is the product and what does it reflect about social concerns and the problems of people in their everyday lives?
4. *Historical Analysis*: How have advertising and its methods evolved over the years? If the advertisement or commercial is part of a campaign, what is the campaign like? Where does this text fit into the campaign? How do advertising texts relate to historical events?
5. *Political Analysis*: What role does the advertisement or commercial have in the political process? What techniques were used? What appeals are made? What effects does it have on an election or some aspect of political decision making?

Figure 8.1

6. *Myth/Ritual Analysis*: What mythical or ritualistic aspects of the text are of interest? How does the advertisement or commercial relate to ancient myths?

I will use many of these techniques in the interpretations of the Fidji advertisement that follow. Since I quoted from Yuri Lotman, a semiotician, at the beginning of this chapter, let me start by discussing the Fidji ad from a semiotic viewpoint.

A SEMIOTIC INTERPRETATION OF THE FIDJI ADVERTISEMENT

Semiotics is defined as the science of signs—a sign being anything that can be used to stand for something else, to deliver some kind of a message, to generate some kind of meaning. There are two dominant systems for analyzing signs—one created by the Swiss linguist Ferdinand de Saussure and the other by the American philosopher C. S. Peirce.

Saussure said signs are made up of *signifiers* (sounds or images) and *signifieds* (concepts or ideas). Our facial expressions, our hair color, our body language, our clothes, our voices—just about everything we do—function as signifiers of something (our moods, feelings, beliefs, religion, and so on). The important thing about the relationship that exists between signifiers and signifieds is that it is arbitrary. That is, it is based on convention and has to be learned; it is not natural and universal.

The other system, Peirce's, includes three kinds of signs: signs that signify by resemblance—what he calls *icons*; signs that signify by some kind of cause-and-effect relationship—what he calls *indexes*; and signs that signify by convention—what he calls *symbols*. A photograph is an icon; smoke coming out of a house is an indexical sign; and a flag, the Star of David, a cross, and so on, are symbolic signs. Each of these systems is rather complex, but just using the fundamental notions of Saussure and Peirce, we can make a decent semiotic analysis of the Fidji advertisement.

Note that the design of the advertisement is formal and has a good deal of empty or white space. See the advertisement for the Bellagio Hotel in Las Vegas for another example of the use of empty space (figure 8.2). This kind of design is typical of expensive, upscale products. In the Fidji advertisement, we only see the bottom of the woman's face. This enables women looking at the advertisement to put themselves into the picture. The woman's lips are full and partially open, suggesting, perhaps, sexual passion or excitement.

We can't be certain, but she seems to be a Polynesian woman—the kind of woman found on Fiji, the kind of woman painted by Paul Gauguin, who "escaped" from France to Polynesia. The lighting is rather extreme, with strong darks and lights; the lighting emphasizes the woman's long neck. She has long, dark hair and is wearing a yellow orchid in it. Dark

Figure 8.2

hair is connected in the American mind (so D. H. Lawrence suggested) with
notions of sexual passion, in contrast to blond hair that is connected with
innocence and sexual coldness and unresponsiveness. And long hair has, for
the popular mind, a sexual dimension to it; in many cosmetic advertisements
(for hair color, and so on) we often see women striding across fields with
their long hair blowing wildly and voluptuously in the wind.

The name of the perfume, Fidji, and the photograph of the Polynesian woman generate a sense that we are in the tropics, where there is heat,
and sexual passion is natural and pervasive. We associate the tropics with
earthy, almost primitive passions and with sexual freedom, for in Fiji and
other tropical islands we have, we believe, escaped from the prohibitions of
civilization.

There is also the use of French—a form of snob appeal that relies on
the stereotype of the French as sexy and not as burdened by Puritanical repression as Americans. French is also a language for sophisticated people,
people who—in America—are cultivated or educated enough to be able to
read the copy, which is all in French.

Saussure explained that we understand what concepts mean only dif-
ferentially. As he put it, "Concepts are purely differential and defined not
by their positive content but negatively with the other terms of the system.
. . . The most precise characteristic of concepts is in being what the others
are not" (1966:117). Thus it is relations that determine meaning, not content per se. Nothing, strictly speaking, has meaning in itself, it is the relationships of concepts to one another that generate meaning, especially
negation. That explains why we find it so easy to make paired oppositions:
rich and poor, happy and sad, dark and light, and so on.

We can use Saussure's insight about the role of oppositions to help
make sense of the Fidji advertisement. It posits two worlds, which are described in table 8.1:

Table 8.1. Polar Oppositions (Implied) in Fidji Advertisement

Fidji	Civilized World
Polynesian Woman	White Woman
Paradise	Hell
Escape	Imprisonment
Dark Hair	Light Hair
Free Sexuality	Repressed Sexuality
Magic	Rationality
Fidji Perfume	Other Perfumes

These are some of the more important signs and meanings generated by these signs found in the Fidji advertisement. There are many others, of course, but my aim here is to give you an idea of what semiotic analysis can do when it is applied to an advertisement, not to do a complete semiotic analysis.

A PSYCHOANALYTIC INTERPRETATION OF THE FIDJI ADVERTISEMENT

One of the most striking elements of the Fidji advertisement is the presence of the snake wound around the woman's neck. In Freudian psychoanalytic theory, snakes are phallic symbols—that is, they represent the penis by nature of their shape—an iconic resemblance, semioticians would say. (In some countries, I should point out, this advertisement appeared without the snake [figure 8.3].)

Snakes and women are part of the Adam and Eve story and are thus known to millions of people. There is, then, a mythological significance to images of snakes and women—one that I explore in more detail later. The snake tempted Eve and she convinced Adam that he should eat from the Tree of the Knowledge of Good and Evil. The results of this act were calamitous for men and women, and snakes also.

There is also anxiety related to snakes and to fears deep in the psyches of some women of being penetrated by men's genitals. Ironically, it could

Figure 8.3

Insights from Advertising Agencies

Advertising agencies search for universal metaphors that people everywhere will be able to understand easily. Account executives are involved, among other things, with developing a creative brief—it tells what the advertisement should accomplish. We ask ourselves, If we could say one thing about the client, what would it be?

---

be argued that perfume is in certain ways seen by women as analogous to venom—a magical substance that has incredible effects. The most important of these effects is to make women irresistible to men. This would be an example of magical thinking—a feeling of being powerful and able to get what you want.

If you think of the snake forming an S, the top of the cover of the Fidji bottle, its two sides and the thin black cording that is used on the bottle forming an E, and the woman's intertwined fingers as forming an X, you have the word *sex* hidden in the advertisement. Even though we may not consciously be aware that we are reading this word, in psychoanalytic theory, seeing it would have some kind of subliminal impact upon our psyches and make us feel more inclined toward sexual activity.

The orchid is also a sexual symbol—flowers being the sexual apparatus of plants. We humans use these flowers to make products that use their smells to excite one another sexually—or so the argument goes. Animals, we know, use smell to determine when females are sexually receptive and fertile. We use the same notions when we use perfumes and aftershave lotions. We try to bring out the animal in those we hope will become our sexual partners, except that the smells we use are not natural, based on our reproductive cycles—but artificial. (Recent scientific studies suggest subtle and hard-to-detect body smells may in fact have a sexual arousal function.)

We can also look at this advertisement, and most advertising, using Freud's structural hypothesis—his suggestion that the psyche has three components: the id, the ego, and the superego. These phenomena are shown in table 8.2. According to Freud, the id can be described as a "cauldron of seething excitement." It is disorganized and seeks, essentially, to satisfy instinctual needs. The superego is the element of the psyche that is always approving or disapproving of acts the id is planning, and it also provides critical self-observation and the need for reparation in cases of wrongdoing. In between these two forces is the ego, trying to keep the psyche in balance. Too much id and a person's life is chaotic; too much superego and a person lacks energy and becomes obsessed with guilt.

Table 8.2. Id/Ego/Superego Applied to Advertising

Id	*Ego*	*Superego*
Drives	Reason	Conscience
"Do it now"	Wait	"Don't do it"
Lust	Balance	Moral precepts
Energy	Survival	Guilt
Desire	Wallet	Fear of debt
Buy it	Limited funds	Do without
Advertising	Budget	Bank account

In terms of advertising, the factors shown in the *Id* column in table 8.2 are the most important. Advertising appeals to the id and tries to evade the strictures of the superego. And the ego tries to control the id's desire to buy everything by suggesting that it might be a good idea to reconsider the desired purchase, by appealing to the superego of limited funds (one's budget) or reminding people that they are maxed out on their credit cards.

In the Fidji advertisement, we are in the tropics, away from civilization, which seeks to curtail our id impulses. That is the point Freud made in *Civilization and Its Discontents*: The price we pay for civilization and culture is repression.

A SOCIOLOGICAL INTERPRETATION OF THE FIDJI ADVERTISEMENT

One thing we might consider when we apply sociological concepts to the Fidji advertisement is its target audience. Who is the advertisement designed to reach and why do the appeals in the Fidji ad sell it to its target audience? On the basis of the woman in the advertisement, one would say it is young women who feel frustrated by the constraints of their everyday lives in contemporary urban societies and who seek, in fantasy, an escape.

This escape involves nature, which is where the Polynesian fantasy takes place, and romantic love—which is why the product is utilized. The target audience is also, we can infer, somewhat sophisticated—in that it knows French—or pseudosophisticated, in that it thinks buying a French perfume shows one has class. That is, users of Fidji think of themselves as elites—if not economically, then in terms of their lifestyles or what might be called their taste culture. Maybe wearing Fidji, a refined perfume (it's French, isn't it?), also indicates one's socioeconomic class. You have to be able to afford it, after all.

Fidji is functional in two ways: First, it is designed either to attract a new sexual partner or stimulate a sexual partner one already has—the main reason for wearing perfume, after all. And second, Fidji consolidates the wearer's sense of herself as sophisticated and desirable. That is, it confers status—or so those who purchase Fidji think. Thus, perfumes in general and Fidji in particular reaffirm the value and importance of romantic love, and wearers of Fidji signify that they are interested in making love.

The fact that the model in the advertisement is a woman of color may signify our sense, a commonplace in American culture, that women of color are more passionate and less inhibited than white women. In America we tend to see blonds as innocent, cold, and frigid and women of color as just the opposite. We assume, of course, that the woman in the advertisement is Polynesian because of the name of the perfume and from what we can see of her face.

A MARXIST INTERPRETATION OF THE FIDJI ADVERTISEMENT

One point a typical Marxist would make about this advertisement is that it reflects, in graphic manner, the exploitation of people of the Third World, the world of people of color, by people in the First World and, in particular, by bourgeois capitalist societies—the kind that encourage capitalist corporations like Fidji's maker, Guy Laroche. According to Marxist theory, capitalism has survived by exporting its problems, and thus the woman in the Fidji advertisement is really an advertisement for capitalist imperialism, not for perfume.

The Fidji advertisement is also a classic example of the excesses of bourgeois consumer culture, which has come to dominate every aspect of our lives, especially our sexuality. Our sexuality can be used against us, so to speak, to encourage us to make ever greater wasteful expenditures in the name of a spurious value—glamour. Advertising is, then, one of the central institutions of contemporary bourgeois cultures and is not to be thought of as merely a form of product entertainment. It has a political mission— to distract us from the breakdown of our civic cultures and focus our attention on private expenditures. We revel in our personal luxuries as our society disintegrates into chaos, and we take refuge in gated communities to escape from the dangers of the social disorganization we have generated.

What advertisements such as the one for Fidji perfume demonstrate is that alienation is very functional for those who own the means of production.

We attempt to assuage our alienation by creating consumer cultures and by continually purchasing things, which creates greater and greater profits for those who own the instruments of production and distribution. That is, alienation leads to consumption and higher profits. And since in recent years bourgeois capitalist societies have sexualized the act of consumption, as W. H. Haug points out, there are even stronger inducements for people to participate in consumer cultures.

One problem with the Marxist analysis of this advertisement and of advertising and consumer cultures is that it is doctrinaire. The party line, so to speak, covers all advertising and just about every other aspect of capitalist societies. In addition Marxism, politically speaking, has imploded, and former Soviet societies are now feverishly consuming, trying, it would seem, to make up for lost time. And while the Marxist critique of bourgeois societies may be logical and even correct, it lacks resonance. Studies have shown that Communist Party members and members of political elites in previously communist societies exploited people terribly and consumed enormous amounts of food and goods in proportion to their numbers.

The bottle of Fidji perfume that the maiden holds so lovingly in her hands might be construed to represent, finally, the domination of bourgeois capitalist cultures over Second and Third World cultures. That is, this advertisement might be seen as a reflection of the cultural imperialism that we find in contemporary society. Because the cost of making media texts is so high, Third World countries import most of the programs they show on their television stations and most of the films they see. The cultural imperialism argument made by Marxists and others is that this First World media is destroying the native cultures found in the Third World, leading to an eventual homogenization of culture, dominated by capitalist bourgeois values.

THE MYTH MODEL AND THE FIDJI ADVERTISEMENT

A number of years ago I developed a myth model that suggested, in essence, that many of the things we do in the contemporary world—or maybe the contemporary secular world would be more accurate—are really tied in curious and interesting ways to ancient myths. Or to be a bit more precise, many of our activities are desacralized manifestations of ancient myths. We have emptied the religious content out of the myths and don't even recognize that what we are doing is, vaguely speaking, a ritual tied to a myth. The myth model attempts to show how ancient myths inform many contemporary activities, whose relation to these myths is beyond our awareness.

The "myth model" has the following categories:

1. The **myth**,
2. A **historical event** related to the myth,
3. A text or work from **elite culture** based on the myth,
4. A text or work for **popular culture** based on the myth, and
5. Some aspects of **everyday life** based on the myth.

We can interpret the Fidji advertisement in terms of this myth model. I would argue that one myth that informs this advertisement is that of Medusa, the mythical creature—a Gorgon—whose hair was made of snakes. If you looked at Medusa, you would turn to stone. Medusa was killed by Perseus, a hero who escaped death by looking at her reflection in his bronze shield and beheading her. What is important is that we have here a woman and a snake intimately connected.

With her hair of snakes she was in psychoanalytic terms a hyperphallic female, since snakes, for Freudians, are phallic symbols. There may also be an element of ambivalence about Medusa in many men: a beautiful female who killed all who looked upon her. (This ambivalence is best reflected in an early churchman's definition of women: *templus supra cloaca*, which means "a temple over a sewer.") A contemporary aspect of the Medusa story is found in the belief some women have that their hair has life and is powerful. Hair color and hairstyle now play an important role in many women's lives. Finally, it might be possible that the fear many men have of snakes is connected, somehow (as this mythic story suggests), to an unconscious unification of snakes and women that leads to seeing women as snakelike. This, in turn, enables us to identify perfume as being like venom.

I interpret myths in conventional terms: They are sacred stories, often dealing with the creation of the world and the activities of various gods, demigods, heroes, and heroines, that provide people with core values and a comprehensive belief system. These beliefs are passed down, according to some anthropological thinkers, in a coded manner and are hidden in various stories and other narratives we learn.

With Medusa as our myth, we can see in table 8.3 the way the rest of the myth model might be filled in. The point, then, is that many of our everyday activities and rituals are intimately connected to ancient myths, though we may not recognize that what we are doing has any connection

Table 8.3. Myth Model and Fidji Advertisement

Myth	Medusa
Historical Act	Cleopatra kills herself with an asp
Elite Culture Text	Shakespeare: *Antony and Cleopatra*
Popular Culture Text	Fidji "Woman with Snake" advertisement
Everyday Life	Woman dabs on Fidji perfume

to myths or to the past. We may think we have escaped from the past and that it is irrelevant, but in more ways than we might imagine, ancient myths inform (though in disguised form) our arts, our media, and our everyday lives. Women and snakes go back, of course, to the story of Adam and Eve in the Garden of Eden. The connection between women and snakes—the beguilers—is ancient and is part of the consciousness of all who have read the Old Testament or heard about it.

A FEMINIST INTERPRETATION OF THE FIDJI ADVERTISEMENT

One of the basic contentions of most contemporary feminist thinkers is that we live in a phallocentric society—one dominated by males and what might be called the invisible power of the phallus. We may not be aware of the power of the phallus but the institutions of society and social relations are shaped, so the argument goes, by the power of males, by male sexuality, and ultimately by the phallus. Males, of course, are blind to their power and to the role of the phallus in the scheme of things; they assume that the power relationships found in any society are logical and natural.

What could be a better expression, then, of the power of the phallus than the image of the woman in the Fidji advertisement with the snake—a phallic symbol—draped around her neck (figure 8.4)? The woman stands there, accessible to the male gaze (the look men give women that reduces

Figure 8.4

them to sex objects). She is holding a bottle of perfume that will make her (and all women who use Fidji, so they think) irresistible to men and thus, without recognizing it, is participating in her own domination and subjugation. In Paradise, we must recall, Adam was given dominion over Eve and all other creatures, whom he named.

> In pain shall you bear children.
> Yet your urge shall be for your husband,
> And he shall rule over you.

Those are the words of God, who speaks them to Adam and Eve as he casts them out of the Garden. Thus, the return to Paradise is in effect a return to being dominated by men. So, not only the image of the maiden with the snake is connected with male sexuality and male domination but also the text of the Fidji advertisement. These images may also be connected in interesting ways with the unconscious fear that some men have of female sexuality and the female genitalia. This advertisement, then, is one that lends itself to feminist analysis.

These interpretations are only a few examples of the many different kinds of analyses that could be made of the Fidji advertisement. Critics and analysts with different areas of knowledge and expertise could find numerous other things to talk about in this advertisement—and in most advertisements and commercials. They are often rich in symbolism and interesting material for those who have the keys—that is, the theories and the conceptual framework—to unlock their meaning. Advertisements and commercials are richer in meaning than we might think, and it takes a good deal of work to understand how they communicate ideas and meanings and, to the extent that they are successful, shape our behavior.

To manufacture a product without at the same time manufacturing a demand has become unthinkable. Today the manufacture of demand means, for most large companies, television—its commercials as well as other program elements. The growing scale of mass production has inevitably made advertising more crucial, but this understates the situation. As society becomes more product-glutted, the pressure on the consumer to consume—to live up to higher and higher norms of consumption— has become unrelenting.

The pressure, as various observers have noted, centers on selling the unnecessary. The merchandising of necessities—which, to some extent, will be bought anyway—can seldom sustain the budgets applied to the unnecessary, unless the necessary is cloaked with mythical supplemental values. The focus is on the creation of emotion-charged values to make the unneeded necessary.

All this is now so taken for granted that it is seldom discussed. The young writer entering advertising assumes that hope and fear are the springs he must touch—hope of success and fear of failure in sex, business, community status. As a dramatic medium that can draw on the resources of every art, and has as its stage the privacy of the home, television has unparalleled opportunity for this psychic pressure.

—Erik Barnouw, *The Sponsor: Notes on a Modern Potentate*

Postmodern advertising—characterized by a rapid succession of visually appealing images (the speed-up effect), repetition, and high-volume, mood-setting music . . . is much more symbolic and persuasive than informative. Advertising is an arena in which conspicuous role display and reversal, preening, and symbolically enticing situations are evident. . . . While modern advertising presented itself as an unquestionable authority figure—a high priest of sorts—postmodern advertising presents itself as an insider, an ally of the common person. Modern advertising uses a paternalistic model; like your physician, it knows what is best for you. Now advertising is trading in the semblance of godlike knowledge for the role of a funny, self-deprecatory chum.

—Anthony J. Cortese, *Provocateur: Images of Women and Minorities in Advertising*

9

ANALYZING TELEVISION COMMERCIALS

The Macintosh "1984" Commercial

Television commercials are much more complex than print advertisements because they can have many more elements in them: a narrative structure, dialogue, music, various kinds of shots, various editing practices, and so on. From Yuri Lotman's perspective, they store a great deal more information than print advertisements with photographs do; that is because they are in essence mini-video or film dramas, and each frame or image in a commercial is, in a sense, similar to a print advertisement with a photograph in it.

In this chapter I offer a list of topics to consider when analyzing commercials and then offer an analysis of the famous "1984" Macintosh commercial, a sixty-second commercial that was recently selected by people in the industry as the second-best television commercial made in the 1980s. What follows is a list of things to consider in a "complex" television commercial—not a simple one in which someone is shown talking

about a product and there's relatively little in the way of production values or narrative line.

1. What is the plot of the narrative in the commercial? That is, what happens to the characters? Are there narrative tricks used—flash-forwards or flashbacks? What dramatic techniques are used?

2. What characters do we find in the commercial? What are they like? What are their ages, genders, educational levels, occupations, and so on? How do they communicate their personalities? What roles do they play? How do they relate to one another?

3. How would you describe the faces of the characters? Their bodies? Their clothing? What about the color of their hair? The way their hair is styled? Their voices? Their use of body language and facial expressions when they see some product or service?

4. What do the characters say to one another? Consider the words they use and the role the dialogue has in the commercial. What arguments, if any, are made? How does the commercial sell people? What do you think the target audience of the commercial is? What techniques of persuasion are used by the characters? What appeals are made? Does the commercial try to scare you? Appeal to your vanity? Provide valuable information? Plead with you?

5. If there's a narrator, is it a male or female (or child or something else)? What role does the narrator have?

6. Where does the commercial take place? What significance does the setting have?

7. Are there any props (objects) used? If so, what are they? Why do you think they were used?

8. How is color used in the commercial?

9. How would you describe the lighting? Does it vary?

10. How is sound used? Is there music? if so, what kind?

11. What kinds of shots are used? Make a list of all the shots found in the commercial and try to determine what significance they have. Are they mostly close-ups or something else?

12. What kind of editing techniques are used? Are there quick cuts, lingering dissolves, zooms? Tie these editing decisions to the dialogue and the goal of the commercial.

13. Are there intertextual references found in the text—parodies, use of famous shots, well-known characters, and so on?
14. In what ways does the commercial rely upon background knowledge on the part of the viewer/listener? How does it relate to widely held ideas, beliefs, notions, myths, values, archetypes, and so on?
15. What role does the product have in society? Who uses it? Why do they use it? What does it tell us about social, economic, and political matters? For example, does it reflect anomie, alienation, anxiety, stereotyping, generational conflict, or boredom?

These questions are ones we should deal with in analyzing commercials. We may not need to cover every part of every question, but we should submit the commercial to as complete an analysis as we can. The nature of the commercial determines the methods and concepts we use to interpret it.

Consider, for example, a "complex" commercial. It may only last sixty seconds, but it may have as many as sixty or seventy different images in it, as well as music, dialogue, print, and human beings with different attributes who use body language and facial expressions to send some message to us about some product or service. Every image is loaded with information, even though we may not realize how much information there is in the image or recognize how the image is impacting on us.

A SYNOPSIS OF THE TEXT

As the commercial begins, the number 1984 appears on the screen (see the storyboard in figure 9.1). The director then cuts to an extreme long shot of vaguely perceived figures marching through a tunnel joining gigantic structures. Next he cuts to a long shot of figures marching. They all have shaved heads and are wearing dull uniforms. The figures have no expression on their faces. Then there is an extreme close-up of their heavy boots. A quick cut shows a blond woman with a white jersey and red shorts running (figure 9.2). We only see her for an instant. The next cut shows the figures again and then there is a cut to a shot of the woman being pursued by stormtroopers. There is cutting back and forth in the commercial between the blond woman and the troopers pursuing her. Then we see another extreme long shot of the inmates of this institution sitting in a huge

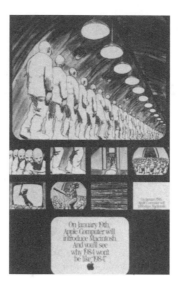

Figure 9.1

room. They are staring at a gigantic television set. A figure wearing glasses is addressing the inmates (figure 9.3), who sit gazing at the television image as if in a hypnotic trance. He is talking about the inmates being free, united, and so on. Then suddenly the blond woman, who is carrying a sledgehammer, enters the room. She hurls her sledgehammer at the television screen and when it hits it there is a gigantic explosion. The explosion creates an image that looks somewhat like that generated by an atomic bomb. The inmates gaze, dazed and openmouthed, at the screen. Then, a message from Apple Computers appears on the screen informing viewers that Apple will be introducing a new computer, the Macintosh, shortly.

Figure 9.2

Figure 9.3

THE BACKGROUND

This commercial, directed by Ridley Scott, the distinguished British filmmaker (*Alien, Blade Runner*), was shown nationally in the United States only once—during the 1984 Super Bowl—though it (or parts of it) also has been aired, from time to time, in news features on advertising and the computer industry. The commercial was created by Apple's advertising agency, Chiat/Day of Los Angeles. According to an advertising executive from Chiat/Day, it cost $500,000 to make and another $600,000 for airtime (sixty seconds).

Apple was hesitant to use it and only decided to do so at the very last minute. An executive in the agency revealed that Apple actually called England to stop production of the commercial, but by that time the commercial had already been shot.

The "1984" commercial is a remarkable text. The actors in the commercial were English skinheads, who were recruited to play the prisoners. (Since 1984, when the commercial was made, skinheads have emerged as a worldwide phenomenon of disaffected youth who are attracted to right-wing neo-Nazi organizations.) The "1984" commercial has a look much different from the average commercial and takes a considerably different approach to the matter of marketing a product than we find with most commercials.

Ridley Scott, the director (auteur), is a distinguished figure in the film world, and the commercial bears his signature—its look, its narrative structure, its message all suggest an art film rather than a television commercial. I believe many "creative" people in the advertising industry are capable of creating aesthetically interesting and artistically pleasing works (and sometimes they do) when they are not prevented from doing so by the companies whose products they are advertising. Of course, a great deal depends

---

Insights from Advertising Agencies

It is imperative not to try too many different ways of solving a problem for a client since this costs the agency a lot of money and confuses our customers. There should be, then, only one campaign suggested; it must be made to seem to be the only answer to the company's problems, so the company's advertising director is sold before he sees the proposed advertisement.

---

on the nature of the product being sold and the nature (that is, the corporate culture) of the company selling the product.

In the remainder of this chapter I discuss some of the most important images from the text and speculate about how these images generate meaning, what that meaning is, and how viewers might be affected by these images. I also discuss the narrative itself.

It is often held that there is no minimal unit in a television text to deal with (unlike film, which has the frame). I don't think this is a major issue as far as our considerations, since one can always isolate important images and scenes to analyze, so even if a television text doesn't have frames, it does have shots, which serve the same function.

GEORGE ORWELL'S *1984* AND RIDLEY SCOTT'S "1984"

The title of this commercial brings to mind George Orwell's novel *1984*, and the text of the commercial is based on the idea of totalitarian anti-utopias or dystopias. The ambience of the "1984" commercial is that of a perverted utopian community, a total institution, in which every aspect of people's lives is controlled—especially their minds. We see "1984," the commercial, in terms of *1984*, the book. Here we have an example of what is known in semiotic literature as intertextuality. That is, we read or interpret one text in terms of another text, or with another text in mind. The events in the commercial would have far less significance if we hadn't read or didn't know about Orwell's classic novel *1984*.

This concept is explained by the Russian literary theorist Mikhail Bakhtin as follows:

> Every extra-artistic prose discourse—in any of its forms, quotidian, rhetorical, scholarly—cannot fail to be oriented toward the "already ut-

tered," the "already known," the "common opinion" and so forth. The dialogic orientation of discourse is a phenomenon that is, of course, a property of *any* discourse. . . . Every word is directed toward an *answer* and cannot escape the profound influence of the answering word that it anticipates. The word in living conversation is directly, blatantly, oriented toward a future answer-word: it provokes an answer, anticipates it and structures itself in the atmosphere of the already spoken, the word is at the same time determined by that which has not been said but which is needed and in fact anticipated by the answering word. Such is the situation in any dialogue. (1981:279–80)

When we write or communicate in any manner we always have an audience in mind, and what we write or say is always connected intimately to thoughts and ideas that have been communicated in the past. Communication of any kind is, then, always dialogic as opposed to monologic and involves a real or imagined audience and the responses the communicator can expect from it. In some cases this dialogical aspect of communication is vague and in the realm of the anticipated; in other cases, it is tied directly to something in the past. This is the case with the Macintosh commercial and the citation of the Orwell novel.

The title of the Macintosh commercial is also connected to a great deal of speculation that occurred in America during the year 1984 about Orwell and his dire predictions. Thus, merely seeing the title generated ambivalent feelings. Would it be about the year 1984 or about the novel *1984*? (Many social commentators have argued that the year 1984 did not by any means bring the kind of society that Orwell imagined.) The title left people in suspense.

THE IMAGE OF THE TOTAL INSTITUTION

The first shot resolved any questions that might have been generated by the title. We see an extreme long shot of gigantic structures connected by a tubular tunnel, in which we can dimly perceive figures marching. The scale of the scene is terrifying. The figures are minute and seemingly irrelevant when contrasted with the huge buildings in which they are incarcerated. One almost thinks of blood flowing through veins.

Thus the spatiality of this scene and the images of control and conformity generated by the columns of figures tell us immediately that the commercial, "1984," is indeed about an Orwellian world. This is reinforced in the next shot, which is a long shot of the prisoners, all with shaved heads and heavy, ill-fitting uniforms, marching sullenly in columns in a long tunnel.

Figure 9.4

THE PRISONERS' BOOTS

A really important shot occurs shortly after the commercial begins when there is a cut to a close-up of the prisoners' boots (figure 9.4). The heavy, thick-soled boots, shown moving in unison, reflect the degree to which the inmates are under the control of their masters. (This is an example of *metonymy*, which confers meaning by association. And, in particular, it is an example of *synecdoche*, in which a part can stand for a whole.)

The shot of the boots is meant to intensify the message. (We may even recall, as another example of intertextuality, the famous shot of the boots in Eisenstein's *The Battleship Potemkin*, though the situation in that film was somewhat different.) Uniforms suggest lack of individuality and depersonalization and, in the content of the "1984" commercial, dehumanization. Thus, the shot of the boots moving in unison strengthens this message by emphasizing one part of the human being and isolating it from the image of the whole human being.

The rather sullen and lethargic nature of their marching and the uniformity of the prisoners' feet as they march suggest these inmates have been reduced to the status of automatons. It is the same kind of reductionism that occurs when we talk about young people being "college material" or football players as "horses," though it is much more exaggerated and intensified here.

THE BLOND AS SYMBOL

Into this scene of marching zombies, of dehumanized and radically depersonalized bodies, there appears for just an instant an image of a beautiful blond woman who is running down a corridor. She wears a white shirt and red shorts. We can see her breasts heaving as she runs directly toward us, the viewers, on the Z-axis of the screen. The blond woman appears for perhaps a second or two, and then we return to the marching bodies and various scenes of totalitarian control.

Who is she? We do not know, but the fact that she exists tells us there must be forces of resistance in this totalitarian society, that not all are enslaved. We see shortly that she is being pursued by a troop of burly policemen who look terribly menacing in their helmets with glass face masks. Her color, her animation, her freedom, even her sexuality, serve to make the situation of the inmates even more obvious and pathetic. Her image functions as a polar opposite to the enslaved men, and even though we only see her the first time for a second or two, her existence creates drama and excitement.

THE BRAINWASHING SCENARIO

In this brainwashing scene we have a long shot of the inmates, sitting in rows, gazing at a gigantic television screen in the front of the auditorium, where a Big Brother figure is shown speaking to them. They are mute, expressionless, and seem almost hypnotized by the figure on the television screen. The message we get from this image is that mind control is an important element in the operation of this totalitarian society.

By implication, of course, control of the media (the gigantic television screen reflects this) is vital for control of the minds of the inmates—and perhaps, by implication, everyone. We must ask ourselves, Is this scene a metaphor for contemporary society, in which we, like the inmates, gaze in a hypnotic stupor at figures who "brainwash" (or try to, at least) us? Is the distance between the world of the "1984" commercial and American society less than we might imagine? Questions like these are raised by this dramatic image.

Is it possible that we are like these prisoners and that we are mind-controlled the way they are? We may not wear their uniform, have shaved heads, or be prisoners (or recognize that we are prisoners, that is) in some kind of a total institution. But that may be because the control is more subtle, the indoctrination less apparent. There may be more control over us than we imagine. That is one of the questions raised by this image.

THE BIG BROTHER FIGURE

We don't see a great deal of the Big Brother figure, only several shots in which we see him spouting ideological gobbledygook to the inmates.

ice of the actor to portray this character is very interesting. He looks like a clerk or minor bureaucrat from some organization. He is in his fifties or sixties, wears glasses, and is definitively portrayed as bland, unanimated, and without much in the way of personality. He speaks in a low, rather monotonous voice. Indeed, for all we know, he may only be a minor functionary in whatever vast organization runs this society.

What we learn from considering this figure is that most totalitarian institutions are essentially bureaucratic, held together not by charismatic individuals but by drab, conformist, rule-following bureaucratic types who do their jobs in a routine manner and do whatever they are told to do. They are not that different from the inmates in many respects, although the control exerted over these figures may be less overt. (There may, of course, be charismatic leaders in totalitarian societies, but we don't see them in this commercial.)

THE BRAINWASHER'S MESSAGE

Here is a transcript of the message the Big Brother figure gives to the inmates. He speaks it, but it is also shown in captions running across the bottom of the screen.

> Today we celebrate the first glorious anniversary of the information purification repentance. We who created from out of this time in all history a garden of pure ideology, where each worker may bloom, secure from the pests purveying contradictory thoughts. Our communication is enormous. It is more powerful than any fleet or army on earth. We are one people with one will, one resolve, one cause. Our enemies shall talk themselves to death and we will bury them with their own confusion. We shall prevail. . . . [At this point television screen is shattered]

Notice the degree to which this rhetoric is garbled and confusing. We have here a good examination of double-talk or baffle-gab: words that don't add up to anything. He talks about events we know nothing of, though we can imagine what might have transpired. The language has the ring of political indoctrination—there is a "glorious revolution" being "celebrated." The language contrasts, starkly, with the scenario in which it is being used. There is talk in this futuristic, oppressive hyper-urban setting of a "garden of pure ideology" and the "security" that the workers should feel from all this.

It is *communication* that is given the major role here—it is a more powerful force than the military, it unites the workers/inmates/prisoners into a collectivity (or is it a mass society?) with "one will, one resolve, one cause." And then there is that wonderfully comic line about the enemies of this society "talking themselves to death." It is the rhetoric of persuasion, and we have the sense that the inmates of this society have been exposed to this kind of talk almost endlessly. That is, they have all been brainwashed by this double-talk.

The language, with phrases such as "information purification repentance," is that of mind control and psychic domination, and the commercial does a wonderful job of imitating it (and perhaps, in a sense, of parodying it). The goal preached is escape from "contradictory thoughts," which enables the inmates to have "one will." In other words, the essentially human function of considering options and alternatives is to be obliterated—or has it been already?

THE BIG EXPLOSION

In the "1984" commercial there are several scenes in which we see the blond woman twirling a sledgehammer (as she prepares to throw it at the screen) and the police racing toward her (figure 9.5). She launches the sledgehammer, and it smashes into the gigantic television screen. There is an enormous explosion, and we see, briefly, an image vaguely similar to that produced by an atomic bomb.

The explosion, which destroys the screen image—and by implication the domination by the mass media of the inmates—is the most significant act in the commercial. With this act a great blow is struck for freedom, and we are led to imagine what might follow. We are shown very little. Implicit in this scenario is the notion that once the control of people's minds by a totalitarian regime is broken, the destruction of that regime more or less

Figure 9.5

follows automatically. This does not have to be spelled out. It is like lancing a boil: When the system of pressure is punctured, healing can take place. The exploding screen signifies, then, the destruction of the totalitarian order that generates mind-controlling images on that screen.

THE INMATES' RESPONSE

After the explosion the commercial cuts to a scene in which the inmates are shown openmouthed, staring in disbelief at what has happened. They are, relatively speaking, emotionless and display no affect other than bewilderment or shock. They have been so brainwashed, we are led to believe, they are incapable of any kind of response. At least, in the immediate present.

We hear a low hissing sound, as if air is escaping from the gigantic television apparatus in the front of the room. The camera pans the inmates as the announcement from Apple rolls onto the screen.

THE MACINTOSH ANNOUNCEMENT

We see the following announcement:

On January 24th, Apple Computers will introduce Macintosh and you will see why 1984 won't be like "1984."

The brevity and simplicity of this announcement, which takes but a few seconds, contrasts with the excitement and visual richness of the rest of the commercial. In this situation the understatement serves to shout at us and to gain a great deal of interest. Not only does Apple tell us it is introducing a new computer, but also that this new computer has enormous political and social implications—for it has the power to save us from ending up like the prisoners, victims of a totalitarian state.

There had been an enormous amount of material about the Macintosh in the press and computer fanzines, so those interested in computers already knew about it. And when the Macintosh computer went on sale, Apple sold approximately 17,000 the first day, a figure far beyond what they had anticipated. People from Chiat/Day talk as if it was the commercial that sold all those computers—an assumption that is very questionable.

THE HEROINE AS MYTHIC FIGURE

In this microdrama, the blond heroine calls to mind several different heroic or mythic figures from our collective consciousness. First, there is something of David and Goliath in this story—a small, seemingly weak, and in this case, female, character brings down a Goliath figure by hurling a stone (sledgehammer) at it. In the commercial there are some close-ups of the Big Brother/Goliath figure, which simulate the size relationships between David and Goliath.

In both cases—the "1984" commercial and the David and Goliath story—it is a missile to the head that does the job. And with the destruction of the evil Goliath figure, of course, the forces of good can prevail. So it seems reasonable to argue that the blond represents a female version of David, and I would imagine many people might see some kind of a resemblance between the David and Goliath story and the events in this commercial. Here we find how intertextual readings can enrich an event and give an image a great deal of cultural resonance.

The woman can also, let me suggest, be interpreted as an Eve figure. The fact that the Apple corporation's symbol is an apple with a bite out of it tells us that. But the blond heroine also functions like Eve, for ultimately what she does is lead to knowledge of good and evil in a reverse Garden of Eden. Before she shattered the image, the inmates were brainwashed and had but "one will, one resolve, one cause." What information these poor souls had was "purified." Their state is vaguely analogous to that of Adam before he ate of the apple. It is the tasting of the fruit that led to Adam and Eve's "eyes being opened," and that is the beginning of human history, one might argue.

The blond heroine, then, is an Eve figure who brings knowledge of good and evil, and by implication, knowledge of reality, to the inmates. We do not see their transformation after the destruction of the Big Brother/Goliath figure—indeed, their immediate reaction is awe and stupefaction—but ultimately we cannot help but assume that something important will happen and they will be liberated.

It is quite possible that this beautiful blond figure may also represent, in our psyches, the Apple corporation. We know that corporations have different images in people's minds—often based on symbolic figures in advertisements and commercials. On the basis of this commercial one might guess that the corporate image we have of Apple is that of a beautiful blond woman (who liberates men from political and psychological domination and ignorance). Much of this would be at the unconscious level, of course.

We can make sense of the image of the blond woman in the 1984 commercial, who is shown running with a sledgehammer into a huge auditorium, at four different levels of meaning:

The Literal Level	the specific image that we see
The Textual Level	the place of the image in the text and its role in the narrative
The Intertextual Level	how it suggests Orwell's 1984 and other dystopias
The Mythic Level	how it calls to mind David & Goliath and other myths and legends.

Images, then, have an enormous amount of resonance and even though we may only glance at a particular image for a second or two, the impact—as we tie this image to information stored in our minds—can be considerable. The responsive chord theory of media suggests that images like this strike responsive chords in our minds that give them a great deal of power. This theory suggests that we shouldn't focus our attention on information transmitted by media but, instead, we should focus our attention on information stored in our minds that media, and advertising in particular, turn on.

It is probably a good image for a computer company to have, since one of the biggest problems computer manufacturers have is fighting anxiety about technology and the difficulties of operating computers—Macintosh's very reason for being, as a matter of fact. If people see Apple computers as beautiful blonds, so much the better for the corporation.

PSYCHOANALYTIC ASPECTS OF THE COMMERCIAL

From a psychoanalytic standpoint, the heroine is an ego figure who mediates between a monstrous and perverted superego figure, Big Brother, and the de-energized and devastated ids of the inmates. The id, as it is commonly defined, involves impulses and desires; the superego involves guilt; and the ego mediates between the two, trying to maintain equilibrium. Ids are needed to give us energy, and superegos are needed to prevent us from becoming creatures of impulse. Both can, I suggest, become perverted.

In the following, we see how the blond is an ego figure.

Id	Ego	Superego
inmates	blond	Big Brother
perverted	normal	perverted
no energy	strong	no heart

As an ego figure, the heroine has to mediate between the inmates, whose ids have been weakened and drained of energy, and the brainwasher, whose superego has become monstrous and distorted. One might see vague elements of an Oedipal conflict, in which a young female and an older, perhaps even "fatherly," figure have a very difficult relationship—to put it mildly.

THE BLOND AS MEDIATOR

One important function of the mythic hero or heroine is to mediate between opposing forces in an attempt to resolve a basic opposition. The text of this commercial is very binary, and the blond heroine serves to identify and highlight the oppositions found in it. There are in essence three characters in this text. First, there are the inmates who function as one character. Then there is the Big Brother character (and the police who are part of him). And there is the blond heroine. Her function is to resolve the oppositions, one way or another, and she does this.

In the list that follows I contrast the inmates and the Big Brother figure. Here we are eliciting the paradigmatic structure of the text, which, according to Claude Lévi-Strauss, tells us its real but hidden meaning (as opposed to the surface meaning, which we get with a syntagmatic or linear narrative analysis).

Inmates	Big Brother
obey	commands
uniforms	regular clothes
hairless	hair
listen	speaks
brainwashed	brainwasher
look at	is looked at

mindless	calculating
dehumanized	dehumanizing
alienated	alienating
emotionless	heartless

The blond heroine, with her gorgeous hair, her vitality, her energy, her force, resolves the dialectic by destroying Big Brother and making it possible (we imagine) for the inmates eventually to regain their humanity. She also makes us aware of the depths to which the inmates have sunk, for unlike them she resists, she has a mind of her own, and she accepts danger.

Thus she contrasts with both the inmates and with Big Brother, whom she destroys. The inmates and Big Brother are reverse images of one another—both drab, depersonalized, and locked into a slave-master relationship that defines each character and on which both may turn out to be dependent.

ALIENATED PROLES

The inmates, workers, prisoners, whatever you wish to call them, reflect with terrifying clarity the power modern bureaucratic states have to destroy humanity and lead people into a state of radical alienation. We have here a classic case (even if somewhat oversimplified and parodied) of, in Marxist terms, a mindless proletariat—maybe a classic example of what Marxists call a *Lumpenproletariat*—being manipulated by a heartless bourgeoisie.

This bourgeoisie rules by virtue of its monopoly of power and its control of the media and the manipulation of the consciousness of the proletariat. The situation in the commercial is one in which the horrors of a capitalist society are shown pushed to their logical conclusion, where workers are now enslaved and brainwashed and the society in which they live has become a totalitarian one.

The blond heroine's actions, then, symbolize revolution. She stands for the role of progressive forces (pushed underground in this society) in leading a stupefied proletariat out of its chains. Since this proletariat has been brainwashed, it is incapable of action and is, perhaps, even reactionary. Hence it remains passive while the revolution takes place, and can only stare in openmouthed wonder at the destruction of the power structure that enslaves it.

In this scenario, the power of the media is shown as central, and when it is put out of action, the rest is almost automatic. Interestingly enough, this message is not too far removed from the overt message of the Apple corporation—that access to user-friendly computers will prevent a totalitarian society from coming into being. Apple thus defines itself as a revolutionary force in the quasitotalitarian world of hard-to-use computers where power will be held by those who know how to function in the information society.

The Macintosh will prevent society from splitting into two groups—those who have access to computers and are part of the information society and those who know nothing about computers and are condemned to menial jobs and will form a class of workers who will have little economic power or status.

Apple is, in our imaginations, the beautiful blond who will prevent a rigid information-based class system from evolving and, by implication, a totalitarian society. The Macintosh brings knowledge of good and evil to humankind—all it takes is a bite (or is it a byte?).

THE BIG BLUE

It is not too far-fetched, I would argue, to suggest that the totalitarian society shown in this commercial is an indirect representation of IBM, International Business Machines. Apple sees itself as a small, humanistic, open corporation battling a gigantic, superpowerful, and highly bureaucratic corporation, IBM. There are two readings to which this insight leads.

Scenario 1: In the first reading, the whole story is about IBM. The Big Brother figure is the corporate leadership, and the inmates are meant to symbolize the IBM workers who are controlled (white shirt and tie, and so on) by IBM. IBM has a reputation for being rather strict about the way its workers and salespeople dress, and this commercial may be alluding to the regimentation identified with IBM.

Scenario 2: The second reading suggests that IBM is the Big Brother and the American public is the inmates—who have been duped and controlled by IBM, but who are about to be liberated by Apple and its revolutionary Macintosh computer.

The battle resolves itself down to one between the beautiful blond heroine and the monolithic monster—a bureaucratic corporation full of faceless nobodies mindlessly following rules and regulations, and enslaving the multitudes. The Macintosh is the sledgehammer which Apple has to throw against IBM—a user-friendly machine that will, democratically, make computing available to all.

A CLEVER MARKETING STRATEGY

Although the "1984" commercial cost a great deal of money to produce (perhaps three or four times as much as a typical high-budget commercial) and air, due to the notoriety it attracted, it ended up being a very good buy. We must remember that it only aired once nationally in the United States—yet it was the subject of a great deal of media attention, and it fascinated the huge audience that was watching the Super Bowl when it was shown.

As someone in the creative department at Chiat/Day explained to me, "Good campaigns end up being relatively inexpensive." A good commercial (and campaign) may cost a great deal to produce and air, but if its impact is sufficiently strong, on attention-per-thousand basis it might work out to be relatively cheap.

Chiat/Day (and Apple) took an unusual approach with this commercial. It focused its attention not so much on the benefits derived from using a Macintosh but instead on the dangers inherent in not using one. The commercial wasn't selling a specific product in a direct manner. Instead, it used indirection to build an image for Apple and Macintosh and, at the same time, cast aspersions on its main rival, IBM.

In the course of sixty seconds it created a memorable microdrama (which is what many commercials are, actually) that worked subtly and indirectly. Like many commercials, it was highly compressed, with neither a beginning nor an ending. (Many commercials don't have a beginning but do show a happy ending, with someone using the product or service advertised.)

The ending implied in the "1984" commercial focused on the avoidance of something hateful rather than the gaining of something desirable. In its own way, there is an element of conditioning involved here; we have a condensed form of *aversion therapy*. The argument, like the commercial, is binary. If there are only two possibilities, Apple and IBM, and IBM (and all that it and its imitators stand for) is shown to be horrible, one is led to choose Apple. One acts not so much to gain pleasure (though that beautiful blond attracts us) as to avert pain—Big Brother and the dystopian world (IBM) that he represents.

The "1984" commercial launched the Macintosh brilliantly. Apple continued to attack conformity in the business world in its 1985 commercial, which showed blindfolded businessmen jumping off a cliff like lemmings. But this ad lacked the polish and aesthetic complexity found in

"1984," and it was followed by a rather meager event, Apple announcing a few minor items in its campaign to get businesses to purchase Macintoshes. The "1984" commercial was a brilliant success, but it did not translate into great business success for Apple for a variety of reasons.

THE "1984" COMMERCIAL AND
A BIT OF SCHOLARLY RESEARCH

In 1991 two communication scholars, Sandra Moriarty and Shay Sayre, presented a paper at the sixteenth annual meeting of the Semiotic Society of America, "A Comparison of Reader Response with Informed Author/Viewer Analysis." The purpose of this research on the Macintosh "1984" commercial was (1991:1) "to find out what meanings an audience can derive from a single showing of a very complex television commercial text, and to test the level of agreement that exists among the author's intention, critic's analysis and reader's response." The sixty-second Macintosh commercial, they point out, had won thirty-four national and international advertising awards and was commonly described as "the commercial that outplayed the game."

The authors say the commercial cost $1.6 million—which differs by a million dollars from what someone in Chiat/Day told me. In any case, they quote Lee Clow, creative director for Chiat/Day, who described the commercial as follows:

> We placed our audience within the context of Orwell's view of society, a place where the dominant computer technology held consumers captive. The intended message was that Mac would set consumer [sic] free from the unfriendly technology of the competition. We gave the message impact with body imagery designed to contrast Apple with the competition. . . . All you have to do is look at IBM's historic approach to computers as something for the few, where they might let you in if you conformed and learned their language, programming. Then look at how Apple makes computers accessible to people. (1991:7)

This, then, is what the advertising agency that was responsible for hiring Ridley Scott wanted to do.

Moriarty and Sayre then describe an earlier version of my "1984" article (upon which this chapter is based) as a representative semiotic interpretation of the "1984" commercial. They go on to describe the methodology used in their research:

> First, the respondents' analyses of the commercial will be compared with the main message points stated by both the creator of the commercial and the semiotic critic to determine if viewers are getting the point of the message. Then the significant images identified by the respondents will be compared with the images noted and interpreted by the critic to determine if the student readings are the same or similar to the reading of an informed viewer. . . . The respondents' level of interpretation also will be analyzed to determine their sophistication in story analysis. . . . Finally, it is expected that differences in the respondents' readings, if any, will be found more in their level of interpretation than in their story focus. (1991:8)

The respondents in this study were 200 undergraduate students taking mass communication courses at two state universities.

The conclusions Moriarty and Sayre reached from analyzing the data from the 200 respondents are quite interesting. As they write:

> In terms of the big question, there is rather high agreement between the student respondents and the critic and creator on the element of the message that focuses on the introduction of the Macintosh computer. This is particularly important since advertising researchers know that the miscomprehension rate of television advertising message points is close to 25 percent. Other elements which the creator and critic thought were important message points were rarely or barely noted, which suggests that a deep reading from a fleeting exposure to a television commercial is probably not realistic. . . . While the *1984* story line was extremely powerful, the Macintosh message was still the focus of their interpretations. While in slightly more than half the cases they were reading and interpreting the stories at a simple level, the number that engaged in a more elaborate decoding with some interpretation beyond simply re-telling was higher than the researchers expected, almost reaching 50 percent. This suggests that viewers of a fast paced, complex commercial may be able to engage in sophisticated interpretation even from a brief exposure. (1991:21–3)

This conclusion is extremely interesting, for it suggests that a relatively high percentage of the students were able to interpret the "1984" commercial—and by implication, all commercials—in a relatively sophisticated manner. The authors suggest that their research indicates how important images (and the codes we use to interpret them) are for generating commercials whose meaning people can understand.

What this research demonstrates is that large numbers of people don't have to know what semiotics is or know the somewhat arcane jargon that semioticians use to get the message in commercials and other mass-mediated texts. And that is because we learn how to decode commercials and everything else as we grow up in a society. We are all semioticians, whether we know it or not. We are always sending messages to others— via the words we use, our facial expressions, our hairstyles, the clothes we wear, our body language, and so on—and interpreting messages others send us. Like the character in one of Molière's plays who didn't realize he was always speaking prose, we are all semioticians, with varying degrees of understanding of certain basic semiotic principles—whether we recognize it or not.

As a society, we are embedded in a culture of consumption. Neil Postman . . . notes that by the age of forty the average American will have seen well over one million commercials and have "close to another million to go before his first social security check." In order to comprehend the impact of all this advertising on society we must learn how to see through advertisements, for they are not just messages about goods and services but social and cultural texts about ourselves.

—Katherine Toland Frith, *Undressing the Ad*

If our material needs are not satisfied, we die from hunger or exposure; if our social needs are not satisfied, we are liable to suffer psychological problems. Now the crucial point is that in our consumption of goods, we satisfy both material and social needs. Various social groups identify themselves through shared attitudes, manners, accents, and habits of consumption—for instance, through the clothes they wear. In this way the objects that we use and consume cease to be mere objects of use; they become carriers of information about what kind of people we are, or would like to be.

—Torben Vestergaard and Kim Schrøder,
The Language of Advertising

10

WHERE NEXT?

W e have covered a great deal of ground in this analysis of advertising and its impact on American character and culture. The soft economy of 2001 and 2002 in the United States meant that companies cut back on the amount of money they spent on advertising, causing great problems for the industry. But when the economy shows signs of improving, things will look up for advertising. When companies have problems, it seems that the first thing they cut is the amount of money they spend on advertising. A good case could be made that they should do just the opposite and spend more on advertising, for it is when the economy is not doing well that organizations need advertising the most.

Where next? we might ask. Let me suggest, here, two areas of considerable importance that are good candidates for further research: drug advertising and advertising to children. They are both quite complicated and the subject of considerable controversy.

DRUG ADVERTISING

Advertising is, as I have suggested all through this book, one of the most interesting, vital, and problematic influences on us as individuals and as American society. Take, for example, prescription drug advertising. In recent years pharmaceutical companies have considerably increased the amount of advertising they do, which has led to a rapid rise in the prices of certain prescription drugs. In addition, patients now demand that their physicians prescribe certain drugs they see advertised, such as Prozac, Allegra, and Viagra. The page spread in figure 10.1, from a many-page advertising insert for a variety of prescription drugs, shows an ad for Lantus insulin, with one page set up to look like a regular article about insulin. The medical profession considers drug advertising to be a nuisance, at best, and a potential menace, at worst.

Insulin: The Modern Miracle

In 1921, Dr. Frederick Banting, a Canadian surgeon, and Charles Best, a medical student, made a landmark discovery: insulin. They learned that injections of insulin — a hormone caused blood sugar levels to drop and and symptoms of diabetes to be mitigated. A year later, insulin made from the pancreas of animals became available.

Thanks to this discovery, millions of people with diabetes are not only living longer, but remain healthy. For those with Type 1, administration of insulin is a matter of day-to-day survival. Because their pancreatic islet cells produce no insulin, injections of insulin are necessary to transform the foods they eat into energy.

Insulin is also used to treat some people

New types of insulin provide options in treatment.

with Type 2 diabetes. Initially, their islet cells produce insulin. But over the years, the amount may become inadequate for the body's needs. Then they may take either insulin or oral diabetes medication alone, or a combination of the two.

According to the Food and Drug Administration, there are now more than 20 types of insulin products in four basic terms. Types vary on how long they begin working (onset), when they work the hardest (peak time) and how long they remain in the body (duration).

The goal of any insulin program is to keep blood glucose close to its normal range, by mimicking normal pancreatic secretions of insulin. The regimen may involve one or two types of insulin that work at different speeds.

In designing a regimen, physicians weigh many factors including the type of diabetes, the patient's daily schedule, meal pattern and exercise level. Other factors, such as where the insulin is injected, illness and stress, may also be considered.

Insulin products are either taken from animals or manufactured in laboratories. Many of the newer insulin products are analogues, modified in structure and reworked in their characteristics than human insulin.

These analogues have facilitated flexible insulin regimens, allowing people with diabetes to adjust their insulin dosages. With a

conventional regimen, insulin is taken at set times, following a strict schedule.

Because they start to work very quickly, rapid-acting insulin analogues allow patients to take injections just before eating, rather than waiting 30 minutes after an injection to eat. Longer-acting insulin analogues have also emerged, providing more consistent blood sugar control. For example, Lantus (glargine) has a 24-hour glucose lowering effect and no distinct peak. Only one injection a day, usually at bedtime, is required, a major advantage for those with erratic schedules.

Insulin cannot be taken orally because it would be destroyed by digestion before it could enter the bloodstream to move glucose from the blood into the cells, for the body's fuel. In addition to syringes, insulin pens, jet injectors and pumps are now available.

Insulin Resistance Syndrome Continued from page 49

was effective for both men and women. About 7.8 percent of the bluroephage group developed prediabetes each year during the study, compared with 11 percent of the group receiving the placebo.

To reduce insulin resistance risk factors, people should lose excess weight; increase physical activity with a goal of at least 30 minutes of moderate-intensity activity, such as brisk walking or bicycling most days of the week, and stay on a healthy diet, including reduced amounts of saturated fat, trans fat and cholesterol.

Two Tests for Diabetes

The NIDDK reports that diabetes and prediabetes can be detected with one of the following tests:

• A fasting glucose test measures your blood glucose after you have gone overnight without eating. This test is most reliable when done in the morning. Fasting glucose levels of 100 to 125 mg/dL are above normal but not high enough to be called diabetes. This condition is called pre-diabetes or impaired fasting glucose

(IFG), and it suggests that you have probably had insulin resistance for some time. IFG is considered a pre-diabetic state, meaning that you are more likely to develop diabetes but do not have it yet.

• A glucose tolerance test measures your blood glucose after an overnight fast and two hours after you drink a sweet liquid provided by the doctor or laboratory. If your blood glucose falls between 140 and 199 mg/dL two hours after drinking the liquid, your glucose tolerance is abnormal but not high enough for diabetes. This condition, also a form of pre-diabetes, is called impaired glucose tolerance and, like IFG, points toward a history of insulin resistance and a risk for developing diabetes.

Figure 10.1

A front-page article in the November 22, 2002, issue of the *New York Times*, "Madison Ave. Plays Growing Role in the Business of Drug Research," deals with this matter and quotes a scientist, Dr. Arnold S. Reiman, a professor emeritus from Harvard Medical School, who said "You cannot separate their advertising and marketing from the science, anymore." Advertising agencies have also bought some companies involved in testing drugs and other areas associated with discovering new drugs.

It seems, then, that advertising agencies are now influencing the kind of research that pharmaceutical companies are doing, suggesting, it must be assumed, which areas would be most fruitful (profitable). Advertising now dominates our politics and is in the process of dominating our medicine. It turns out that there is also a relationship between pharmaceutical companies and political advertising. Pharmaceutical companies have formed a lobbying association, the Pharmaceutical Researchers and Manufacturers of America (PhRMA). It gave a great deal of money to an organization with strong Republican leanings, the United Seniors Association, which paid for ads in a number of campaigns, generally supporting Republican candidates whose interests were close to those of the pharmaceutical industry. Major drug companies are also behind Citizens for Better Medicare, which spent $50 million in the 2000 election on television commercials in twenty-six congressional districts. They also gave the United States Chamber of Commerce $10 million and spent another $27 million in individual campaign contributions, 70 percent of which went to Republican candidates. This investment paid off handsomely for the pharmaceutical industry, which now has an administration that is very receptive to its wishes. (This material comes from an article by Tom Hamburger, "Drug Industry Ads Aid GOP," in the *Wall Street Journal*, June 18, 2002.)

In 1970 I appeared before a subcommittee of the United States Senate and gave a presentation on drug advertising. My argument was that drug advertising follows what I call a "pain-pill-pleasure" model. Someone has a terrible headache, takes a pill, and in no time flat, is better. I also pointed out that a large percentage of advertising in the United States is for drugs of one kind or another—alcohol, nicotine, caffeine, aspirin, and so on, ad infinitum. We are, it can be argued, an over-the-counter and prescription-drug culture and we learn, from the many advertisements and commercials we are exposed to, that if there is a problem, there is always a drug to solve that problem, as if by magic.

It's not difficult to see how people might move from legal, over-the-counter drugs for minor problems and prescription drugs for health problems to illegal drugs such as heroin, cocaine, and crack for other problems.

The pain–pill–pleasure model still works, except that there are side effects to be considered to using illegal drugs, such as addiction or related problems like getting AIDS from sharing needles, and destroying one's life.

CHILDREN AND ADVERTISING

We're used to subjecting children to advertising here in the United States, but in Sweden and some other countries, advertising directed toward children is forbidden. There is, I would suggest, an ethical problem of subjecting children to advertising. Until the age of seven or eight, they often do not understand what advertising is and can't distinguish between advertising and regular content. Should we subject these children to advertising? Personally speaking, I would say no.

One effect of subjecting children to advertising is to turn them into whiners. People in the advertising industry call the kind of nagging children do, to get something they see on television and want, "pester power." An article by Martha Irvine in the Associated Press points out that when parents say "no," children nag them an average of nine times before they give in. Some children nag fifty times. These figures come from children from twelve to seventeen who were interviewed for a survey on children

and advertising. The survey, commissioned by the Center for the New American Dream, revealed that 60 percent of the children said that even before they reached the first grade they knew how to manipulate their parents for small things.

Young children, we must realize, have a great deal of spending power, and also influence the spending habits of their parents for everything from new cars to kinds of vacations to take. As Underhill notes:

> The marketplace wants kids, needs kids, and they're flattered by the invitation and happy to oblige. They idolize licensed TV characters the way children once were taught to worship patron saints, and manage to suss out the connection between brand name and status at a very early age. . . . You no longer need to stay clear of the global marketplace just because you're three-and-a-half-feet tall, have no income to speak of and are not permitted to cross the street without Mom. You're an economic force, now and in the future, and that's what counts. (2000:142)

The following shows the projected evolution of spending power for children ages four to twelve:

Year	Amount of Income
1994	$17 billion
2002	$40 billion
2006	$52 billion

The survey by the Center for the New American Dream also revealed that children who didn't have the right kind of clothes felt they wouldn't be able to have any friends and would be rejected by other children.

In recent years, as the problem of obesity has exploded in the United States (and other countries as well), consumer groups have been attacking cereal makers and fast food restaurant companies for contributing to the obesity epidemic in young children. They have accused advertisers of using commercials that sell cereals and other food products to children that are full of sugar and of luring children into eating foods full of fat, such as hamburgers and French fries.

Increasingly larger numbers of young children now are suffering from Type 2, so-called "Adult Onset" Diabetes, and the arteries of some adolescents are similar, in terms of the fat blockages in them, to those of middle-aged men. In addition, there is a diabetes epidemic in the United States and various consumer groups have argued that the advertising industry is a major contributor to this and other medical problems. The burden of our unhealthy eating habits on our medical system and the costs of treating people with these diseases are growing to astronomical levels.

It is impossible to pin all the blame for our problems with obesity and diabetes and other medical diseases only on the advertising agencies, but there is little question that the commercials to which young children are exposed have played a major contributing role in the spread of these diseases.

BATTLING FOR PEOPLE'S ATTENTION

There is a kind of imperialism inherent in the advertising industry; it has a methodology for shaping desire and seeks to use its methods and powers everywhere. So there is good reason to investigate advertising and consider what role it's been playing, and may play in the future, in America and elsewhere.

There is, ironically, a countervailing force affecting advertising and that is the work of other agencies, which are engaged in an endless battle for people's attention—the first step in getting people to buy something—and which seem to be willing to do almost anything to get it. Advertising agencies are battling one another, and as this battle intensifies, it creates more and more clutter. This means that ordinary people, deluged by commercials, become victims of information overload, which leads them to become confused and turned off, so to speak.

So there may be a point of diminishing returns that the advertising industry faces, though, for the moment, as we are subjected to thousands and thousands of print advertisements and television commercials, we have no way of knowing when a particular advertisement will become a tipping point, a straw that will break the advertising camel's back, metaphorically speaking. It is conceivable, on the other hand, that we can be taught to process an almost infinite number of commercial messages, though I tend to doubt that this is possible. Eventually, there will be a turning point, and people will be unable to react the way advertising agencies want them to. New technology may also play a role; with the development of TiVo and other hard disks that store television programs and delete the commercials, many people are finding ways to avoid commercials in their television viewing. So things are in considerable flux, and much research is needed on advertising's role in politics, in the lives of children and teenagers, in medicine—topics I have discussed in this book. The list of possible subjects goes on and on.

APPENDIX: USEFUL WEB SITES

For those who wish to pursue their investigations of advertising, let me list some useful web sites to access. Some of these sites will enable you to find books and periodicals of interest. These web sites and others available on the Internet can be found by using Google or other search engines, and will enable anyone interested in doing research on advertising to find a wealth of materials.

Adbusters (www.adbusters.com)

This site attempts to counter advertising's influence on American culture and society. It and other similar sites attack advertising and often parody some of the most famous campaigns.

***Advertising Age* (www.AdAge.com)**

This is the web site of one of the more important publications dealing with the advertising industry. It has news about every aspect of the industry, from campaigns that are getting under way to matters involving the consolidation of the advertising industry.

Advertising Educational Foundation (www.aef.com)

This site has access to a scholarly journal, *Advertising and Society Review*, about many aspects of advertising. The Advertising Educational Foundation made it possible for me to spend three weeks at Goldberg Moser O'Neill in San Francisco a number of years ago, where I had the opportunity to interview many people who worked in various positions in the agency.

***AdWeek* (www.adweek.com)**

This is another important site for information about the advertising industry. Between this site and AdAge.com it is possible to keep up-to-date on the advertising industry.

Amazon (www.amazon.com)
Barnes & Noble (www.bn.com)

These web sites lists a huge number of books that deal with advertising. You can ask them to list books in terms of date of publication, features, and popularity, among other things. In addition, you can often examine a given book's table of contents and some sample pages.

Google (www.google.com)

This search engine can help you find an enormous number of sites that deal with various aspects of advertising. It is the most important, most comprehensive, most useful, and fastest search engine. There are many organizations involved in the business of advertising and assessing its social consequences that can be found on the Internet. There's also a good deal of scholarly research—in the form of articles and data—that can be accessed using Google.

Media Education Foundation (www.mediaed.org)

The Media Education Foundation sells videos and DVDs and provides study guides on topics such as advertising, gender, diversity, race, health, and politics.

New York Times **(www.nytimes.com)**

This web site has many different features, including Stuart Elliott/In Advertising, which it e-mails, free of cost, to anyone who wishes to receive it. Stuart Elliott covers advertising for the *New York Times* and is very knowledgeable about the industry.

GLOSSARY

Aberrant Decoding The notion that audiences decode or interpret texts such as television commercials and print advertisements in ways that differ from the ways the creators of these texts expect them to be decoded. Aberrant decoding is the rule rather than the exception when it comes to the mass media, according to the semiotician Umberto Eco. It has been estimated that about 25 percent of advertisements and commercials are decoded aberrantly, that is, not the way the creators of the texts expected them to be decoded.

Advertisement The word *advert* means "to call attention to something," and thus an advertisement is, for our purposes, a kind of text—carried by electronic or print media—that attracts attention to, stimulates desire for, and in some cases leads to the purchase of a product or service. The convention is that commercial messages in print are called advertisements and those in electronic media are called commercials.

Aesthetics Aesthetics involves the way technical matters such as lighting, sound, music, kinds of shots and camera work, and editing affect the way audiences react to commercials or print advertisements.

Alienation In Marxist theory, capitalist societies can create huge amounts of consumer goods, but they also inevitably generate alienation and feelings of estrangement from oneself and others in the society. Alienation is functional for those who own the means of production and distribution, since alienation leads to consumer cultures—ones characterized by endless and frantic consumption, which people use as an escape from their feelings of alienation. In capitalist societies, therefore, advertising plays a central role in maintaining the status quo. See also **Consumer Cultures**.

Archetype According to Carl Jung, archetypes are images found in dreams, myths, works of art, and religions all over the world. They are not transmitted by culture but are somehow passed on in a collective unconscious. We are not conscious of them directly, but they reveal themselves in our dreams and works of art. One of the most important archetypes is the hero. Archetypal heroes and heroines are commonly used in advertising since they resonate so strongly with people.

Artist   We will consider an artist to be not only someone who writes, paints, sculpts, or plays musical instruments, but anyone involved in the creation or performance of a text. The creative people in advertising agencies are copywriters, artists, typographers, designers, and so on. Generally speaking, a creative director in an advertising agency assembles teams of creative artists to work on particular campaigns. Many artists nowadays do not know how to draw particularly well, but are adept at using the computer for creating visual images.

Attitudes   *Attitude*, as social psychologists use the term, refers to a person's relatively enduring state of mind about some phenomenon or aspect of experience. Attitudes generally are either positive or negative, have direction, and involve thoughts, feelings, and behaviors. I suggest in this book that advertising should be examined in terms of its impact on culture in general rather than being dealt with in terms of attitude change in individuals or groups.

Audience   Audiences are generally defined as collections of individuals who watch a television program, listen to a radio show, attend a film

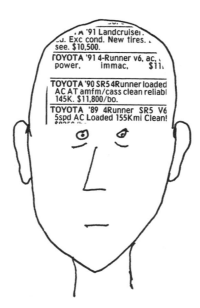

or some kind of live artistic performance (symphony, rock band, and so on). The members of the audience may be together in one room or, in the case of television, each watching from his or her own set. In technical terms, audiences are addressees who receive mediated texts sent by an addresser. For advertisers, securing the right audiences is crucial because it doesn't pay to advertise to people who either aren't interested or can't afford the product or service being advertised. The media, in economic terms, can be held to deliver audiences to advertisers.

Blogs Web logs that individual use to place their ideas on the Internet. Some blogs are strictly personal and are a form of electronic diary or journal while others deal with politics and other topics.

Branding Creating emotional ties between individuals and certain products or services who will purchase them over the course of their lives. From a semiotic perspective, brands are signs people use to display their taste or wealth and to help them fashion an identity. The fact that certain companies prominently attach their logos to what they make helps users solidify their sense of style and discrimination and their identities.

Broadcast We use the term *broadcast* to deal with texts that are made available over wide areas via radio or television signals. Broadcasting differs from other forms of distributing texts such as cablecasting, which uses cables, and satellite transmission, which requires dishes to capture signals sent by the satellites.

Claritas A market research company which argues that there are sixty-six different kinds of consumers in the United States, each of which tends to be found in certain Zip codes. They argue that "birds of a feather flock together" and give each of the groupings jazzy names such as "Blue Blood Estates" and "Shotguns and Pickups."

Class From a linguistic standpoint, a class is any group of things that have something in common. We use the term to refer to social classes, or more literally, socioeconomic classes: groups of people who share income and lifestyle. Marxist theorists argue that there is a ruling class, which shapes the ideas of the proletariat, the working classes. Advertisers are interested in socioeconomic classes and lifestyles because these phenomena are held to be the key to selling products and services.

Codes Codes are systems of symbols, letters, words, sounds, whatever, that generate meaning. Language, for example, is a code. It uses combinations of letters that we call words to mean certain things. The relation between the word and the thing the word stands for is arbitrary, based on convention. In some cases, the term *code* is used to describe hidden meanings and disguised communications. Audiences have to decode texts correctly, so advertising strives to create print advertisements and commercials that are easy to understand. Despite the best intentions of those who create advertisements, approximately one quarter of the people decode them aberrantly.

Cognitive Dissonance Dissonance refers to sounds that clash with one another. According to psychologists, people wish to avoid ideas that challenge the ones they hold, which creates conflict and other disagreeable feelings. Cognitive dissonance refers to ideas that conflict with ones people hold and generate psychological anxiety and displeasure. Advertisers strive to avoid dissonance and to reinforce beliefs people already hold, as a means of selling products and services.

Collective Representations Emile Durkheim used this concept to deal with the fact that people are both individuals pursuing their own aims, and social animals guided by the groups and societies in which they find themselves. Collective representations are, broadly speaking, texts that reflect the beliefs and ideals of collectivities. Advertisements are designed, one could say, as collective representations that will appeal to people and help advertisers shape people's behavior.

Communication There are many different ways of understanding and using this term. For our purposes, communication is a process that involves the transmission of messages from senders to receivers. We often make a distinction between communication using language, verbal communication, and communication using facial expressions, body language, and other means, or nonverbal communication. In advertisements and television commercials, both verbal and nonverbal communication play very important roles.

Consumer Cultures Consumer cultures are characterized by widespread personal consumption rather than socially conscious and useful investment in the public sphere. The focus is on private expenditure and leisure pursuits, and this leads to privatism, self-centeredness, and a reluctance to allocate resources for the public realm. Advertising is held by many critics to be a primary instrument of those who own the means of production in generating consumer lust and consumer cultures and distracting people from social and public matters. Social scientists Aaron Wildavsky and Mary Douglas suggest that there are four political cultures, which also function as consumer cultures: hierarchical or elitist, individualist, egalitarian, and fatalist. See also **Political Cultures**.

CPM CPM is an acronym for cost per thousand, the way advertising is traditionally measured. It is the number of viewers reached that is critical, not the absolute cost of running the advertisement. Thus a print advertisement in a newspaper that costs $10,000 to run, which reaches 500,000 people, is much more expensive, on a CPM basis, than a commercial that costs $100,000 to run but which reaches 20 million people.

Critical Research Critical research refers to approaches to media that are essentially ideological, that focus on the social and political dimensions of the mass media and the way they are used by organizations and others allegedly to maintain the status quo rather than to enhance equality. This contrasts with administrative research. Many books about the advertising industry written by scholars can be described as examples of critical research—including this book.

Cultivation Theory This theory argues that television dominates the symbolic environment of its audiences and gives people false views of reality. That is, television "cultivates" or reinforces certain beliefs in its viewers, such as the notions that society is permeated by violence, that there are hardly any older people, and that everyone is living in upper-middle-class splendor. Advertising plays a significant role in cultivating the American public.

Cultural Criticism The term *cultural criticism* refers to the analysis of texts and various aspects of everyday life by scholars in various disciplines who use concepts from their fields of expertise to interpret mass-mediated texts, the role of the mass media, and related concerns. The focus is on what impact these texts and the media that carry them have on individuals, society, and culture. Cultural criticism involves the use of literary theory, media analysis, philosophical thought, communication theory, and various interpretive methodologies.

Cultural Homogenization When people use the term *cultural homogenization*, they mean that the media of mass communication are destroying Third World cultures and regional cultures in specific countries, leading to a cultural sameness, standardization, and homogenization. For example, McDonald's has affected the eating habits of many Asian countries and McDonald's uses advertising to attract patrons, so advertising plays a role in this cultural homogenization process.

Cultural Imperialism (also Media Imperialism) The theory of cultural imperialism describes the flow of media products (such as songs, films, and television programs) and popular culture from the United States and a few other capitalist countries in Western Europe to the Third World. Along with these texts and popular culture, it is alleged that values and beliefs (and bourgeois capitalist ideology) are also being transmitted, leading to the domination of these people.

Culture   There are hundreds of definitions of culture. Generally speaking, from the anthropological perspective, it involves the transmission from generation to generation of specific ideas, arts, customary beliefs, ways of living, behavior patterns, institutions, and values. When applied to the arts, it generally is used to specify "elite" kinds of artworks, such as operas, poetry, classical music, and serious novels. The argument in this book is that advertising is an important institution and has an enormous impact upon our culture.

Defense Mechanisms   Defense mechanisms are methods used by the ego to defend itself against pressures from the id or impulsive elements in the psyche and superego, such as conscience and guilt. Some of the more common defense mechanisms are *repression* (barring unconscious instinctual wishes, memories, and so on from consciousness), *regression* (returning to earlier stages in one's development), *ambivalence* (a simultaneous feeling of love and hate for a person, thing, or concept), and *rationalization* (offering excuses to justify one's actions). I've explained how the ego mediates between id-dominated desires to purchase products and services and superego attempts to avoid spending money.

Demographics   The term *demographics* refers to similarities found in groups of people in terms of race, religion, gender, social class, ethnicity, occupation, place of residence, age, and so on. Demographic information plays an important role in the creation of advertising and the choice of which media to use to deliver this advertising.

Dysfunctional   In sociological thought, something is dysfunctional if it contributes to the breakdown or destabilization of the entity in which it is found. Some critics of advertising argue that it is dysfunctional in that it diverts the attention of people from public problems to private desires.

Egalitarians   They stress that everyone is equal in terms of certain needs, such as for food, shelter, and access to health care. Egalitarians function as critics of the two dominant political/consumer cultures—elitist and individualist.

Ego   In Freud's theory of the psyche, the ego functions as the executant of the id and as a mediator between the id and the superego (conscience). The ego is involved in the perception of reality and the adaptation to reality. One aspect of the ego, I argue, is in helping the superego to restrain compulsive spending, which the id wishes to do.

Emotive Functions   According to Roman Jakobson, messages have a number of functions. Some of them are emotive functions, which involve expressing feelings by the sender of a message. (Other functions are referential and poetic.) Advertising is an art that makes great use of the emotive functions of actors to generate emotional responses in audiences to convince people to purchase products and services being advertised. See also **Poetic Functions, Referential Functions**.

Enclavists   See **Egalitarians**.

Ethical Critics   Ethics involve our sense of what is moral and correct. Ethical critics deal with texts such as advertisements in terms of the moral aspects of what happens in these texts and the possible impact of these advertisements on those exposed to these texts and on others.

False Consciousness   In Marxist thought, false consciousness refers to mistaken ideas that people have about their class, status, and economic possibilities. These ideas help maintain the status quo and are of great use to the ruling class, which wants to avoid changes in the social structure. Karl Marx argued that the ideas of the ruling class are always the ruling ideas in society. Marxists would argue that the belief many Americans have that they are "elites" because they can consume at a relatively high level is an example of false consciousness.

Fatalists   They are at the bottom rungs of society—they have little political or consumer power and can only escape their status as a result of luck or chance.

Feminist Criticism   Feminist criticism focuses on the roles given to women and the way they are portrayed in texts of all kinds, including one of the worst offenders—advertising. Feminist critics argue that women are typically used as sexual objects and are portrayed stereotypically in advertisements and other texts, and this has negative effects on both men and women.

Focal Points   Focal points are the five general topics or subject areas we can concentrate upon in studying mass communication. These are: (1) the work of art or text, (2) the artist, (3) the audience, (4) America or the society, and (5) the media.

Formula   A formula in narrative theory refers to a text with conventional characters and actions that audiences are familiar with. Genre texts, such as detective stories, Westerns, science-fiction adventures, and romances are highly formulaic. Many advertisements and commercials are also formulaic, because this facilitates easy comprehension by audience members.

Functional   In sociological thought, the term *functional* refers to the contribution an institution makes to the maintenance of society or an institution or entity. Something functional helps maintain the system in which it is found. Defenders of advertising argue that it is functional in that it facilitates consumption, innovation, and general economic well-being.

Functional Alternative   Functional alternative refers to something that takes the place of something else. For example, professional football can be seen as a functional alternative to religion. I argue in this book that a department store can be seen as a modern functional alternative to medieval cathedrals.

Gender   Gender is the sexual category of an individual: male or female, and the behavioral traits connected with each category.

Genre   Genre is a French word that means "kind" or "class." As we use the term, it refers to the kind of formulaic texts found in the mass media such as commercials and print advertisements, soap operas, news shows, sports programs, horror shows, and detective programs. I have dealt with this topic at length in my book *Popular Culture Genres* (1992).

Global   Marshall McLuhan suggested, many years ago, that as a result of new developments in technology the world was becoming a "global" village. The term suggests that as the result of the growth of the Internet and other media of communication, people everywhere are linked together like people in a small village. The advertising industry is now global with giant mega-agencies that own hundreds of other agencies all over the world.

Google   The most important search engine which has used its technological prowess to become a major force in contemporary American society, as far as technology is concerned. By selling advertisements on its search engine, Google has become a very wealthy and powerful company.

Grid-Group Theory   This theory is based on the work of social-anthropologist Mary Douglas, who argued that there are four (and only four) consumer cultures or lifestyles in modern societies, based on the degree to which the groups have weak or strong boundaries and whether members have few or many rules and prescriptions to follow.

Hierarchical Elitists   These people are at the top of the economic and power pyramid and believe that hierarchy is needed for society to run smoothly. They have a sense of obligation to those beneath them.

Hypodermic Needle Theory of Media   This theory, generally discredited now, holds that all members of an audience "read" a text the same way and get the same things out of it. Media is seen as a hypodermic needle, injecting its messages into one and all. The fact that a relatively high percentage of people decode mass-mediated texts aberrantly suggests that the hypodermic needle theory is too simplistic.

Id The id in Freud's theory of the psyche (technically known as his *structural hypothesis*) is that element of the psyche that is the representative of a person's drives. In *New Introductory Lectures on Psychoanalysis*, Freud called it "a chaos, a cauldron of seething excitement." It also is the source of energy, but lacking direction, it needs the ego to harness it and control it. In popular thought, it is connected to impulse, lust, and "I want it all now" behavior. Many advertisements appeal to id elements in our psyches.

Ideology An ideology is a logically coherent, integrated explanation of social, economic, and political matters that helps establish the goals and direct the actions of a group or political entity. People act (and vote or don't vote) on the basis of an ideology they hold, even though they may not have articulated it or thought about it. Some critics argue that advertising is an ideological tool that members of the ruling class use to distract people from their problems and convince them that the political order is worth supporting.

Image Defining images is extremely difficult. In my book *Seeing Is Believing: An Introduction to Visual Communication,* I define an image as "a collection of signs and symbols—what we find when we look at a photograph, a film still, a shot of a television screen, a print advertisement, or just about anything." The term is used for mental as well as physical representations of things. Images often have powerful emotional effects on people and historical significance. Advertisers use the power of images to sell products and services.

Individualists Individualists believe that the basic function of government is to prevent crime and invasion by foreign powers. They are competitive and stress the importance of individual initiative.

Intertextuality This theory argues that texts (works of art) of all kinds, are influenced to varying degrees by texts that preceded them. Sometimes, as in the case of parody, the relationship is overt but in many cases, creators of texts are influenced by stylistic practices or thematic ones from earlier works. We can say, then, that intertextuality involves making allusions to, imitating, modifying, or adapting previously created texts and styles of expression.

Isolates See **Fatalists**.

Lasswell Formula Harold Lasswell was a prominent political scientist. Considered by some scholars to be the most famous formula in communication theory, the Lasswell formula goes as follows: Who? Says what? In which channel? To whom? With what effect?

Latent Functions   Latent functions are hidden, unrecognized, and unintended results of some activity, entity, or institution. They are contrasted by social scientists with manifest functions, which are recognized and intended. Some critics suggest that the latent function of advertising is to support the political order, while the manifest function of advertising is to sell goods and services. See also **Manifest Functions**.

Lifestyle   Literally style of life, lifestyle refers to the way people live—to the decisions they make about how to decorate their homes (and where they are located), the cars they drive, the clothes they wear, the foods they eat, the restaurants they visit, and where they go for vacations. Lifestyles tend to be coherent or logically connected, and they play an important part in market research.

Limited Effects (of Media)   Some mass communication theorists argue that the mass media have relatively minor effects on the scheme of things. They cite research that shows, for example, that media effects don't tend to be long lasting and argue that mass media's strong effects have not been demonstrated. When they testify before governmental agencies, advertisers argue that advertisements and commercials have limited effects, and when dealing with clients they argue that they have powerful effects.

Manifest Functions   The manifest functions of an activity, entity, or institution are those that are obvious and intended. Manifest functions contrast with latent functions, which are hidden and unintended. The manifest function of advertising is to sell products and services; the latent function is to sell the political order. See also **Latent Functions**.

Mass   For our purposes, "mass" as in "mass communication" refers to a large number of people who are the audience for some communication. There is considerable disagreement about how to understand

the term *mass*. Some theorists say a mass comprises individuals who are heterogeneous, do not know one another, are alienated, and do not have a leader. Others attack these notions, saying they are not based on fact but on theories that are not correct and have not been proven in experiments.

Mass Communication Mass communication refers to the transfer of messages, information, and texts from a sender (for our purposes, an advertising agency) to a receiver, a large number of people, a mass audience. This transfer is done through the technologies of the mass media—newspapers, magazines, television programs, films, records, computers, the Internet, and CD-ROMs. The sender is often a person in a large media organization, the messages are public, and the audience tends to be large and varied.

Medium (plural: Media) A medium is a means of delivering messages, information, or texts to audiences. There are different ways of classifying the media. One of the most common ways is as follows: print (newspapers, magazines, books, billboards), electronic (radio, television, computers, CD-ROMs, the Internet), and photographic (photographs, films, videos). Various critics have suggested that the main function of the commercial media is to deliver audiences to advertisers, and that everything else the media does is of secondary importance.

Metaphor A metaphor is a figure of speech that conveys meaning by analogy. It is important to realize that metaphors are not confined to poetry and literary works but, according to some linguists, are the fundamental way in which we make sense of things and find meaning in the world. A simile is a weaker form of metaphor that uses either "like" or "as" in making an analogy. Metaphors are an important element in advertising. For example, Fidji perfume had a campaign that was explicitly metaphoric: Woman is an island.

Metonymy According to linguists, metonymy is a figure of speech that conveys information by association and is, along with metaphor, one of the most important ways people convey information to one another. We tend not to be aware of our use of metonymy, but whenever we use association to get an idea about something (Rolls-Royce = wealthy) we are thinking metonymically. A form of metonymy that involves seeing a whole in terms of a part or vice versa is called synecdoche. Using the White House to stand for the presidency is an example of synecdoche. Metonymy is another important technique used by advertisers to generate information and emotional responses to advertisements.

Mimetic Theory of Art (and Mimetic Desire)   This theory, dating from Aristotle's time, suggests that art is an imitation of reality. Mimesis means "imitation." The theory of mimetic desire, developed by René Girard, is that people imitate the desire of others and that advertising uses this mimetic desire to sell people products and services.

Model   Models, in the social sciences, are abstract representations that explain a phenomenon. Theories are typically expressed in language, but models tend to be graphic or statistical or mathematical. Denis McQuail and Sven Windahl define *model* in *Communication Models: For the Study of Mass Communication* (1993:2) as "a consciously simplified description in graphic form of a piece of reality. A model seeks to show the main elements of any structure or process and the relationships between these elements."

Motivation Research   Practitioners of motivation research argue that it is necessary to determine and understand people's unconscious and unrecognized attitudes in order to persuade them to purchase products and services. Ernest Dichter was one of the founding fathers of motivation research, which, he argued, could be used also for many socially valuable purposes.

Myth   Myths are conventionally understood to be sacred stories about gods and cultural heroes (and in more recent years, mass-mediated heroes and heroines) that are used to transmit a culture's basic belief system to younger generations and to explain natural and supernatural phenomena. According to Mark Shorer (1968:355), "Myths are instruments by which we continually struggle to make our experiences intelligible to ourselves. A myth is a large, controlling image that gives philosophical meaning to the facts of ordinary life."

Narrowcasting   A medium such as radio with stations that focus on discrete groups of people is called narrowcasting. It contrasts with broadcasting, which tries to reach as many people as possible. Advertisers use broadcasting, but they aim most of their advertisements at the 18–45 segment of the population.

Nonfunctional   In sociological thought, something is nonfunctional if it is neither functional nor dysfunctional, but plays no role in the entity in which it is found.

Nonverbal Communication   Our body language, facial expressions, styles of dress, and hairstyles are examples of our communicating feelings and attitudes (and a sense of who we are) without words. In advertising, a great deal of the communication is done nonverbally. In some commercials, almost all the information or meaning is communicated nonverbally. You can see this if you turn off the sound and watch commercials. Notice how in many commercials, facial expressions and body language are used to sell the product.

Objective Theory of Art   This theory argues that art is like a lamp and projects a reality (that of the artist) rather than being like a mirror and imitating reality.

Opinion Leader   People whose opinions affect those of others are opinion leaders. The notion that there are opinion leaders is part of the two-step flow theory of communication. We can adapt this theory and suggest that some people are fashion and lifestyle opinion leaders, who can be used to sell products and services. See also **Two-Step Flow**.

Phallic Symbol   An object that resembles the penis either by shape or function is described as a phallic symbol. Symbolism is a defense mechanism of the ego that permits hidden or repressed sexual or aggressive thoughts to be expressed in a disguised form. For a discussion of this topic see Freud's book *An Interpretation of Dreams*.

Phallocentric   The term *phallocentric* is used to suggest societies that are dominated by males, and the ultimate source of this domination, that which shapes our institutions and cultures, is the male phallus. In this theory, a link is made between male sexuality and male power.

Poetic Functions   In Roman Jakobson's theory, poetic functions are those which use literary devices such as metaphor and metonymy. Poetic functions differ, Jakobson suggests, from emotive functions and referential functions. In this book I discuss the pseudo-poetic aspects of some advertisements meant to convince people they are having a profound experience. See also **Emotive Functions**, **Referential Functions**.

Political Cultures   According to political scientist Aaron Wildavsky, there are four political cultures in every democratic society. They are: hierarchical or elitist (based on the notion that hierarchy is important and on a sense of obligation of those at the top for those beneath them), individualist (based on the notion that individuals are of primary importance and government should do as little as possible, except for maximizing individual initiative), egalitarian (based on the notion that everyone has certain needs that have to be taken care of), and fatalist (based on the notion that some people are at the lowest rungs of society and are controlled by those above them. They can only escape their situation as a result of chance or luck). See also **Consumer Cultures**.

Popular   Popular is one of the most difficult terms used in discourse about the arts and the media. Literally, the term means "appealing to a large number of people." It comes from the Latin *popularis*, "of the people." Separating the popular and elite arts has become increasingly problematic in recent years. For example, is an opera shown on television an example of elite or popular culture?

Popular Culture   *Popular culture* is a term that identifies certain kinds of texts that appeal to a large number of people. But mass communication theorists often identify (or should I say confuse?) "popular" with "mass" and suggest that if something is popular, it *must* be of poor quality, appealing to the mythical "lowest common denominator." Popular culture is generally held to be the opposite of elite culture—arts that require certain levels of sophistication and refinement to be appreciated, such as ballet, opera, poetry, and classical music. Many critics now question this popular culture/elite culture polarity.

Postmodernism   This theory states that a new kind of culture has developed in the United States and elsewhere, since approximately 1950, which rejected the values and beliefs of the modernist society that had been dominant until that time. One theorist of postmodernism argued that it involves "incredulity toward metanarratives," by which he meant the rejection of the overarching religious, social, political, aesthetic, and moral theories of the modernist period that have shaped people's thinking and their lives. Postmodernism is associated with stylistic eclecticism, a rejection of the split between elite and popular culture. The theory is very controversial and important facets of it are explored in my books *Postmortem for a Postmodernist* (a postmodern mystery) and *The Portable Postmodernist*.

Pragmatic Theory of Art   This theory holds that art must do something, have certain consequences that are held to be desirable. Thus art should teach or indoctrinate or perform some function. Advertising is a good example of a pragmatic art: It exists to do something—namely sell goods, services, and at times, politicians and political parties.

Product Placement   Because so many people are using TiVo and other similar devices to fast-forward through commercials, or are avoiding them in other ways, advertising agencies are now paying money to have their products placed in television programs and films, where the audiences for these texts will not or cannot fast-forward them out. In addition, advertisers get a "halo" effect since their products become identified with actors and celebrities.

Psychoanalytic Theory   Sigmund Freud can be said to be the founding father of psychoanalytic theory. He argued that the human psyche had three levels: consciousness, preconsciousness, and the unconscious, which is the largest area of the psyche and an area not able to be accessed by individuals. What is important is that the unconscious shapes and affects our mental functioning and our behavior. Another of his theories posited three forces in the psyche: the id (desire), the ego (reason), and the superego (guilt), which were continually battling with one another for domination. Freud believed that sexuality and what he called "the Oedipus Complex" play a dominant role in human behavior, even if their presence is not recognized.

Psychographics   In marketing the term *psychographics* is used to deal with groups of people who have similar psychological characteristics or profiles. It differs from demographics, which marketers use to focus upon social and economic characteristics that people have in common.

Public   Instead of popular culture, we sometimes use the terms *public arts* or *public communication* to avoid the negative connotations of "mass" and "popular." A public is a group of people, a community. We can contrast public acts—those meant to be known to the community—with private acts, which are not meant to be known to others.

Rationalization   In Freudian thought, a rationalization is a defense mechanism of the ego that creates an excuse to justify an action (or inaction when an action is expected). Ernest Jones, who introduced the term, used it to describe logical and rational reasons that people give to justify behavior that is really caused by unconscious and irrational determinants. We often use rationalizations to justify purchases that are unwise and unnecessary.

Reader Response Theory (also Reception Theory)   This theory suggests that readers (a term used very broadly to cover people who read books, watch television programs, go to films, listen to texts on the radio, and so on) play an important role in the realization of texts. Texts such as advertising, then, function as sites for the creation of meaning by readers, and different readers interpret a given text differently.

Referential Functions   In Roman Jakobson's theory, the referential function of speech deals with the way it helps speakers relate to their surroundings. He contrasts it with the emotive and poetic functions of speech. See also **Emotive Functions**, **Poetic Functions**.

Role   Sociologists describe a role as a way of behavior that we learn in a society and that is appropriate to a particular situation. A person generally plays many roles with different people during the hours of a day, such as *parent* (family), *worker* (job), and *spouse* (marriage). We also use the term to describe the parts actors have in mass-mediated texts, including commercials.

Sapir-Whorf Hypothesis   This hypothesis argues that language is not something transparent that merely conveys information from one person to another, but something that affects the way people think and act. Language—for our purposes, language used in print advertisements and radio and television commercials—is not like a windowpane but more like a prism.

Secondary Modeling Systems   Language, according to Yuri Lotman, is our primary modeling system. Works of art, which use phenomena such as myths and legends, function as secondary modeling systems; they are secondary to language, that is. Lotman also argued that every element in a text is important and that texts are so incredibly complex they can be mined continually for new meanings.

Selective Attention (or Selective Inattention)   We have a tendency to avoid messages that conflict with our beliefs and values. One way we do this is through selective attention—avoiding or not paying attention to messages that would generate cognitive dissonance. Thus, we tend to ignore information that would counsel us not to buy something that we want to buy.

Semiotics   Literally, the term *semiotics* means "the science of signs." *Semeion* is the Greek term for sign. A sign is anything that can be used to stand for anything else. According to C. S. Peirce, one of the founders of the science, a sign "is something which stands to somebody for something in some respect or capacity." My book *Signs in Contemporary Culture: An Introduction to Semiotics* (1999) discusses many of the more important semiotic concepts and shows how they can be applied to popular culture.

Sign   The basic concept in semiotics, the science of signs (from the Greek word *semeion,* sign) that deals with how we find meaning in images and other kinds of communication. Ferdinand de Saussure, one of the founding fathers of semiotics, argued that a sign is made up of a signifier (a sound or object) and a signified (a concept). The relation between the signifier and signified is arbitrary and not natural. C. S. Peirce, another founding father of semiotics, had a different notion. He said a sign is "something which stands to somebody for something in some respect or capacity." His theory of signs is dealt with in the discussion of symbols.

Social Controls   Social controls are ideas, beliefs, values, and mores people get from their societies that shape their beliefs and behavior. People are both individuals with certain distinctive physical and emotional characteristics and desires and at the same time members of societies.

And people are shaped to a certain degree by the institutions found in these societies. The question this book considers is, What impact do advertising in general and specific advertising texts have upon societies and individuals?

Socialization   Socialization refers to the processes by which societies teach individuals how to behave: what rules to obey, roles to assume, and values to hold. Socialization was traditionally done by the family, educators, religious figures, and peers. The mass media in general and advertising in particular seem to have usurped this function to a considerable degree nowadays, with consequences that are not always positive.

Socioeconomic Class   A socioeconomic class is a categorization of people according to their incomes and related social status and lifestyles. In Marxist thought, there are ruling classes that shape the consciousness of the working classes, and history is, in essence, a record of class conflict.

Stereotypes   Stereotypes are commonly held, simplistic, and inaccurate group portraits of categories of people. Stereotypes can be positive, negative, or mixed, but generally they are negative. Stereotyping involves making gross overgeneralizations. (All Mexicans, Chinese, Jews, African-Americans, WASPS, Americans, lawyers, doctors, professors, and so on, are held to have certain characteristics, usually negative.) Stereotypes are used in advertising because they are thought to facilitate understanding by audiences.

Subculture   Any complex society is made up of numerous subcultures that differ from the dominant culture in terms of such matters as ethnicity, race, religion, sexual orientation, beliefs, values, and tastes. Often members of subcultures are marginalized and victimized by members of the dominant culture. One problem advertisers face is in trying to reach and persuade members of these subcultures to purchase products and services designed for members of the dominant culture.

Superego   In Freud's structural hypothesis, the superego is the agency in our psyches related to conscience and morality. The superego is involved with processes such as approval and disapproval of wishes on the basis of their morality, critical self-observation, and a sense of guilt over wrongdoing. The functions of the superego are largely unconscious and are opposed to id elements in our psyches. Mediating between the two and trying to balance them are our egos. The superego, in my application of Freud's theory to advertising, is what tells the ego (and the id) that some product or service that the id longs for is not needed. The id says, "I want to buy it!" The superego says, "Don't buy that!" And the ego helps the superego deal with the id.

Suspension of Disbelief   It was the English critic Samuel Coleridge who first used the phrase "suspension of disbelief" to describe what happens to people when they become involved with works of art and start identifying with characters in these texts. Thus, in plays, films, television shows, and commercials, they forget or "suspend" their recognition of the fact that they are members of an audience and become involved with the characters they are observing.

Symbol   Literally speaking, a symbol is something that stands for something else. The term comes from the Greek word *symballein* which means "to put together." Advertisers use symbols because they have powerful emotional effects on people. Think, for example, of all that is found in three symbols: the cross, the Star of David, and the crescent. In C.S. Peirce's theory of semiotics, there are three kinds of signs: icons, which communicate by resemblance; indexes, which communication by cause and effect; and symbols, whose meaning must be learned. Advertisers make use of symbols because of their power to affect human emotions.

Taste Cultures   Sociologist Herbert Gans's theory that there are a number of taste cultures in America, "each with its own art, literature, music, and so forth, which differ mainly in that they express different aesthetic standards." Basic to his argument is the idea that all taste cultures are of equal worth.

Teleculture   The concept of teleculture suggests that television has become a dominant influence on society and helps shape both individual behavior and cultural institutions. Our culture used to be passed on through books, parents, teachers, and others, but they have been supplanted by the characters we see on television or in other media.

Text   For our purposes, a text is, broadly speaking, any work of art in any medium. Critics use the term *text* as a convenience—so they don't have to name a given work all the time or use various synonyms. There are problems involved in deciding what the text is when we deal with serial texts, such as soap operas or comics. In this book I use the term to stand for print advertisements, radio and television commercials, and any other kind of advertising or commercial messages carried by any medium.

Theory   *Theories*, as I use the term, are expressed in language and systematically and logically attempt to explain and predict phenomena being studied. They differ from concepts, which define phenomena that are being studied, and from models, which are abstract, usually graphic in nature, and explicit about what is being studied.

Two–Step Flow   This refers to a theory of how mass communication reaches and affects people. According to this theory, in the first step the media influence opinion leaders, and in the second step the opinion leaders influence others. Applied to advertising, this suggests that large numbers of people are influenced by certain style and fashion leaders. People identify with others, which is why celebrities, supermodels, and actors are often used in advertising. See also **Opinion leaders**.

Typology   We will understand a typology to be a system of classification of things that is done to clarify matters.

Uses and Gratifications   This sociological theory argues that researchers should pay attention to the way audiences use the media (or certain texts or genres of texts, such as print advertisements or radio and television commercials) and the gratifications they get from their use of these texts and the media. Uses and gratifications researchers focus, then, on how audiences use the media and not on how the media affect audiences.

Values   Values are abstract and general beliefs or judgments about what is right and wrong, and what is good and bad, that have implications for individual behavior and for social, cultural, and political entities. There are a number of problems with values from a philosophical point of view. First, how does one determine which values are correct and good and which aren't? That is, how do we justify values? Are values objective or subjective? Second, what happens when there is a conflict between groups, each of which holds a central value that conflicts with that of another group? Values are part of the VALS—values and lifestyles—marketing system.

Youth Culture   Youth cultures are subcultures formed by young people around some area of interest, usually connected with leisure and entertainment, such as rock music, computer games, hacking, and so on. Typically, youth cultures adopt distinctive ways of dressing and develop institutions that cater to their needs. Simon Frith discusses this topic at length in his book *Sound Effects: Youth, Leisure, and the Politics of Rock and Roll* (1981). Youth cultures and young people, though they may have "antiestablishment beliefs," are particularly susceptible to the entrapments of advertising.

ANNOTATED BIBLIOGRAPHY

In this section I deal with a number of books that offer different approaches to the matter of interpreting advertisements and understanding their social, cultural, and ideological significance. Many of the books use and apply semiotic theory, often in combination with other approaches, since it has become the most important means of deconstructing particular advertising texts and campaigns. There are many books on advertising that I could have cited. I've chosen those that I feel are accessible and that offer a variety of approaches to the subject. The regular bibliography (which follow this section) lists hundreds of books that students interested in the subject can consult.

Anthony J. Cortese. *Provocateur: Images of Women and Minorities in Advertising*, Second Edition. 2004. Rowman & Littlefield.
    Cortese deals with important themes such as the semiotics of advertising in social life, postmodernism and advertising, and the representation of marginalized groups in America (such as blacks, women, Latinos, Asians, Native Americans, gays and lesbians). He offers a systematic methodology for a sociological analysis of advertising.

Marcel Danesi, *Interpreting Advertisements: A Semiotic Guide*. 1995. Legas.
    In this slender volume of 111 pages, Marcel Danesi offers an overview of semiotic theory and then applies it to analyze a number of advertisements, showing how semiotics can be used to "deconstruct" advertisements and find all kinds of interesting things in them.

Stuart Ewen. *Captains of Consciousness: Advertising and the Social Roots of the Consumer Culture.* 1976. McGraw-Hill.
    This important book deals with advertising's impact on social life in America and its functions as an instrument of social control. It has sections on "Advertising as Social Production," "The Political Ideology of Consumption," and "*Mom, Dad and the Kids:* Toward a Modern Architecture of Daily Life."

Katherine Toland Frith, ed. *Undressing the Ad: Reading Culture in Advertising.* 1997. Peter Lang.
    As the subtitle of this book suggests, it is focused on the relationship between advertising and culture. It contains theoretical chapters on advertising and others that deal with specific advertisements for products such as those for Diesel jeans.

Robert Goldman and Stephen Papson. *Sign Wars: The Cluttered Landscape of Advertising.* 1996. Guilford.

The authors of this volume argue that advertising can be seen as involving "sign wars" or "sign competitions," which suggests a semiotic and sociological approach to the industry. They argue that advertising agencies are involved in a brutal war with other agencies to make their signs and advertisements—whether for sneakers or any other product—dominant. The book combines semiotic theory and sociological analysis of the advertising industry and of particular advertising campaigns.

Wolfang Fritz Haug. *Critique of Commodity Aesthetics: Appearance, Sexuality and Advertising in Capitalist Society.* 1986. University of Minnesota Press.

As the subtitle of the book suggests, Haug offers a Marxist interpretation of the advertising industry and an indictment of its use of sexuality as a means of exploiting those who are exposed to advertising. Haug's focus is upon capitalism and its imperatives in "bourgeois" societies as they relate to advertising.

Montague Kern. *30-Second Politics: Political Advertising in the Eighties.* 1989. Praeger.

An excellent overview and explanation of how political advertising has evolved with a focus on some important and controversial political campaigns in the United States in the 1980s.

Paul Messaris, *Visual Persuasion: The Role of Images in Advertising.* 1997. Sage Publications.

Thus book is useful because it focuses upon visual phenomena and the role they play in advertising. Thus it provides an important theoretical perspective involving applied media aesthetics on how images can be used to persuade people and to affect their emotions.

Marshall McLuhan. *The Mechanical Bride: Folklore of Industrial Man.* 1967. Beacon.

McLuhan's book was first published in 1951 and can be regarded as a path breaking work, a true classic, that focused attention on the role popular culture played in American culture. The book deals mostly with advertisements though it does discuss some comic strips and other aspects of popular culture. What McLuhan does is to use the tools of literary analysis and aesthetics to analyze the cultural significance of several dozen advertisements. His style is jazzy and his insights are penetrating.

William M. O'Barr. *Culture and the Ad: Exploring Otherness in the World of Advertising.* 1994. Westview.

O'Barr's book is the same size as McLuhan's and the design of the book and analytical focus suggests a similarity with McLuhan's. His focus is on the way advertising presents "others" to the world, especially in travel advertising and advertising dealing with people in other cultures, and on explicating the social ideologies found in this advertising. O'Barr describes himself as being heavily influenced by Marxism and semiotic theory.

Greg Myers. *Ad Worlds: Brands/Media/Audiences.* 1999. Arnold.

Myers covers a wide range of topics such as how ads work, brands, globalization, the Internet, audience research, and promotional culture. It was written for British readers but its insights can be adapted to advertising in the United States and other countries.

Torben Vestergaard and Kim Schrøder. *The Language of Advertising*. 1985. Basil Blackwell.

The focus in this book is on linguistic communication in print advertising, but the authors are aware of the importance of visual images and deal with them as well. Among the topics covered are verbal and visual messages, the structure of advertisements, strategies for dealing with sex and class differences, and ideological aspects of advertising.

BIBLIOGRAPHY

Altstiel, Tom, and Jean Grow. 2005. *Advertising Strategy: Creative Tactics from the Outside In.* Thousand Oaks: Sage.

Ansolabehere, Stephen, and Shanto Iyengar. 1995. *Going Negative: How Political Advertisements Shrink and Polarize the Electorate.* New York: Free Press.

Bakhtin, Mikhail. 1981. *The Dialogic Imagination.* Ed. M. Holmquist; Trans. C. Emerson and M. Holmquist. Austin: University of Texas Press.

Barnouw, Eric. 1979. *The Sponsor: Notes on a Modern Potentate.* New York: Oxford University Press.

Baudrillard, Jean. 1968. *The System of Objects.* Trans. James Benedict. London: Verso.

———. 1998. *The Consumer Society: Myths & Structures.* London: Sage.

Beckett, Jamie. "Ad Pitches Popping Up in Unusual Places." *San Francisco Chronicle*, July 17, 1989.

Berger, Arthur Asa. "Don't Go Away, We'll Be Back with More Ads." *The Chronicle Review, Chronicle of Higher Education*, November 13, 1978.

———. 1998. *Media Analysis Techniques.* Second edition. Thousand Oaks, Calif: Sage.

———. 1998. *Seeing Is Believing: An Introduction to Visual Communication.* Second edition. Mountain View, Calif: Mayfield.

———. 1999. *Signs in Contemporary Culture: An Introduction to Semiotics.* Second edition. Salem, Wisc.: Sheffield.

———. 2002. *The Agent in the Agency.* Cresskill, NJ: Hampton.

Berger, John. 1972. *Ways of Seeing.* London: British Broadcasting System and Penguin Books.

Bogart, Leo. 1967. *Strategy in Advertising.* New York: Harcourt Brace.

Bulkeley, William M. *The Wall Street Journal*; Eastern edition; Jun 23, 2005; B.1.

"Coca-Cola Turns to Pavlov," *Wall Street Journal*, January 19, 1984.

Cortese, Anthony J. 2004. *Provocateur: Images of Women and Minorities in Advertising*, Second Edition. Lanham, Md.: Rowman & Littlefield.

Danesi, Marcel. 1995. *Decoding Advertisements: A Semiotic Guide.* Toronto: Legas.

Danesi, Marcel. 1995. *Interpreting Advertisement: A Semiotic Guide.* New York: Legas.

Diamond, Edwin, with Stephen Bates. 1992. *The Spot: The Rise of Political Advertising on Television.* Cambridge, Mass.: MIT Press.

Dichter, Ernest. 1960. *The Strategy of Desire.* Garden City, N.Y.: Doubleday.

Douglas, Mary. 1997. "In Defense of Shopping," in Pasi Falk and Colin Campbell, eds. *The Shopping Experience.* London: Sage.

Elliott, Stuart. "The Media Business: Advertising." New York Times, December 7, 2004.

———. "Advertising." New York Times, January 7, 1993.

Enzensberger, Hans Magnus. 1974. The Consciousness Industry: On Literature, Politics, and the Media. New York: Seabury.

Ewen, Stuart. 1976. Captains of Consciousness: Advertising and the Social Roots of the Consumer Culture. New York: McGraw-Hill.

Ewen, Stuart, and Elizabeth Ewen. 1982. Channels of Desire: Mass Images and the Shaping of American Consciousness. New York: McGraw-Hill.

Falk, Pasi, and Colin Campbell, eds. 1997. The Shopping Experience. London: Sage Publications.

Farrell, Greg. "Marketers Put a Price on Your Life." USA Today, July 7, 1999.

Featherstone, Mike. 1991. Consumer Culture and Postmodernism. London: Sage.

Foerster, Norman, ed. 1957. American Poetry and Prose, Part One. Fourth edition. Boston: Houghton Mifflin.

Freud, Sigmund. 1963. "Psychoanalysis," in Sigmund Freud, Character and Culture (ed. Philip Rieff). New York: Collier Books.

———. 1965. New Introductory Lectures on Psychoanalysis. Trans. James Strachey. New York: Norton.

Frith, Katherine Toland, ed. 1997. Undressing the Ad: Reading Culture in Advertising. New York: Peter Lang.

Frith, Simon. 1981. Sound Effects: Youth, Leisure, and the Politics of Rock and Roll. New York: Pantheon.

Gans, Herbert. 1974. Popular Culture and High Culture. New York: Basic Books.

Garber, Marjorie. "Joe Camel, an X-rated Smoke." New York Times, March 20, 1992.

Girard, René. 1991. A Theater of Envy. New York: Oxford University Press.

Goffman, Erving. 1976. "Gender Advertisements." Studies in the Anthropology of Visual Communication, volume 3, number 2.

Goldman, Robert, and Stephen Papson. 1996. Sign Wars: The Cluttered Landscape of Advertising. New York: Guilford.

Greer, Germaine. 1971. The Female Eunuch. New York: McGraw-Hill.

Hackley, Chris. 2005. Advertising and Promotion. Thousand Oaks, CA: Sage.

Hall, Trish. "The Young Are Getting and Spending, Too." New York Times, August 23, 1990.

Hamburger, Tom. "Drug Industry Ads Aid GOP." Wall Street Journal, June 18, 2002.

Haug, W. F. 1986. Critique of Commodity Aesthetics: Appearance, Sexuality, and Advertising in Capitalist Society. Trans. Robert Bock. Minneapolis: University of Minnesota Press.

Haug, Wolfgang Fritz. 1987. Commodity Aesthetics, Ideology and Culture. New York: International General.

Henry, Jules. 1963. Culture Against Man. New York: Vintage Books.

Herman-Cohen, Valli. "Primping or Pimping." San Francisco Chronicle, September 26, 2000.

Hinsie, L. E., and Campbell, R. J. 1970. Psychiatric Dictionary. New York: Oxford University Press.

Howard, Niles. "A New Way to View Consumers." Dun's Review, August 1981.

Huizinga, Johan. 1924. The Waning of the Middle Ages. Garden City, N.Y.: Anchor.

Irvine, Martha. "Survey: More Young People Nagging." Associated Press, June 17, 2002.

Itow, Laurie. "What Your Values Tell Advertisers You'll Buy." San Francisco Sunday Examiner and Chronicle, June 27, 1982.

Jamieson, Kathleen Hall. 1992. Dirty Politics: Deception, Distraction, and Democracy. New York: Oxford University Press.

————. 1996. *Packaging the Presidency*. Third edition. New York: Oxford University Press.

Jones, John Philip. 2004. *Fables, Fashions and Facts About Advertising*. Thousand Oaks, CA: Sage.

Jung, Carl. 1968. *Man and His Symbols*. New York: Dell.

Kern, Montague. 1989. *30-Second Politics: Political Advertising in the Eighties*. New York: Praeger.

Key, Wilson Bryan. 1973. *Subliminal Seduction*. New York: Signet.

Klein, Melanie, and Joan Riviere. 1967. *Love, Hate, and Reparation*. New York: Norton.

Kotler, Philip, Ned Roberto, and Nancy Lee. 2002. *Social Marketing: Improving the Quality of Life*. Thousand Oaks, CA: Sage.

Kurtz, Bruce. 1977. *Spots: The Popular Art of American Television Commercials*. New York: Arts Communications.

Lakoff, George, and Mark Johnson. 1980. *Metaphors We Live By*. Chicago, IL: University of Chicago Press.

Lefebvre, Henri. 1984. *Everyday Life in the Modern World*. New Brunswick, NJ: Transaction.

Lotman, Yuri. 1977. *The Structure of the Artistic Text*. Trans. G. Lenhoff and R. Vroon. Ann Arbor: Michigan Slavic Contributions.

Lyotard, Jean-François. 1984. *The Postmodern Condition: A Report on Knowledge*. Trans. Geoff Bennington and Brian Massumi. Minneapolis: University of Minnesota Press.

Marshand, Roland. 1986. *Advertising and the American Dream*. Berkeley, CA: University of California Press.

McAllister, Matthew P. 1996. *The Commercialization of American Culture: New Advertising, Control, and Democracy*. Thousand Oaks, Calif.: Sage.

McFall, Liz. 2004. *Advertising: A Cultural Economy*. Thousand Oaks, CA: Sage.

McLuhan, Marshall. 1951. *The Mechanical Bride*. Boston: Beacon.

McQuail, Denis, and Sven Windahl. 1993. *Communication Models: For the Study of Mass Communication*. Second edition. New York: Longman.

Messaris, Paul. 1997. *Visual Persuasion: The Role of Images in Advertising*. Thousand Oaks, Calif: Sage.

Mooij, Marieka de. 2003. *Consumer Behavior and Culture: Consequences for Global Marketing and Advertising*. Thousand Oaks, CA: Sage.

Moriarty, Sandra, and Shay Sayre. 1991. "A Comparison of Reader Response with Informed Author/Viewer Analysis." Unpublished Paper.

Myers, Greg. 1994. *Words in Ads*. London: Edward Arnold.

————. 1999. *Ad Worlds: Brands/Media/Audiences*. London: Arnold.

Nixon, Sean. 2003. *Advertising Cultures: Gender, Commerce, Creativity*. Thousand Oaks, CA: Sage.

O'Barr, William O. 1994. *Culture and the Ad: Exploring Otherness in the World of Advertising*. Boulder, CO: Westview.

Packard, Vance. 1957. *The Hidden Persuaders*. New York: David McKay.

Patai, Raphael. 1972. *Myth and Modern Man*. Englewood Cliffs, NJ: Prentice-Hall.

Peterson, Melody. "Madison Ave. Plays Growing Role in the Business of Drug Research." *New York Times*, November 22, 2002.

Potter, David M. 1954. *People of Plenty: Economic Abundance and the American Character*. Chicago, Ill.: University of Chicago Press.

Riviere, Joan. 1967. "Hate, Greed and Aggression," in Melanie Klein and Joan Riviere, eds. *Love, Hate, and Reparation*. New York: Norton.

Rotzoll, Kim, and James E. Haefner. 1986. *Advertising in Contemporary Society: Perspectives Toward Understanding.* Cincinnati, OH: South-Western Publishing.

Saussure, Ferdinand de. 1966. *A Course in General Linguistics.* Trans. W. Baskin. New York: McGraw-Hill.

Scholes, Robert. 1974. *Structuralism in Literature: An Introduction.* New Haven, Conn.: Yale University Press.

Schwartz, Barry. 2004. *The Paradox of Choice.* New York: Harper Collins.

Sheehan, Kim Bartel. 2004. *Controversies in Contemporary Advertising.* Thousand Oaks, CA: Sage.

Shorer, Mark. 1968. "The Necessity of Myth," in H. A. Murray, ed. *Myth and Mythmaking.* Boston: Beacon.

Solomon, Jack. 1990. *The Signs of Our Times: The Secret Meanings of Everyday Life.* New York: Harper & Row.

Solomon, Michael, Gary Barmossy, and Soren Askegaard. 2002. *Consumer Behavior: A European Perspective.* Second edition. Harlow, England: Financial Times/Prentice Hall.

Solow, Martin. 1988. "The Case of the Closet Target," in Arthur Asa Berger, ed., *Media USA: Process and Effect.* New York: Longman.

Tellis, Gerard J. 2004. *Effective Advertising: Understanding When, How, and Why Advertising Works.* Thousand Oaks, CA: Sage.

Tharp, Marye C. 2001. *Marketing and Consumer Identity in Multicultural America.* Thousand Oaks, CA: Sage.

Thompson, Michael, Richard Ellis, and Aaron Wildavsky. 1990. *Cultural Theory.* Boulder, Colo.: Westview Press.

Twitchell, James. 1996. *Adcult USA: Advertising in American Culture.* New York: Columbia University Press.

Underhill, Paco. 2000. *Why We Buy: The Science of Shopping.* New York: Touchstone/Simon & Schuster.

Van Duyn, Aline. "Bloggers' New Brand Starts to Click with Advertisers." *Financial Times,* March 28, 2005.

Vestergaard, Torben, and Kim Schrøder. 1985. *The Language of Advertising.* Oxford, U.K.: Basil Blackwell.

Walters, Dan. "A State of Gray." *Wall Street Journal,* October 24, 2002.

Weiss, Michael. 1988. *The Clustering of America.* New York: Harper & Row.

Wernick, Andrew. 1991. *Promotional Culture: Advertising, Ideology and Symbolic Expression.* London: Sage.

West, Darrell M. 1997. *Air Wars: Television Advertising in Election Campaigns.* Washington, D.C.: Congressional Quarterly.

Whiting, Sam. "Your ZIP Code Tells All About You." *San Francisco Chronicle,* November 23, 1988.

Wildavsky, Aaron. 1989. "A Cultural Theory of Preference Formation" in Arthur Asa Berger, ed., *Political Culture and Public Opinion.* New Brunswick, NJ: Transaction.

Williamson, Judith. 1978. *Decoding Advertisements: Ideology and Meaning in Advertising.* London: Marion Boyars.

Zukin, Sharon. 2005. *Point of Purchase: How Shopping Changed American Culture.* New York: Routledge.

INDEX